The Best of
COUNTRY COOKING
2008

Senior Vice President, Editor in Chief: Catherine Cassidy
Vice President, Executive Editor/Books: Heidi Reuter Lloyd
Creative Director: Ardyth Cope
Senior Editor/Books: Mark Hagen
Art Director: Gretchen Trautman
Layout Designer: Emma Acevedo
Content Production Supervisor: Julie Wagner
Proofreader: Linne Bruskewitz
Editorial Assistant: Barb Czysz

Food Director: Diane Werner RD
Test Kitchen Manager: Karen Scales
Recipe Editors: Sue A. Jurack (Senior), Mary King, Christine Rukavena
Recipe Asset System Manager: Coleen Martin
Photographers: Rob Hagen (Senior), Dan Roberts, Jim Wieland, Lori Foy
Food Stylists: Sarah Thompson (Senior), Tamara Kaufman
Assistant Food Stylists: Kaitlyn Besasie, Alynna Malson, Shannon Roum, Leah Rekau
Set Stylists: Jenny Bradley Vent (Senior), Stephanie Marchese (Senior),
Melissa Haberman, Dee Dee Jacq
Photo Studio Coordinator: Kathy Swaney

Chief Marketing Officer: Lisa Karpinski
Vice President/Book Marketing: Robert Graham Botta
Creative Director/Creative Marketing: James Palmen

THE READER'S DIGEST ASSOCIATION, INC.
President and Chief Executive Officer: Mary G. Berner
President, RDA Food & Entertaining: Suzanne M. Grimes

Taste of Home Books
©2008 Reiman Media Group, Inc.
5400 S. 60th St., Greendale WI 53129

International Standard Book Number (10): 0-89821-601-X
International Standard Book Number (13): 978-0-89821-601-1
International Standard Serial Number: 1097-8321
All rights reserved. Printed in U.S.A.

For additional copies of this book and other *Taste of Home* titles and products,
visit our Web site at *www.ShopTasteofHome.com*.

PICTURED ABOVE AND ON FRONT COVER: Sugar Snap Pea Stir-Fry (p. 86),
Peach Melba Mountain (p. 113) and Herb-Crusted Pork Roast (p. 48). Photography by
Jim Wieland. Food styled by Sue Draheim. Set styled by Jenny Bradley Vent.

Hundreds of Homemade Specialties Done Right!

COME AND GET IT! It's time to dig into the down-home flavor of country cooking. Barbecued chicken, corn bread, grilled steaks, apple dumplings and rustic loaves of freshly baked breads…you'll find all of these family favorites in this mouth-watering collection.

In fact, *The Best of Country Cooking 2008* offers 351 finger-licking delights. Best of all, nearly all of the recipes were shared by cooks from coast to coast in recent issues of *Country Woman*, *Country*, *Country EXTRA*, *Reminisce* and *Reminisce EXTRA* magazines.

Page through this colorful collection and you'll find dozens of bubbling casseroles, farm-fresh veggie dishes, creamy soups and enough cakes, pies and goodies to satisfy your sweet tooth any time of the year.

Consider the chapter, "Snacks & Beverages." There you'll discover perfect party bites such as Sweet Sausage Puffs (p. 5) and Marinated Mushrooms and Cheese (p. 11). Looking for something special to ring in the holidays? See page 12 for an appetizer buffet that's merry and bright. In addition, this chapter offers simple nibbles and after-school staples such as Almond Snack Cake (p. 18) and Chunky Fruit 'n' Nut Fudge (p. 7).

You can't go wrong with the items in the "Soups, Salads & Sandwiches" chapter…particularly when you need to set a meal on the table fast. Just mix and match the recipes for effortless menu planning. We've even selected a few specialties for picnics (p. 28), and we've highlighted some change-of-pace gelatins (p. 36) that you've simply got to try.

"Main Dishes" is jam-packed with supper ideas…61 entrees in all! If you are looking for a weeknight supper, try Hamburger Stroganoff (p. 49) or Easy Chicken Fajitas (p. 66). For weekend guests, consider Herb-Crusted Pork Roast (p. 48) or Biscuit Ham Spirals (p. 70).

Round out dinners with any of the heart-warming items in "Side Dishes & Condiments." In addition to cheesy potato bakes, good-for-you veggies and savory rice favorites, you can count on Spice Cranberry Sauce (p. 77), Kentucky Spoon Bread (p. 83) and a host of hearty side dish casseroles (p. 84). And because nothing represents a country kitchen like the aroma of oven-fresh loaves and biscuits, the comforting chapter "Breads & Rolls" offers plenty of golden baked goods.

Speaking of baking, you'll want to check out the 22 recipes in "Cookies, Bars & Brownies." Whether looking for simple classroom snacks, bake-sale items or additions to Christmas cookie trays, this is one chapter you'll turn to time and again. Double Frosted Brownies (p. 103) and Chocolate Almond Logs (p. 109) will surely become household favorites.

In addition, *The Best of Country Cooking 2008* features more than 45 impressive after-dinner delights. See "Dazzling Desserts" for incredible recipes, including Mocha Chip Pie (p. 114) and Pumpkin Spice Torte (p. 131). A special section featuring frosty sensations (p. 118) and ideas that take pears from ordinary to extraordinary (p. 128) are included as well.

You'll also find the standbys you've come to expect from this handy collection…including 16 complete meals.

Cooking for Two—Dishes and dinners that are sized right for a pair.

Meals in Minutes—Four suppers that require a minimum of prep work.

Most Memorable Meals—A total of 24 recipes divided into six unforgettable menus.

Be sure to watch for the blue ribbon symbol at right as you thumb through *The Best of Country Cooking 2008*. It identifies prize winners—the recipes that earned high honors in national cooking contests sponsored by one of our magazines.

You'll also see "restricted diet" recipes marked with the check at right. These ☑ dishes use less fat, salt or sugar. Some of them even include Diabetic Exchanges.

So what are you waiting for? Grab a fork and dig in! It won't be long before you realize why these dishes are simply the best in the country.

CONTENTS

MUNCH *to your heart's content with this yummy assortment of easy appetizers, after-school snacks, swift sweets and thirst-quenching beverages.*

FIESTA OF FLAVORS. Greek Salsa (p. 5).

GREEK SALSA
(Pictured at left)

Heidi Mitchell, Cornwall, Prince Edward Island

Color, texture and a fantastic blend of flavors—this salsa has it all. It's easy to adapt to the taste preferences of your family or guests. I've made it dozens of times, and it's foolproof.

✓ Uses less fat, sugar or salt. Includes Nutrition Facts.

    1 tablespoon white balsamic vinegar
    2 tablespoons olive oil, *divided*
2-1/2 teaspoons Greek seasoning, *divided*
    1 garlic clove, minced
    1 cup grape tomatoes, quartered
  3/4 cup chopped cucumber
  1/2 cup crumbled feta cheese
  1/2 cup chopped red onion
    1 can (2-1/4 ounces) sliced ripe olives, drained
    1 package (12 ounces) whole wheat pita breads

In a small bowl, combine the vinegar, 1 tablespoon oil, 1-1/2 teaspoons Greek seasoning and garlic; set aside.

In a large bowl, combine the tomatoes, cucumber, feta cheese, onion and olives. Drizzle with vinegar mixture and toss to coat. Chill until serving.

Cut each pita bread into eight wedges. Place on an ungreased baking sheet. Brush with remaining oil; sprinkle with remaining Greek seasoning. Bake at 400° for 6-8 minutes or until crisp. Serve with salsa. **Yield:** 2-3/4 cups salsa and 40 pita chips.

Nutrition Facts: 1/4 cup equals 120 calories, 4 g fat (1 g saturated fat), 3 mg cholesterol, 445 mg sodium, 18 g carbohydrate, 3 g fiber, 4 g protein.

FRUITY SANGRIA

Your party will get off to a great start when you welcome guests with glasses of sangria. Our staff liked it just as well using nonalcoholic red wine and orange juice in place of the wine and Triple Sec.

    1 bottle (750 milliliters) dry red wine
    1 can (11.3 ounces) peach nectar
    1 cup orange juice
  1/2 cup Triple Sec *or* additional orange juice
  1/2 cup lemon juice
    2 cups lemon-lime soda, chilled
    1 medium peach *or* nectarine, sliced
    1 cup sliced fresh strawberries
    1 cup cubed seedless watermelon

In a pitcher, combine the first five ingredients. Cover and refrigerate until chilled. Just before serving, stir in the soda and fruit. **Yield:** 12 servings.

SWEET SAUSAGE PUFFS

Gloria Butler, Plain City, Ohio

A homemade pecan syrup is a sweet complement to the mini sausages I wrap and bake in buttery dough. It's a hearty appetizer that everyone seems to enjoy.

  1/2 cup butter
    1 cup packed brown sugar
    2 tablespoons water
  1/2 cup finely chopped pecans
    1 tube (12 ounces) refrigerated flaky buttermilk biscuits
   40 miniature smoked sausages

For syrup, in a heavy saucepan, melt butter. Stir in the brown sugar and water. Bring to a boil. Stir in pecans. Remove from the heat; set aside.

Flatten each biscuit into a 3-in. circle; cut into quarters. Place a sausage on each piece of dough; wrap dough around sausage and seal edge. Place seam side down in a greased 15-in. x 10-in. x 1-in. baking pan. Pour syrup over bundles.

Bake at 375° for 15-20 minutes or until golden brown. Transfer to a chafing dish or slow cooker; cover and keep warm over low heat. **Yield:** 40 appetizers.

ADDING GARDEN-FRESH FLAIR

Lend some color and a bit of fun to veggie-and-dip trays with this easy idea. Simply cut the top off of a red, green or yellow bell pepper. Scoop out the seeds and membrane and use the pepper to hold the tray's dip.

BLACK FOREST HAM PINWHEELS
(Pictured above)

Kate Dampier, Quail Valley, California

My popular pinwheels wow guests at holiday parties. People like the smokiness of the ham and the sweet surprise of the cherries. I appreciate the make-ahead convenience the recipe offers.

    1 package (8 ounces) cream cheese, softened
    4 teaspoons minced fresh dill
    1 tablespoon lemon juice
    2 teaspoons Dijon mustard
Dash salt and pepper
  1/2 cup dried cherries, chopped
  1/4 cup chopped green onions
    5 flour tortillas (10 inches)
  1/2 pound sliced deli Black Forest ham
  1/2 pound sliced Swiss cheese

In a small mixing bowl, beat the cream cheese, dill, lemon juice, mustard, salt and pepper until blended. Stir in the cherries and onions. Spread over each tortilla; layer with ham and cheese.

Roll up tightly; wrap in plastic wrap. Refrigerate for at least 2 hours. Cut into 1/2-in. slices. **Yield:** about 3-1/2 dozen.

PASTRAMI ARTICHOKE SPREAD

Donna Plarman, Elgin, Illinois

Chopped pastrami adds a tasty twist to this artichoke spread, but it's the wonderful blend of flavors that'll make you want to serve it often. I'm a caterer, and this is an absolute hors d'oeuvre staple for many of my customers. It's also wonderful served warm.

☑ Uses less fat, sugar or salt. Includes Nutrition Facts.

    1 can (14 ounces) water-packed artichoke hearts, rinsed, drained and chopped
    1 cup (8 ounces) sour cream
    1 cup mayonnaise
    6 ounces thinly sliced deli pastrami, chopped
  1/4 cup shredded Parmesan cheese
    1 tablespoon prepared horseradish
    1 teaspoon dill weed
Snack rye bread

In a bowl, combine the artichokes, sour cream, mayonnaise, pastrami, Parmesan cheese, horseradish and dill. Serve with snack rye. Refrigerate leftovers. **Yield:** 3 cups.

Nutrition Facts: 1/4 cup equals 210 calories, 19 g fat (5 g saturated fat), 29 mg cholesterol, 346 mg sodium, 3 g carbohydrate, trace fiber, 5 g protein.

🎗 HEARTY RYE MELTS
(Pictured below)

Melanie Schlaf, Edgewood, Kentucky

When we moved from the Midwest to Kentucky, we were invited to a neighborhood gathering, where this appetizer was served.

- 1/2 pound lean ground beef
- 1/2 pound bulk pork sausage
- 1-1/2 teaspoons chili powder
- 8 ounces process cheese (Velveeta), shredded
- 24 slices snack rye bread
- **Fresh parsley sprigs, stems removed**

In a large skillet, cook the beef and sausage over medium heat until no longer pink; drain. Add chili powder and cheese; cook and stir until cheese is melted. Spread a heaping tablespoonful onto each slice of bread. Place on a baking sheet.

Bake at 350° for 12-15 minutes or until edges of bread begin to crisp. Garnish with parsley. Serve warm. **Yield:** 2 dozen.

🎗 CHUNKY FRUIT 'N' NUT FUDGE
(Pictured above right)

Allene Bary-Cooper, Ramona, Oklahoma

Variations on this fudge are endless, but this recipe is my favorite. Besides five types of chips, it includes everything from dried fruit to nuts. Every bite is packed with flavor and crunch.

✓ Uses less fat, sugar or salt. Includes Nutrition Facts.

- 1 package (11 ounces) dried cherries
- 1 cup dried cranberries
- 1-1/2 teaspoons plus 3/4 cup butter, softened, *divided*
- 1 can (14 ounces) sweetened condensed milk
- 1 package (12 ounces) miniature semisweet chocolate chips
- 1 package (11-1/2 ounces) milk chocolate chips
- 1 package (10 to 11 ounces) butterscotch chips
- 1 package (10 ounces) peanut butter chips
- 3 tablespoons heavy whipping cream
- 1 jar (7 ounces) marshmallow creme
- 1/2 teaspoon almond *or* rum extract
- 1-1/2 cups unsalted cashew halves
- 1 package (11-1/2 ounces) semisweet chocolate chunks

In a large bowl, combine cherries and cranberries. Add enough warm water to cover; set aside. Line a 15-in. x 10-in. x 1-in. pan with foil and grease the foil with 1-1/2 teaspoons butter; set aside.

In a large heavy saucepan, melt remaining butter. Stir in the milk, chips and cream. Cook and stir over low heat for 15-20 minutes or until chips are melted and mixture is smooth and blended (mixture will first appear separated, but continue stirring until fully blended). Remove from the heat; stir in marshmallow creme and extract.

Drain cherries and cranberries; pat dry with paper towels. Stir the fruit, cashews and chocolate chunks into chocolate mixture. Spread into prepared pan. Let stand at room temperature until set.

Using foil, lift fudge out of pan. Discard foil; cut fudge into 1-in. squares. **Yield:** 6-3/4 pounds.

Nutrition Facts: 1 piece equals 92 calories, 5 g fat (3 g saturated fat), 4 mg cholesterol, 23 mg sodium, 12 g carbohydrate, 1 g fiber, 1 g protein.

BRIE WITH APRICOT TOPPING
(Pictured below)

Folks will think you fussed over this pretty appetizer, but it took our Test Kitchen only minutes to top a round of smooth and creamy Brie with warm sweet apricots. This is one easy recipe that's certain to make any occasion special.

    1/2 cup chopped dried apricots
      2 tablespoons brown sugar
      2 tablespoons water
      1 teaspoon balsamic vinegar
Dash salt
    1/2 to 1 teaspoon minced fresh rosemary *or*
          1/4 teaspoon dried rosemary, crushed
      1 round Brie cheese (8 ounces)
Assorted crackers

In a small saucepan, combine the apricots, brown sugar, water, vinegar and salt. Bring to a boil. Reduce heat to medium; cook and stir until slightly thickened. Remove from the heat; stir in rosemary.

    Remove rind from top of cheese. Place in an ungreased ovenproof serving dish. Spread apricot mixture over cheese. Bake, uncovered, at 400° for 10-12 minutes or until cheese is softened. Serve with crackers. **Yield:** 6-8 servings.

NUTTY CARAMEL APPLE DIP
(Pictured above)

Darlene Brenden, Salem, Oregon

Looking for a standout appetizer that could double as a dessert? Try this fast, no-fuss favorite that mixes up in a pinch. It's a fun change of pace for traditional munchies and a simple way to get folks to snack on more fruit.

      1 package (8 ounces) cream cheese, softened
    1/2 cup apple butter
    1/4 cup packed brown sugar
    1/2 teaspoon vanilla extract
    1/2 cup chopped salted peanuts
      3 medium apples, sliced

In a small mixing bowl, beat the cream cheese, apple butter, brown sugar and vanilla until combined. Stir in the peanuts. Serve with apple slices. Refrigerate leftovers. **Yield:** 2 cups.

    Editor's Note: This recipe was tested with commercially prepared apple butter.

GARLIC EGGPLANT SPREAD

Brenda Martin, Greenwood, Indiana

What a mouth-watering mix of flavors and textures in this delicious spread! Mild eggplant makes a perfect backdrop for the blend of fresh garlic, dill and salty capers. It's also terrific on pita sandwiches.

✓ Uses less fat, sugar or salt. Includes Nutrition Facts.

      1 medium eggplant
      2 tablespoons olive oil
      1 to 2 tablespoons dill weed

1 tablespoon capers, drained
2 garlic cloves, minced
3/4 teaspoon salt
Baked pita chips

Pierce eggplant thoroughly; place in an 8-in. square baking dish. Bake at 400° for 60-65 minutes or until tender.

Drain. Cut eggplant in half and scoop out the pulp. In a bowl, mash the pulp. Add oil, dill, capers, garlic and salt; mix well. Serve with pita chips. **Yield:** 1-1/3 cups.

Nutrition Facts: 3 tablespoons equals 57 calories, 4 g fat (1 g saturated fat), 0 cholesterol, 293 mg sodium, 5 g carbohydrate, 2 g fiber, 1 g protein.

CRANBERRY MOUSSE
(Pictured below)

Pauline Tucker, Baldwinville, Massachusetts

We live about 100 miles from Cape Cod, which is known for its cranberries. When we spent a weekend there, we toured the Cranberry World Visitors Center, which is where I found this recipe. You'll be surprised at how easily the four ingredients come together.

1 can (16 ounces) jellied cranberry sauce
1 cup cranberry juice
1 package (3 ounces) cranberry *or* raspberry gelatin
1 cup heavy whipping cream, whipped

In a large saucepan, bring the cranberry sauce and juice to a boil; cook and stir until smooth. Stir in the gelatin until dissolved. Cool slightly; transfer to a bowl. Refrigerate for 1 hour or until mixture begins to thicken.

Fold in the whipped cream. Spoon into dessert dishes. Chill mixture for 3-4 hours or until firm. **Yield:** 6 servings.

RASPBERRY APPLE CAKE
(Pictured above)

Pinkie Mosteller, Lincolnton, North Carolina

This recipe won first prize at the annual Apple Festival in Lincoln County, North Carolina! It's not your usual apple cake—you spread raspberry jam over the crust, then cover that with apple pie filling and a sour cream topping. I hope it's a winner in your home, too.

1/3 cup butter, softened
1/3 cup packed brown sugar
1 egg
1 cup all-purpose flour
1/2 teaspoon baking powder
1/4 teaspoon salt
1/4 cup seedless raspberry jam
1 can (21 ounces) apple pie filling
4 tablespoons sugar, *divided*
1/2 teaspoon ground cinnamon
1 cup (8 ounces) sour cream
1 teaspoon vanilla extract

In a small mixing bowl, cream butter and brown sugar until fluffy. Beat in egg. Combine the flour, baking powder and salt; beat into the creamed mixture.

Spread into a greased 9-in. square baking pan. Bake at 350° for 20-25 minutes or until lightly browned.

Remove cake; leave oven on. Spread with jam and top with pie filling. Combine 1 tablespoon sugar and the cinnamon; sprinkle over filling. Combine the sour cream, vanilla and remaining sugar; spread over top.

Bake 10 minutes longer or until topping is set. Cool on a wire rack for 1 hour. Refrigerate for 3 hours or until chilled. **Yield:** 6 servings.

Curried Vegetable Dip

(Pictured above)

Lois Kodada, Northfield, Minnesota

The combination of curry powder and honey gives this dip a sweet, spicy flavor. It's a nice change from onion and ranch vegetable dips.

1-1/2 cups mayonnaise
2 tablespoons finely chopped onion
2 tablespoons lemon juice
2 tablespoons honey
2 tablespoons ketchup
1 teaspoon curry powder
2 to 4 drops hot pepper sauce
Assorted fresh vegetables

In a small bowl, combine the first seven ingredients. Cover and refrigerate for at least 1 hour. Serve with vegetables. **Yield:** 1-2/3 cups.

A Chilly Solution

To keep dips cool, fill a large serving bowl with ice. Fill a smaller bowl with the dip and set it on top of the ice. Replace the ice as it melts. If you're taking the dip to an outing, spoon the dip into a bowl, cover with plastic wrap, and put it in a cooler. Assemble the ice-filled serving bowl when you arrive at the picnic.

Poppy Seed Coffee Cake

(Pictured below)

Carla Granger, Big Horn, Wyoming

I tasted this cake while visiting a friend in South Dakota. The memory of it stayed with me for years, until I finally called and asked her for the recipe. It was her mother's, and she was glad to share it.

2/3 cup butter, softened
1 cup sugar
3 eggs, *separated*
1 teaspoon vanilla extract
2-1/2 cups all-purpose flour
3 tablespoons poppy seeds
3/4 teaspoon baking powder
1/2 teaspoon baking soda
1/2 teaspoon salt
1 cup buttermilk

FILLING:

1/3 cup packed brown sugar
4 teaspoons ground cinnamon
1/2 teaspoon instant coffee granules

In a large mixing bowl, cream butter and sugar. Beat in egg yolks and vanilla. Combine the flour, poppy seeds, baking powder, baking soda and salt; add to creamed mixture alternately with buttermilk.

In a small mixing bowl, beat egg whites until stiff peaks form; fold into batter. Pour half of the batter into a greased 13-in. x 9-in. x 2-in. baking pan.

Combine filling ingredients; sprinkle over batter. Carefully top with remaining batter. Bake at 350° for 35-40 minutes or until a toothpick inserted near the center comes out clean. Cool on a wire rack. **Yield:** 12-15 servings.

Marinated Mushrooms and Cheese

(Pictured above)

Kim Marie Van Rheenen, Mendota, Illinois

I like to serve these savory mushrooms alongside sliced baguettes and crackers. They're so versatile that you can vary the cheese or add olives, artichokes or even a little basil. The recipe is ideal for fancy cocktail parties as well as casual get-togethers.

1/2 cup sun-dried tomatoes (not packed in oil), julienned
1 cup boiling water
1/2 cup olive oil
1/2 cup white wine vinegar
2 garlic cloves, minced
1/2 teaspoon salt
1/2 pound sliced fresh mushrooms
8 ounces Monterey Jack cheese, cubed

In a small bowl, combine the tomatoes and water. Let stand for 5 minutes; drain.

In a large resealable plastic bag, combine the oil, vinegar, garlic and salt; add the tomatoes, mushrooms and cheese. Seal bag and toss to coat. Refrigerate for at least 4 hours before serving. Drain and discard marinade. **Yield:** 12-14 servings.

Westerfield Wassail

Jim and Marilyn Westerfield, Freeburg, Illinois

Cranberry juice cocktail and a little red wine make it easy to stir up this comfy beverage. It's great after a day of winter fun with friends.

✓ Uses less fat, sugar or salt. Includes Nutrition Facts.

32 ounces cranberry juice cocktail
2 cups apple juice
1 cup sugar
1 lemon, sliced
2 cinnamon sticks
3/4 teaspoon whole cloves
12 to 24 whole allspice
2 cups red wine, optional

In large saucepan, combine cranberry juice, apple juice and sugar. Fill a square of cheesecloth with the lemon slices, cinnamon sticks, cloves and allspice; tie closed and place in the saucepan. Bring to a boil. Reduce heat; cover and simmer for 30 minutes.

Remove spice-filled cheesecloth and discard. Stir in wine, if desired, and heat through (do not boil). Serve warm. **Yield:** 12-1/2 cups.

Nutrition Facts: 1 cup equals 113 calories, trace fat (trace saturated fat), 0 cholesterol, 3 mg sodium, 29 g carbohydrate, trace fiber, trace protein.

A Buffet That's Merry and Bright

HOLIDAYS mean lots of friendly get-togethers that feature incredible finger foods. This year, deck the halls with the following items, each sure to bring guests plenty of comfort and joy.

FONTINA ASPARAGUS TART
(Pictured at far right)

Heidi Meek, Grand Rapids, Michigan

This lemony cheese and veggie appetizer is easy to make but looks pretty impressive. Be advised...your guests will be vying for the last slice.

    1 pound fresh asparagus, trimmed
    1 sheet frozen puff pastry, thawed
1/2 pound fontina cheese, shredded, *divided*
    2 tablespoons lemon juice
    1 tablespoon olive oil
    1 teaspoon grated lemon peel
1/4 teaspoon salt
1/4 teaspoon pepper

In a large skillet, bring 1 in. of water to a boil; add asparagus. Cover and cook for 3-5 minutes or just until crisp-tender; drain.

On a lightly floured surface, roll out pastry into a 12-in. x 16-in. rectangle; transfer to a parchment paper-lined baking sheet. Bake at 400° for 10 minutes or until golden brown.

Sprinkle 1-1/2 cups cheese over pastry. Arrange asparagus on top; sprinkle with remaining cheese. Combine the lemon juice, oil, lemon peel, salt and pepper; sprinkle over top. Bake 10-15 minutes longer or until asparagus is tender and cheese is melted. Slice and serve warm. **Yield:** 1 tart (about 24 appetizers).

BUFFALO WING POPPERS
(Pictured above, far right)

Barbara Nowakowski, Mesa, Arizona

The taste of buffalo wings and peppers pair well in this appealing idea. The bites will disappear fast, so make a double batch, and have copies of the recipe handy.

   20 jalapeno peppers
    1 package (8 ounces) cream cheese, softened
1-1/2 cups (6 ounces) shredded part-skim mozzarella cheese
    1 cup diced cooked chicken
1/2 cup blue cheese salad dressing
1/2 cup buffalo wing sauce

Cut peppers in half lengthwise, leaving stems intact; discard seeds. In a small mixing bowl, combine the remaining ingredients. Pipe or stuff into pepper halves.

Place in a greased 15-in. x 10-in. x 1-in. baking pan. Bake, uncovered, at 325° for 20 minutes for spicy flavor, 30 minutes for medium and 40 minutes for mild. **Yield:** 40 appetizers.

Editor's Note: When cutting or seeding hot peppers, use rubber or plastic gloves to protect your hands. Avoid touching your face.

SPICY PORK BAGUETTE BITES
(Pictured at right)

Virginia Anthony, Jacksonville, Florida

Here's an interesting twist on mini cocktail sandwiches. Lime mayonnaise provides a cool counterpoint to the nicely spiced pork, and toasted baguette slices contribute crunch.

    1 teaspoon paprika
1/2 teaspoon salt
1/2 teaspoon dried oregano
1/2 teaspoon ground cumin
1/4 teaspoon garlic powder
1/4 teaspoon cayenne pepper
1/4 teaspoon pepper
    1 pork tenderloin (1 pound)
LIME MAYONNAISE:
1/2 cup mayonnaise
    1 tablespoon lime juice
1/2 teaspoon grated lime peel
    1 French bread baguette (1 pound), sliced and toasted
Additional grated lime peel, optional

In a small bowl, combine the first seven ingredients; rub over tenderloin. Place in a large resealable plastic bag; seal and refrigerate overnight.

Place tenderloin on a rack in a foil-lined shallow roasting pan. Bake, uncovered, at 425° for 30-35 minutes or until a meat thermometer reads 160°. Let stand for 5 minutes.

Meanwhile, in a small bowl, combine the mayonnaise, lime juice and peel. Thinly slice the pork; serve on toasted bread with a dollop of lime mayonnaise. Sprinkle with additional lime peel if desired. **Yield:** 20-24 appetizers.

APPETIZER-BUFFET BASICS

Hosting an appetizer buffet is a cinch, but to make things truly manageable, prepare items with make-ahead appeal. Be sure to offer a variety of flavors to please your guests' palates, and choose a few bites that can be picked up and eaten without a plate, such as cubed sausage and cheese. Remember to set out bowls of nuts and snack mixes in other rooms, too.

 WARM CRAB DIP
(Pictured below)

Colleen Taliaferro, Woodbine, Maryland

Maryland's Chesapeake Bay is known for crabs, and they're a big favorite of ours. When fresh crabmeat is available, we'll use it in this dip, but we think canned works just as well.

> 1 package (8 ounces) cream cheese, cubed
> 1/2 cup mayonnaise
> 1 tablespoon lemon juice
> 2 teaspoons Worcestershire sauce
> 1/2 teaspoon sherry, optional
> 2 cans (6 ounces *each*) lump crabmeat, drained
> 1 tablespoon chopped green onion
> Assorted crackers *or* baked pita chips

In a heavy saucepan, heat the cream cheese, mayonnaise, lemon juice, Worcestershire sauce and sherry if desired over low heat, stirring often. Stir in crab and onion; heat through. Serve warm with crackers. **Yield:** 2-1/4 cups.

MANGO TANGO SMOOTHIES
(Pictured above right)

With a cup of milk and a half cup of yogurt, this smoothie is rich in calcium, and an excellent choice for breakfast on the run. For added convenience, our home economists suggest purchasing mango chunks that are already peeled and chopped.

> 1 cup chopped peeled mango
> 1 medium ripe banana, frozen, peeled and sliced
> 1 cup fat-free milk
> 1/2 cup reduced-fat plain yogurt
> 1/2 cup unsweetened pineapple juice

In a blender, combine all ingredients; cover and process until smooth. Pour into chilled glasses; serve immediately. **Yield:** 2 servings.

EGGNOG TRUFFLE CUPS

Terrie Malsom, Vermillion, South Dakota

If you like homemade eggnog, you'll love these elegant, little truffle cups. To save time, I often use small, premade chocolate cups.

✓ Uses less fat, sugar or salt. Includes Nutrition Facts.

> 1 cup (6 ounces) semisweet chocolate chips
> 2 teaspoons shortening
> 6 tablespoons eggnog
> 1 package (10 to 12 ounces) vanilla *or* white chips
> 1/2 teaspoon rum extract
> 1/4 to 3/4 teaspoon ground nutmeg

In a microwave-safe bowl, melt semisweet chips and shortening; stir until smooth. Using a narrow pastry brush, brush the inside of 1-in. foil candy liners with 1/2 teaspoon melted chocolate. Freeze for 45 minutes or until firm.

Using 1/4 teaspoon chocolate mixture for each cup, brush on another layer of chocolate. Freeze until firm.

In a small saucepan, bring eggnog to a boil

over low heat. Remove from the heat; stir in vanilla chips until melted. Remove from the heat; stir in extract. Refrigerate for 30 minutes or until filling begins to set.

Spoon or pipe 1-1/2 teaspoons of filling into each cup. Freeze until firm. Carefully remove and discard foil cups. Cover and store truffles in an airtight container in the refrigerator. Just before serving, sprinkle with nutmeg. **Yield:** 3 dozen.

Nutrition Facts: 1 truffle equals 71 calories, 4 g fat (3 g saturated fat), 3 mg cholesterol, 9 mg sodium, 8 g carbohydrate, trace fiber, 1 g protein.

Editor's Note: This recipe was tested with commercially prepared eggnog.

CHORIZO-QUESO EGG ROLLS

Kari Wheaton, Beloit, Wisconsin

Little bites deliver big flavor in this combination of tangy sausage and creamy cheese. The recipe is an appetizing take-off on my favorite Mexican entree.

      1/2 cup mayonnaise
      1/2 cup sour cream
        2 ounces cream cheese, softened
        2 tablespoons minced fresh cilantro
        1 tablespoon chopped chipotle pepper in adobo sauce
        6 ounces uncooked chorizo *or* bulk spicy pork sausage
        2 cups crumbled queso fresco
      1/4 cup enchilada sauce
      1/4 cup chopped green chilies
        1 package (12 ounces) wonton wrappers
Oil for frying

For dipping sauce, in a small bowl, combine the mayonnaise, sour cream, cream cheese, cilantro and chipotle peppers. Cover and refrigerate until serving.

In a large skillet, cook chorizo over medium heat until no longer pink; drain. Stir in the queso fresco, enchilada sauce and chilies.

Position a wonton wrapper with one point toward you. Place 2 teaspoons of filling in the center. Fold bottom corner over filling; fold sides toward center over filling. Roll toward the remaining point. Moisten top corner with water; press to seal. Repeat with remaining wrappers and filling.

In an electric skillet, heat 1 in. of oil to 375°. Fry egg rolls in batches for 1-2 minutes on each side or until golden brown. Drain on paper towels. Serve warm with dipping sauce. **Yield:** 4 dozen.

Editor's Note: Fill wonton wrappers a few at a time, keeping the others covered with a damp paper towel until ready to use.

FAUX CHICKEN NUGGETS
(Pictured below)

Here's a recipe from our Test Kitchen for "chicken nuggets" that are poultry-free. It calls for pound cake in place of chicken that is rolled in a "batter" of chopped peanuts. Kids will think they are having dinner for dessert.

        1 loaf (10-3/4 ounces) frozen pound cake, thawed
    1-1/2 cups confectioners' sugar
        2 tablespoons water
    4-1/2 teaspoons light corn syrup
        1 tablespoon butter, softened
      1/4 teaspoon vanilla extract
        2 cups finely chopped salted peanuts
GOLDEN DIPPING SAUCE:
        2 snack-size cups (3-1/2 ounces *each*) vanilla pudding
        2 teaspoons dark corn syrup
        2 drops yellow food coloring, optional

Cut cake into 12 slices; cut each slice in half. Cut into irregular nugget-shaped pieces; set aside.

In a small mixing bowl, combine the confectioners' sugar, water, corn syrup, butter and vanilla; beat on low speed until sugar is moistened. Beat on high until smooth. Dip cake pieces into glaze, then roll in peanuts. Let stand until set.

In a small bowl, combine the sauce ingredients. Serve with nuggets. **Yield:** 2 dozen (1 cup sauce).

CURRIED CHICKEN TURNOVERS

Mary Kisinger, Calgary, Alberta

You'll want to try these party-perfect turnovers. My guests enjoy the delicious curried chicken. Plus, the puff pastry makes for an elegant snack.

    1/2 cup finely chopped celery
    1/4 cup finely chopped onion
    1/4 cup finely chopped carrot
      2 teaspoons butter
      1 tablespoon all-purpose flour
1-1/2 teaspoons curry powder
    1/4 teaspoon salt
    1/2 cup chicken broth
1-1/2 cups diced cooked chicken
    1/4 cup sour cream
    1/4 cup plain yogurt
      1 package (17.3 ounces) frozen puff
        pastry, thawed
      1 egg yolk
      1 teaspoon water

In a large skillet, saute the celery, onion and carrot in butter for 4-6 minutes or until tender. Stir in the flour, curry powder and salt until blended. Add broth. Bring to a boil; cook and stir for 1 minute or until thickened. Remove from the heat. Stir in the chicken, sour cream and yogurt.

On a lightly floured surface, roll each pastry sheet into a 12-in. x 10-in. rectangle. With a floured 3-in. round cookie cutter, cut out 12 circles from each rectangle. Place 2 teaspoons chick-en mixture on one side of each circle. Moisten edges with water; fold dough over filling. Press edges with a fork to seal.

Place 1 in. apart on a greased baking sheet. In a small bowl, beat egg yolk and water; brush over pastry. Bake at 400° for 17-20 minutes or until golden brown. Serve warm. **Yield:** 2 dozen.

FESTIVE BAKED BRIE
(Pictured above)

Genny Derer, Madison, Wisconsin

In this recipe, rich, smooth Brie cheese accented with caramelized onions is reminiscent of fondue. With a red and green tomato and herb topping, it's quite a showpiece on a buffet table.

      1 large onion, halved and thinly sliced
      2 tablespoons butter
      2 tablespoons olive oil
    1/2 cup oil-packed sun-dried tomatoes,
        drained and chopped
    1/4 cup minced fresh parsley
      2 tablespoons minced fresh basil
Dash pepper
      1 round (8 ounces) Brie *or* Camembert
        cheese
Assorted crackers

In a large skillet over medium heat, cook onion in butter and oil for 15-20 minutes or until golden brown, stirring frequently; set aside.

In a small bowl, combine the tomatoes, parsley, basil and pepper. Remove rind from the top of the Brie; place Brie in an ungreased oven-proof serving dish. Top with tomato mixture and onion mixture.

Bake, uncovered, at 400° for 10-12 minutes or until cheese is softened. Serve warm with crackers. **Yield:** 6-8 servings.

WASSAIL BOWL PUNCH
(Pictured below)

Margaret Harms, Jenkins, Kentucky

All ages enjoy my heartwarming punch. The blend of spices, fruit and citrus flavors is scrumptious. You can assemble it before heading out for a winter activity and sip away the chill when you return. It's ready whenever you are.

✓ Uses less fat, sugar or salt. Includes Nutrition Facts.

    4 cups hot brewed tea
    4 cups cranberry juice
    4 cups unsweetened apple juice
    2 cups orange juice
    1 cup sugar
  3/4 cup lemon juice
    3 cinnamon sticks (3 inches)
   12 whole cloves

In a 5-qt. slow cooker, combine the first six ingredients. Place the cinnamon sticks and cloves on a double thickness of cheesecloth; bring up corners of cloth and tie with string to form a bag. Add to slow cooker. Cover and cook on high for 1 hour or until punch begins to boil. Discard spice bag. Serve warm. **Yield:** 3-1/2 quarts.

Nutrition Facts: 1 cup equals 143 calories, trace fat (trace saturated fat), 0 cholesterol, 6 mg sodium, 36 g carbohydrate, trace fiber, 1 g protein.

SESAME SALMON SPREAD
(Pictured above)

Sandy Sanford, Anchorage, Alaska

Alaska is known for its salmon, and this is one of our favorite appetizers. I pack the spread and crackers in our picnic lunch when my husband and I head out to harvest wood, which we do several times a year.

    1 package (8 ounces) cream cheese,
      softened
    2 tablespoons lemon juice
    1 can (14-3/4 ounces) salmon, drained,
      bones and skin removed
  1/4 cup sour cream
    1 garlic clove, minced
    2 tablespoons sesame seeds
    2 teaspoons Liquid Smoke, optional
    1 teaspoon minced fresh cilantro
    1 teaspoon minced fresh parsley
  1/4 teaspoon dill weed
  1/4 teaspoon salt
  1/8 teaspoon pepper
Assorted crackers

In a small mixing bowl, beat cream cheese and lemon juice until fluffy. Add the salmon, sour cream, garlic, sesame seeds, Liquid Smoke if desired, cilantro, parsley, dill, salt and pepper; stir until blended. Cover and refrigerate for at least 2 hours. Serve with crackers. Refrigerate leftovers. **Yield:** 2-1/2 cups.

WARM UP TO STEAMY SIPPERS

For hot beverages, avoid shattering your serving bowl by making sure the bowl is heat-resistant. Consider warming the bowl with warm water before adding the hot punch.

 MOCHA FONDUE
(Pictured below)

Karen Boehner, Glen Elder, Kansas

At our friends' 25th anniversary celebration, several couples had fun enjoying this chocolate fondue. With fresh fruit, marshmallows, pretzels and vanilla wafers as their dippers, everyone dove into dessert.

    2 cups (12 ounces) semisweet chocolate
      chips
  1/4 cup butter
    1 cup heavy whipping cream
    3 tablespoons strong brewed coffee
  1/8 teaspoon salt
    2 egg yolks, beaten
Cubed pound cake, sliced bananas and fresh
      strawberries and pineapple chunks

In a heavy saucepan, melt the chocolate chips, butter, cream, coffee and salt. Stir 1/2 cup into egg yolks; return all to the pan. Cook and stir until mixture reaches 160°. Transfer to a fondue pot and keep warm. Serve with cake and fruit. **Yield:** 10 servings.

ALMOND SNACK CAKE
(Pictured above)

Mary Lou Crabill, Peyton, Colorado

My oldest son was allergic to chocolate, so I had to find goodies to make without it. These treats filled the bill. In fact, my son is 47 now, so I've been making this recipe for a long time! With its great almond flavor, this snack cake is also popular at bake sales.

    4 eggs
2-1/4 cups sugar, *divided*
    1 cup butter, melted
    2 cups all-purpose flour
  1/4 teaspoon salt
1-1/2 teaspoons almond extract
  1/2 cup sliced almonds

In a mixing bowl, beat the eggs until light and lemon-colored. Gradually add 2 cups sugar, beating until combined. Stir in the butter, flour, salt and extract. Spread into a greased 13-in. x 9-in. x 2-in. baking pan. Sprinkle with almonds and remaining sugar.

Bake at 350° for 25-30 minutes or until a toothpick inserted near the center comes out clean. Cool on a wire rack. **Yield:** 24 servings.

MOCHA FIRESIDE COFFEE

Gladys Goldstone, Nanaimo, British Columbia

Warm up on a cold day with this coffee mix. You can prepare it in advance and just add boiling water when you want a tasty mugful. It also makes a nice gift.

 Uses less fat, sugar or salt. Includes
Nutrition Facts.

18   Snacks & Beverages

2-1/2 cups powdered nondairy creamer
2 cups hot cocoa mix
1 cup instant coffee granules
1 cup Ovaltine chocolate drink mix
1/4 cup sugar
2 teaspoons ground cinnamon
1/2 teaspoon ground nutmeg

Mix all ingredients. Store in an airtight container. To serve, add 1 tablespoon mix to 3/4 cup boiling water. **Yield:** 6 cups mix (96 servings).

Nutrition Facts: 1 cup equals 43 calories, 1 g fat (1 g saturated fat), trace cholesterol, 20 mg sodium, 9 g carbohydrate, trace fiber, trace protein.

CRANBERRY CAMEMBERT PIZZA
(Pictured below)

Heidi Mellon, Waukesha, Wisconsin

After I'd tasted this quick, yummy pizza at a party, I just knew I had to have the recipe. I've been serving it at my house for years, and it always disappears in a few minutes.

1 tube (13.8 ounces) refrigerated pizza crust
8 ounces Camembert *or* Brie cheese, rind removed and cut into 1/2-inch cubes
3/4 cup whole-berry cranberry sauce
1/2 cup chopped pecans

Unroll crust onto a lightly greased 12-in. pizza pan; flatten dough and build up edges slightly. Bake at 425° for 10-12 minutes or until light golden brown.

Sprinkle cheese over crust. Spoon cranberry sauce evenly over crust; sprinkle with pecans. Bake 8-10 minutes longer or until cheese is melted and crust is golden brown. Cool for 5 minutes before cutting. **Yield:** 12-14 slices.

ARTICHOKES WITH LEMON-MINT DRESSING
(Pictured above)

Here's a light green, fresh-tasting dressing that's simply perfect with steamed artichokes. Our Test Kitchen staff even suggests making a double batch of the dressing to use with leafy greens.

4 medium artichokes
1 package (12.3 ounces) silken firm tofu
4 teaspoons minced fresh mint *or* 1-1/4 teaspoons dried mint
4 teaspoons lemon juice
1 tablespoon olive oil
2-1/2 teaspoons honey mustard
1 teaspoon grated lemon peel
3/4 teaspoon salt
1/4 teaspoon curry powder
1/4 teaspoon pepper

Place the artichokes upside down in a steamer basket; place in a saucepan over 1 in. of boiling water. Cover and steam for 20-25 minutes or until tender.

Meanwhile, for dressing, combine the remaining ingredients in a blender or food processor; cover and process until smooth. Serve with artichokes. **Yield:** 4 servings (1 cup dressing).

ENJOYING ARTICHOKES

Eating whole artichokes is a tasty experience! Start on the outside of the artichoke, removing petals, one at a time. Pull each petal through your teeth to remove the soft, pulpy portion. Discard petals. The fuzzy, center portion is the "choke" and shouldn't be eaten. The meaty bottom, or heart, is completely edible.

SAVOR *the goodness of a hearty bowl of soup, a sandwich piled-high with deli favorites or a salad loaded with garden-fresh appeal. It's easy with this chapter!*

CHASING CHILLS. Three Meat Chili (p. 21).

THREE MEAT CHILI

(Pictured at left)

Jan Pinard, Sabattus, Maine

A combination of pork tenderloin, ground turkey and ground beef makes this chili unique. Instead of pinto beans, you can use kidney beans, white beans or black beans. It makes a big batch, but don't worry if you have leftovers—the chili is even better the next day.

1-1/2 pounds pork tenderloin, cubed
1 large onion, chopped
1 medium green pepper, chopped
3 tablespoons olive oil
1 pound ground turkey
1 pound ground beef
2 cans (15 ounces *each*) pinto beans, rinsed and drained
2 cans (14-1/2 ounces *each*) diced tomatoes, undrained
1 can (28 ounces) baked beans
3 garlic cloves, minced
1/4 cup chili powder
1 tablespoon all-purpose flour
2 to 3 teaspoons ground cumin
1 teaspoon salt
1/2 teaspoon crushed red pepper flakes
1/4 teaspoon pepper

In a Dutch oven or soup kettle, cook the pork, onion and green pepper in oil over medium heat until meat is no longer pink.

Meanwhile, in a large skillet, cook turkey and beef over medium heat until no longer pink; drain. Drain pork mixture; add turkey and beef.

Stir in the remaining ingredients. Bring to a boil. Reduce heat; cover and simmer for 1 hour or until flavors are blended. **Yield:** 12 servings (3 quarts).

EASY SAUERKRAUT SALAD

Diane Hays, Morris, Minnesota

Five ingredients are all you need for a tasty, change-of-pace salad. It's nutritious, simple and folks always come back for more.

 Uses less fat, sugar or salt. Includes Nutrition Facts.

1 can (27 ounces) sauerkraut, rinsed and drained
1 cup finely chopped celery
1 cup finely chopped onion
1 jar (2 ounces) chopped pimientos, drained
1 cup sugar

In a large bowl, combine the first four ingredients. Pour sugar over and mix well. Cover and refrigerate overnight. Serve chilled. **Yield:** 8-10 servings.

Nutrition Facts: 1 cup equals 101 calories, trace fat (trace saturated fat), 0 cholesterol, 518 mg sodium, 25 g carbohydrate, 3 g fiber, 1 g protein.

GREEN BEAN-TOMATO SALAD

Ann Ingalls, Gladstone, Missouri

This deliciously different way to dress up green beans is sure to become a favorite at your house. The snappy dressing enhances the fresh flavor of beans, tomatoes and onions.

1 pound fresh green beans, trimmed and halved
2 medium tomatoes, sliced
1 small onion, sliced
1/3 cup olive oil
3 tablespoons red wine vinegar
1 teaspoon Dijon mustard
1/4 teaspoon salt
1/8 teaspoon pepper

Steam green beans for 6 minutes or just until crisp-tender. Immerse in cold water; drain.

Place beans in the center of a large plate. Arrange tomato and onion slices around beans. Whisk together remaining ingredients and pour over vegetables. Chill until ready to serve. **Yield:** 4-6 servings.

BUYING GREEN BEANS

Select green beans with slender green pods that are free of bruises or brown spots. Store unwashed fresh green beans in a resealable plastic bag for up to 4 days. Wash just before using, removing strings and ends if necessary.

■▪■▪■▪■▪■▪■▪■

CANTALOUPE CHICKEN-ORZO SALAD
(Pictured above)

Too hot to cook? Then try a main-dish salad served on cool, refreshing cantaloupe wedges. Our home economists enjoyed the salad alongside grainy muffins.

✓ Uses less fat, sugar or salt. Includes Nutrition Facts and Diabetic Exchanges.

1/2 cup uncooked orzo pasta
1 snack-size cup (4 ounces) pineapple tidbits
1/2 cup fat-free mayonnaise
1/3 cup fat-free plain yogurt
4 teaspoons lemon juice
1 teaspoon minced fresh mint
1 teaspoon grated lemon peel
1 teaspoon honey
1/4 teaspoon salt
1/8 teaspoon pepper
2 cups cubed cooked chicken breast
1/2 cup chopped celery
1/3 cup chopped sweet red pepper
1/4 cup chopped green onions
1 small cantaloupe, quartered and seeded
1/4 cup unsalted cashews

Cook pasta according to package directions. Meanwhile, drain pineapple, reserving juice; set pineapple aside. In a small bowl, whisk the mayonnaise, yogurt, lemon juice, mint, lemon peel, honey, salt, pepper and pineapple juice until smooth.

Drain pasta and rinse in cold water. Place in a large bowl; add the chicken, celery, red pepper, onions and pineapple. Add mayonnaise mixture and toss to coat. Serve on cantaloupe wedges. Sprinkle with cashews. **Yield:** 4 servings.

Nutrition Facts: 1 serving equals 345 calories, 8 g fat (2 g saturated fat), 58 mg cholesterol, 473 mg sodium, 43 g carbohydrate, 4 g fiber, 27 g protein. **Diabetic Exchanges:** 3 very lean meat, 2 starch, 1 fruit, 1 fat.

■▪■▪■▪■▪■▪■▪■

SPICED-UP CHICKEN SALAD
(Pictured below)

Iola Egle, Bella Vista, Arkansas

A unique combination of basil and mint in the dressing adds fresh appeal to this outstanding salad. The recipe comes with my tried-and-true approval.

1/3 cup lime juice
2 tablespoons brown sugar
1 tablespoon minced fresh basil *or* 1 teaspoon dried basil
1 tablespoon minced fresh mint *or* 1 teaspoon dried mint
1 tablespoon soy sauce
1-1/2 teaspoons minced garlic, *divided*
1/4 teaspoon ground ginger
1/4 cup olive oil
1-1/2 pounds boneless skinless chicken breasts, cut into strips
1 jalapeno pepper, seeded and chopped
1/4 teaspoon salt
1/8 teaspoon white pepper
1/8 teaspoon paprika
1 package (5 ounces) spring mix salad greens
2 large sweet red peppers, julienned
1 small cucumber, halved and sliced

In a small saucepan, combine the lime juice, brown sugar, basil, mint, soy sauce, 1/2 teaspoon garlic and ginger. Slowly whisk in oil; set aside.

In a large nonstick skillet coated with cooking spray, saute chicken until no longer pink. Add the jalapeno, salt, white pepper, paprika and remaining garlic; saute 1 minute longer.

Place salad greens on a large platter; top with red peppers, cucumber and chicken. Bring lime juice mixture to a boil; drizzle over salad. Serve immediately. **Yield:** 6 servings.

Editor's Note: When cutting or seeding hot peppers, use rubber or plastic gloves to protect your hands. Avoid touching your face.

ANTIPASTO SALAD PLATTER

Webbie Carvajal, Alpine, Texas

This salad is made for nights when it's just too hot to cook. I used to work in a pizza and sub shop, where this platter was popular.

- 1/2 pound fully cooked ham, diced
- 1 jar (10 ounces) pimiento-stuffed olives, drained and sliced
- 1 can (3.8 ounces) sliced ripe olives, drained
- 1 package (3-1/2 ounces) sliced pepperoni, quartered
- 8 cups shredded lettuce
- 10 to 12 cherry tomatoes, quartered
- 1 cup Italian salad dressing
- 1-1/2 cups (6 ounces) shredded part-skim mozzarella cheese

In a bowl, combine the ham, olives and pepperoni. On a platter or individual salad plates, arrange the lettuce, olive mixture and tomatoes. Drizzle with dressing; sprinkle with cheese. **Yield:** 8 servings.

RICH BROCCOLI CREAM SOUP

Carol Macagno, Fresno, California

Go ahead and indulge in a bowl of this rich and creamy soup…it's deliciously thick, flavorful and full of broccoli. Homemade soup never tasted so good!

- 4 celery ribs, chopped
- 1 large onion, chopped
- 3 tablespoons butter
- 2 bunches broccoli, trimmed and coarsely chopped (about 8 cups)
- 1-1/2 cups chicken broth
- 2 teaspoons garlic salt
- 1/2 teaspoon pepper
- 2 tablespoons cornstarch
- 1/4 cup water
- 1 pint heavy whipping cream

In a saucepan, saute celery and onion in butter until tender. Add broccoli, broth, garlic salt and pepper; bring to a boil. Reduce heat; cover and simmer for 45 minutes or until broccoli is tender.

In a small bowl, combine cornstarch and water until smooth. Stir into soup. Bring to a boil; cook and stir for 2 minutes or until thickened. Reduce heat to low. Stir in the cream; cook 10 minutes longer or until the soup is heated through. **Yield:** 6-8 servings.

BEEF-STUFFED FRENCH BREAD
(Pictured above)

Erin Gee, Fort Collins, Colorado

A wonderful lady in Spanish Fork, Utah shared this recipe with me—it fed her large farm family, and now I serve it to my family and friends. Using Colorado beef and an Idaho potato makes this hearty sandwich a real Western meal! If you have a leftover baked potato from dinner, this is a perfect way to use it.

- 1 pound ground beef
- 1/2 cup chopped onion
- 1 large baked potato, peeled and cubed
- 1 can (10-3/4 ounces) condensed cream of mushroom soup, undiluted
- 1 can (4 ounces) mushroom stems and pieces, drained
- 1 teaspoon dried parsley flakes
- 1/4 teaspoon garlic powder
- 1/8 teaspoon pepper
- Dash hot pepper sauce
- 1 loaf (1 pound) French bread
- 1 cup (4 ounces) shredded cheddar cheese

In a large skillet, cook the beef and onion over medium heat until meat is no longer pink; drain. Add the potato, soup, mushrooms, parsley, garlic powder, pepper and hot pepper sauce; cover and simmer for 10 minutes.

Meanwhile, cut the loaf of bread in half lengthwise. Hollow out bottom of loaf, leaving a 3/4-in. shell; set aside. Place the removed bread in a blender; cover and process until crumbled. Add 1 cup of crumbs to beef mixture (save remaining crumbs for another use). Stir in cheese.

Spoon beef mixture into bread shell; replace bread top. Wrap in heavy-duty foil; place on a baking sheet. Bake at 350° for 20 minutes. Let stand for 5 minutes before slicing. **Yield:** 6-8 servings.

MARINATED MOZZARELLA TOSSED SALAD
(Pictured below)

Pam Bremson, Kansas City, Missouri

Here's a special salad that's made with mozzarella cheese, grape tomatoes and a flavorful homemade dressing from balsamic vinegar and apricot nectar.

✓ Uses less fat, sugar or salt. Includes Nutrition Facts and Diabetic Exchanges.

- 2 tablespoons balsamic vinegar
- 2 tablespoons apricot nectar
- 1 garlic clove, minced
- 1/4 teaspoon salt
- 1/4 teaspoon *each* dried basil, oregano and thyme
- 1/8 teaspoon pepper
- 2 tablespoons olive oil
- 4 ounces part-skim mozzarella cheese, cut into 1/2-inch cubes
- 6 cups torn romaine
- 1 cup grape tomatoes, halved

In a small bowl, whisk the vinegar, apricot nectar, garlic, salt, basil, oregano, thyme and pepper. Slowly whisk in the oil. Add cheese cubes and toss to coat. Cover and refrigerate for 1 hour.

Just before serving, toss the romaine, tomatoes and cheese mixture in a large salad bowl. **Yield:** 6 servings.

Nutrition Facts: 1 cup equals 113 calories, 8 g fat (3 g saturated fat), 10 mg cholesterol, 206 mg sodium, 5 g carbohydrate, 1 g fiber, 6 g protein. **Diabetic Exchanges:** 1 lean meat, 1 vegetable, 1 fat.

RAG DOLL SALAD
(Pictured above)

Donna Van Horn, Inverness, Florida

Both kids and adults alike will enjoy lunching with these cutie-pie dolls. They make having a delicious salad both healthy and fun...so, go ahead and play with your food!

- 1 hard-cooked egg, cut lengthwise in half
- 2 tablespoons carrot curls
- 4 whole cloves
- 2 pimiento strips
- 1 medium tomato, halved
- 2 pitted ripe olives, halved
- 2/3 cup chicken *or* tuna salad
- 2 lettuce leaves
- 8 baby carrots
- 1 teaspoon mayonnaise

For each salad, place an egg half at the top of a plate for doll's head. Arrange carrot curls around egg for hair. Insert cloves for eyes; position a pimiento strip for mouth.

Place a tomato half below the egg; add olive halves for buttons. Spoon chicken salad below tomato; place a lettuce leaf over salad for skirt. For arms and legs, place baby carrots on either side of tomato and below the lettuce.

Place mayonnaise in a small pastry or plastic bag; cut a small hole in a corner of bag. Pipe stripes on carrot legs for stockings. Discard cloves before eating. **Yield:** 2 servings.

SPINACH SALAD

Paula Crabtree, Alma, Arkansas

This leafy salad is accented with bacon, hard-cooked eggs, bean sprouts, water chestnuts and an easy homemade dressing. It was a hit when I served it at the National Spinach Conference last year.

☑ Uses less fat, sugar or salt. Includes Nutrition Facts.

1/3 cup sugar
1/3 cup white vinegar
1/3 cup ketchup
1/3 cup vegetable oil
1 tablespoon Worcestershire sauce
SALAD:
1 pound fresh baby spinach
1 can (14 ounces) canned bean sprouts, drained
1 can (8 ounces) sliced water chestnuts, drained
2 medium onions, sliced
2 hard-cooked eggs, sliced
1/4 cup real bacon bits

In a jar with a tight-fitting lid, combine the sugar, vinegar, ketchup, oil and Worcestershire sauce; shake well. Cover and refrigerate until serving.

In a large bowl, combine the spinach, bean sprouts, water chestnuts, onions and eggs. Just before serving, shake dressing and pour over salad; toss to coat. Sprinkle with bacon. Serve immediately. **Yield:** 12 servings.

Nutrition Facts: 2 cups equals 136 calories, 7 g fat (1 g saturated fat), 37 mg cholesterol, 218 mg sodium, 15 g carbohydrate, 3 g fiber, 4 g protein.

BERRY PEACH TOSSED SALAD

Maryvonne Martin, Orangevale, California

Loaded with fresh peaches and berries, this salad perfectly summarizes summer eating. It is a wonderful accompaniment to grilled meats, poultry or seafood.

3 tablespoons olive oil
3 tablespoons orange juice
3 tablespoons lemon juice
1/4 teaspoon salt
1/4 teaspoon pepper
3 romaine hearts, torn
1 medium red onion, halved and thinly sliced
1/2 cup crumbled feta cheese
2 medium peaches, thinly sliced
1 cup fresh raspberries
1 cup fresh blackberries

For dressing, in a small bowl, whisk the first five ingredients. In a large salad bowl, combine the romaine, onion, feta cheese and peaches. Drizzle with dressing and toss gently. Sprinkle with raspberries and blackberries. Serve immediately. **Yield:** 6 servings.

CREAMY TOMATO BASIL SOUP
(Pictured below)

Linda Manuszak, Clinton Township, Michigan

I created this soup while trying to duplicate one I enjoyed at a restaurant in Philadelphia. It isn't exactly right, but it's close! My husband and I love it on cold nights with grilled cheese sandwiches.

2 tablespoons chopped green onion
2 garlic cloves, minced
1-1/2 teaspoons olive oil
1 can (28 ounces) crushed tomatoes
1 can (10-1/2 ounces) condensed chicken broth, undiluted
1-1/3 cups water
1/4 teaspoon pepper
3/4 cup heavy whipping cream
2 tablespoons sherry *or* additional chicken broth
2 tablespoons minced fresh basil
2 teaspoons sugar

In a large saucepan, saute onion and garlic in oil until tender. Add the tomatoes, broth, water and pepper. Bring to a boil. Reduce heat; simmer for 10 minutes.

Stir in the cream, sherry or additional broth, basil and sugar. Cook for 1 minute or until heated through (do not boil). **Yield:** 6 servings.

FRUITY APPLE SALAD
(Pictured above)

Carol Forcum, Marion, Illinois

Lots of apples are grown in southern Illinois, and this is one of my favorite ways to use them. I like Golden Delicious, or a combination of Golden and Red Delicious for pretty color, but you can use whatever type of apple you prefer. The cooked dressing gives the salad an old-fashioned feel.

☑ Uses less fat, sugar or salt. Includes Nutrition Facts.

1/4 cup sugar
1/4 cup packed brown sugar
1 tablespoon all-purpose flour
2/3 cup water
1 egg, lightly beaten
1 teaspoon white vinegar
1-1/2 teaspoons butter
3 medium apples, diced
2 medium firm bananas, sliced
1/3 cup diced celery
1/2 cup seedless red grapes, halved
1/2 cup fresh pineapple chunks
1/3 cup chopped cashews

For dressing, in a small saucepan, combine the sugars, flour and water until blended. Bring to a boil over medium heat; cook and stir for 2 minutes or until thickened. Remove from the heat.

Stir a small amount into the egg; return all to the pan. Cook and stir until mixture reaches 160° and coats the back of a metal spoon. Remove from the heat; gently stir in vinegar and butter. Cool mixture completely.

In a large bowl, combine the apples, bananas, celery, grapes, pineapple and cashews. Drizzle with dressing and toss to coat. Cover and refrigerate until chilled. Serve with a slotted spoon. **Yield:** 8 servings.

Nutrition Facts: 3/4 cup equals 172 calories, 4 g fat (1 g saturated fat), 28 mg cholesterol, 59 mg sodium, 34 g carbohydrate, 3 g fiber, 2 g protein.

ZIPPY CHICKEN WRAPS
(Pictured below)

Jackie Smulski, Lyons, Illinois

This is a nice sandwich for hot summer days or picnics. If you're in a hurry, you can use precooked chicken tenders.

1/2 pound boneless skinless chicken breast, cut into thin slices
1 tablespoon butter
1 garlic clove, minced
1 teaspoon chili powder
1/2 teaspoon ground cumin
Dash cayenne pepper
1 package (3 ounces) cream cheese, softened
1/2 cup shredded cheddar cheese
1/4 cup sour cream
1 can (10 ounces) diced tomatoes and green chilies, drained
2 green onions, thinly sliced
4 flour tortillas (8 inches)
Sliced avocado, sliced ripe olives and salsa

In a large skillet, saute the chicken in butter until no longer pink. Add the garlic, chili powder, cumin and cayenne; cook and stir until heated through. Remove from the heat; cool.

In a small mixing bowl, beat the cream cheese, cheddar cheese and sour cream. Stir in the chicken, tomatoes and onions.

Spoon 1/2 cup chicken mixture down the center of each tortilla; top with avocado and olives. Fold sides over filling and secure with a toothpick if desired. Serve with salsa. **Yield:** 4 servings.

CHUNKY CRANBERRY SALAD

Joyce Butterfield, Nancy, Kentucky

I found this recipe while taking a cooking class. Full of mixed fruit, celery and nuts, it's a lively alternative to jellied cranberry sauce.

    4 cups fresh *or* frozen cranberries
3-1/2 cups unsweetened pineapple juice
    2 envelopes unflavored gelatin
  1/2 cup cold water
    2 cups sugar
    1 can (20 ounces) unsweetened pineapple tidbits, drained
    1 cup chopped pecans
    1 cup green grapes, chopped
  1/2 cup finely chopped celery
    2 teaspoons grated orange peel

In a large saucepan, combine the cranberries and pineapple juice. Cook over medium heat until berries pop, about 15 minutes.

Meanwhile, in a small bowl, sprinkle gelatin over cold water; let stand for 5 minutes. In a large bowl, combine the berry mixture, sugar and softened gelatin. Chill until partially set.

Fold in the pineapple, pecans, grapes, celery and orange peel. Pour into individual serving dishes. Chill until firm. **Yield:** 12 servings.

COUNTRY SAUSAGE SOUP

Grace Meyer, Galva, Kansas

Savory pork sausage, two kinds of beans and diced tomatoes make this soup one I prepare time and again. It's a hearty fix for when I don't know what to prepare for supper.

  3/4 pound bulk pork sausage
    1 can (14-1/2 ounces) diced tomatoes, undrained
    1 can (14-1/2 ounces) chicken broth
    1 teaspoon dried thyme
  3/4 to 1 teaspoon dried rosemary, crushed
  1/4 teaspoon pepper
    1 can (15-1/2 ounces) great northern beans, rinsed and drained
    1 can (15 ounces) garbanzo beans *or* chickpeas, rinsed and drained

In a large saucepan, cook sausage over medium heat until no longer pink; drain. Stir in the tomatoes, broth, thyme, rosemary and pepper. Bring to a boil. Stir in the beans; heat through. **Yield:** 4 servings.

AVOCADO-ORANGE SPINACH TOSS

Margaret O'Bryon, Bel Air, Maryland

Baby spinach, mandarin oranges and avocado are teamed in this refreshing springtime salad. You can also substitute fresh orange slices for the can of mandarin oranges.

☑ Uses less fat, sugar or salt. Includes Nutrition Facts and Diabetic Exchanges.

  1/4 cup orange juice
4-1/2 teaspoons lemon juice
    1 tablespoon sugar
    1 tablespoon white wine vinegar
    1 tablespoon canola oil
  1/4 teaspoon grated orange peel
Dash salt
    6 cups fresh baby spinach
    1 can (11 ounces) mandarin oranges, drained
    1 small cucumber, thinly sliced
  1/2 medium ripe avocado, peeled and sliced

For dressing, in a small bowl, combine the first seven ingredients.

Place the spinach in a large salad bowl; top with the oranges, cucumber and avocado. Drizzle with the dressing and gently toss to coat. **Yield:** 8 servings.

Nutrition Facts: 1-1/4 cups equals 71 calories, 4 g fat (trace saturated fat), 0 cholesterol, 38 mg sodium, 9 g carbohydrate, 1 g fiber, 1 g protein. **Diabetic Exchanges:** 1 fat, 1/2 fruit.

Salads Are Summer Picnic Staples

WHEN planning a picnic, backyard barbecue or even a warm-weather reunion, make sure to add a few of these must-try salads to the menu.

SUMMER BEAN SALAD

Roberta Freedman, Mesilla Park, New Mexico

I've been making this recipe for over 30 years, and it always seems to be a favorite. This isn't your average bean salad, though—the mandarin oranges make it unique and refreshing.

> 2 cans (11 ounces *each*) mandarin oranges, drained
> 1 can (16 ounces) kidney beans, rinsed and drained
> 1 can (15 ounces) garbanzo beans *or* chickpeas, rinsed and drained
> 1 medium green pepper, chopped
> 1/2 cup chopped red onion
> 1/4 cup minced fresh parsley
> 1/2 cup vegetable oil
> 1/4 cup red wine vinegar
> 1 teaspoon sugar

In a large bowl, combine the oranges, beans, green pepper, onion and parsley. In a jar with a tight-fitting lid, combine the oil, red wine vinegar and sugar; shake well.

Pour over salad and toss to coat. Cover and refrigerate for at least 4 hours before serving. **Yield:** 6 servings.

CONFETTI BROCCOLI SLAW
(Pictured at right)

Kathy Murphy, Fort Thomas, Arizona

With its flavorful dressing and flecks of tomato and green pepper, my pretty coleslaw is great for a variety of summertime meals. Instead of purchasing the broccoli coleslaw mix, you can use broccoli stalks—just peel them, then shred in a food processor. You'll want about 3 cups for this recipe.

> 1 package (12 ounces) broccoli coleslaw mix
> 1 medium green pepper, chopped
> 1 medium tomato, seeded and chopped
> 1 small onion, finely chopped
> 1/2 teaspoon salt
> 1/4 teaspoon pepper
> DRESSING:
> 1/2 cup mayonnaise
> 1/3 cup sugar
> 2 tablespoons cider vinegar
> 2 tablespoons ketchup
> 1 tablespoon vegetable oil
> 1-1/2 teaspoons prepared mustard
> 1 teaspoon lemon juice
> 1/8 teaspoon paprika
> 1/8 teaspoon pepper
> 1/8 teaspoon salt
> Dash garlic powder
> Dash hot pepper sauce

In a large bowl, combine the coleslaw mix, green pepper, tomato, onion, salt and pepper. In a blender or food processor, combine the dressing ingredients; cover and process until blended. Pour over coleslaw and toss to coat. Cover and refrigerate for at least 2 hours before serving. **Yield:** 6 servings.

3 cups uncooked spiral pasta
1 pound ground beef
1 envelope taco seasoning
1-1/4 cups mayonnaise
2 to 3 tablespoons milk
3-3/4 teaspoons cider vinegar
3-3/4 teaspoons sugar
1 tablespoon ground mustard
7 cups torn iceberg lettuce
1 to 2 medium tomatoes, chopped
2 cups (8 ounces) shredded cheddar cheese
1 to 2 cups crushed nacho tortilla chips

Cook pasta according to package directions. Meanwhile, in a large skillet, cook beef over medium heat until no longer pink; drain. Stir in taco seasoning; heat through.

In a small bowl, combine the mayonnaise, milk, vinegar, sugar and mustard; set aside. Drain pasta; place in a large bowl. Add beef and mayonnaise mixture; toss to coat. Add lettuce, tomatoes and cheese; toss to combine. Sprinkle with tortilla chips. **Yield:** 12-14 servings.

COLORFUL CAULIFLOWER SALAD
(Pictured above)

Dorothy Joiner, Warsaw, Missouri

Bacon, cheese, tomatoes and olives really dress up plain old cauliflower. Even my husband admits that this salad is delicious!

6 cups fresh cauliflowerets
3 plum tomatoes, chopped
1 cup thinly sliced green onions
1 cup (4 ounces) shredded cheddar cheese
1/2 cup sliced pimiento-stuffed olives
1/2 cup mayonnaise
12 bacon strips, cooked and crumbled

In a large bowl, combine the cauliflower, tomatoes, onions, cheese and olives. Add mayonnaise; toss to coat. Cover and refrigerate for at least 1 hour. Just before serving, sprinkle with bacon. **Yield:** 10 cups.

TACO PASTA SALAD

Mary Bergen, Winnipegosis, Manitoba

I've taken this dish to 4-H potlucks and such. It's a tasty salad with a little spunk!

DILLY COLESLAW

Carrie Roberts, Porterville, California

When I took this coleslaw to a church function, I came home with an empty bowl! With chopped dill pickles and a sweet-tart dressing made of pickle juice, it's not your typical slaw.

8 cups shredded cabbage
1/2 cup chopped dill pickles
1/4 cup finely chopped onion
1/2 cup sugar
1/2 cup mayonnaise
1/4 cup milk
1/4 cup dill pickle juice
1 teaspoon salt
1/4 teaspoon garlic powder
1/4 teaspoon pepper

In a large bowl, combine the cabbage, pickles and onion. In a small bowl, whisk the remaining ingredients until smooth.

Pour over cabbage mixture and toss to coat. Cover and refrigerate for at least 2 hours. Serve with a slotted spoon. **Yield:** 8 servings.

SMOTHERED ONION PATTY MELTS
(Pictured below)

Margie Jarvis, Decatur, Tennessee

Looking for a new twist on burgers? Try this patty melt that's loaded with onions and Swiss cheese. You can even create the melts with ground turkey if you like.

          2 medium onions, sliced
          1 teaspoon vegetable oil
      1/8 teaspoon plus 1/2 teaspoon salt, *divided*
      1/4 teaspoon pepper, *divided*
          2 teaspoons Dijon mustard
          1 garlic clove, minced
      1/4 teaspoon dried thyme
      1/4 teaspoon dried oregano
          1 pound ground beef *or* turkey
          8 slices rye bread, toasted
          4 slices Swiss cheese

In a large nonstick skillet, saute onions in oil for 3 minutes. Sprinkle with 1/8 teaspoon salt and 1/8 teaspoon pepper. Reduce heat; cover and simmer for 25-30 minutes or until onions are tender.

Meanwhile, in a large bowl, combine the mustard, garlic, thyme, oregano and remaining salt and pepper. Crumble beef over mixture and mix well. Shape into four patties.

Grill patties, covered, over medium-hot heat for 6-8 minutes on each side or until a meat thermometer reads 160°. Place each patty on a slice of toast; top with cheese, onions and remaining toast. **Yield:** 4 servings.

GRANDMA'S SPINACH SALAD

Shelley Riebel, Armada, Michigan

This was my grandma's favorite salad. It's colorful and has a sweet-sour blend to tempt any taste buds. Even my kids like it…regardless of the spinach!

      1/2 cup sugar
      1/2 cup vegetable oil
      1/4 cup white vinegar
      1/2 teaspoon celery seed
          1 package (10 ounces) fresh baby spinach
          1 small red onion, thinly sliced
      1/2 pound sliced fresh mushrooms
          5 hard-cooked eggs, sliced
          8 bacon strips, cooked and crumbled

In a jar with a tight-fitting lid, combine the sugar, oil, vinegar and celery seed; shake well. In a large salad bowl, layer half of the spinach, onion, mushrooms and eggs. Repeat layers. Top with bacon. Drizzle with dressing. **Yield:** 8 servings.

ITALIAN VEGETABLE SOUP

Phyllis Eismann Schmalz, Kansas City, Kansas

With macaroni, kidney beans, tomatoes, zucchini and lots of other veggies, this flavorful soup is hearty enough for dinner with corn bread or hot rolls. It really hits the spot on a cold day.

          2 medium carrots, diced
          1 small onion, chopped
          2 garlic cloves, minced
          1 tablespoon olive oil
          2 cans (14-1/2 ounces *each*) beef broth
          1 can (14-1/2 ounces) diced tomatoes, undrained
          2 cups water
          1 small zucchini, diced
          1 teaspoon dried basil
          1 teaspoon salt
      1/2 teaspoon dried oregano
      1/4 teaspoon pepper
          2 to 3 drops hot pepper sauce
          1 can (16 ounces) kidney beans, rinsed and drained
          1 cup chopped fresh spinach
      3/4 cup uncooked elbow macaroni
          2 tablespoons minced fresh parsley
      1/2 cup shredded Parmesan cheese

In a soup kettle or large saucepan, saute the carrots, onion and garlic in oil until tender. Stir in the broth, tomatoes, water, zucchini, basil, salt, oregano, pepper and hot pepper sauce. Bring to a boil. Re-

duce heat; cover and simmer for 15 minutes.

Stir in the kidney beans, spinach, macaroni and parsley. Cover and cook 15 minutes longer or until macaroni is tender. Garnish with Parmesan cheese. **Yield:** 6-8 servings.

⬛⬜⬛⬜⬛⬜⬛⬜⬛⬜⬛⬜⬛⬜

BLACK BEAN ASPARAGUS SALAD
(Pictured above)

Laurie Jackson, Falcon, Colorado

Do you like asparagus, but want something beyond plain, steamed asparagus? Try this refreshing idea. The black beans, red pepper, cilantro and cumin give it a Southwest twist.

 Uses less fat, sugar or salt. Includes Nutrition Facts and Diabetic Exchanges.

> 1 pound fresh asparagus, trimmed and cut into 1-inch pieces
> 1 can (15 ounces) black beans, rinsed and drained

1 medium sweet red pepper, cut into 1/2-inch pieces
1 tablespoon finely chopped onion
3 tablespoons olive oil
2 tablespoons cider vinegar
1 tablespoon minced fresh cilantro
1 garlic clove, minced
1/2 teaspoon salt
1/2 teaspoon ground cumin
Dash pepper

Place 1/2 in. of water in a large saucepan; add asparagus. Bring to a boil. Reduce heat; cover and simmer for 4-5 minutes or until crisp-tender. Drain.

In a bowl, combine the asparagus, beans, red pepper and onion. In a small bowl, whisk the oil, vinegar, cilantro, garlic, salt, cumin and pepper. Pour over vegetables and toss to coat. Cover and refrigerate for at least 2 hours before serving. **Yield:** 8 servings.

Nutrition Facts: 1/2 cup equals 100 calories, 5 g fat (1 g saturated fat), 0 cholesterol, 252 mg sodium, 10 g carbohydrate, 3 g fiber, 3 g protein. **Diabetic Exchanges:** 2 vegetable, 1 fat.

Sour Cream Potato Salad
(Pictured above)

Veda Luttrell, Sutter, California

Italian dressing and horseradish make this creamy potato salad different from most, plus those ingredients really add some zip! It's perfect for picnics, potlucks or block parties.

- 2 pounds medium red potatoes
- 1/2 cup Italian salad dressing
- 4 hard-cooked eggs
- 3/4 cup sliced celery
- 1/3 cup thinly sliced green onions
- 1 cup mayonnaise
- 1/2 cup sour cream
- 1-1/2 teaspoons prepared horseradish
- 1-1/2 teaspoons prepared mustard
- 1-1/2 teaspoons celery seed
- 3/4 teaspoon salt

Place potatoes in a large saucepan and cover with water. Bring to a boil. Reduce heat; cover and cook for 20-30 minutes or until tender. Drain.

When cool enough to handle, peel and slice potatoes. Place in a large bowl; add salad dressing and toss gently. Cover and refrigerate for 2 hours.

Slice eggs in half; remove yolks and set aside. Chop egg whites; add to the potatoes with the celery and onions.

In a small bowl, combine the mayonnaise, sour cream, horseradish, mustard, celery seed and salt. Crumble egg yolks; add to mayonnaise mixture and whisk until blended. Spoon over potatoes; toss gently to coat. Cover and refrigerate for at least 2 hours before serving. **Yield:** 8 servings.

Wild Rice Salad
(Pictured below)

Kathi Saari, Ames, Iowa

Wild rice is native to the Midwest, so this recipe is perfect for our area. We eat it cold or warmed just enough to soften the cheese and further blend the flavors. It can be served as a main dish or as a accompaniment to chicken or turkey.

- 1 cup uncooked wild rice
- 3 cups water
- 1 tablespoon instant chicken bouillon granules
- 1 cup julienned fully cooked ham
- 1 cup julienned Monterey Jack cheese
- 1 cup julienned sweet red pepper
- 1 cup broccoli florets
- 1/2 cup thinly sliced carrots
- 1/2 cup thinly sliced green onions with tops

DRESSING:
- 2 tablespoons lemon juice
- 2 tablespoons white vinegar
- 1/2 teaspoon ground mustard
- 1/2 to 1 teaspoon curry powder

Salt and pepper to taste
- 1/2 cup vegetable oil

In a medium saucepan, bring rice, water and bouillon to a boil. Reduce heat; cover and simmer for 1 hour or until the rice is tender. Drain if necessary; cool.

In a large bowl, toss rice with ham, cheese, red pepper, broccoli, carrots and green onions. For dressing, combine lemon juice, vinegar, mustard, curry powder, salt and pepper in a blender or food processor. With machine on high, slowly add oil through the feeder cap until well mixed; dressing will thicken slightly.

Pour over salad and toss to coat. Cover and chill several hours or overnight. **Yield:** 6-8 servings.

BAKED HAM 'N' CHEESE CROISSANTS

Ann Chrysler, Adrian, Michigan

You just can't go wrong with these heartwarming sand-wiches. They're a true delight on a cold, winter day.

3 large onions, sliced
1/2 cup butter, cubed
3 tablespoons Dijon mustard
1 tablespoon poppy seeds
1 tablespoon lemon juice
8 croissants, split
2 pounds shaved deli ham
1/2 pound sliced baby Swiss cheese

Place onions and butter in a large microwave-safe bowl; cover and microwave on high for 2-3 minutes or until onions are tender. Stir in the mustard, poppy seeds and lemon juice. Cover and microwave on high for 1 minute or until heated through.

Spread onion mixture over cut sides of crois-sants. On bottom halves, layer ham and cheese; replace tops.

Wrap each sandwich in foil. Place on a bak-ing sheet. Bake at 350° for 20-25 minutes or un-til cheese is melted. **Yield:** 8 servings.

Editor's Note: This recipe was tested in a 1,100-watt microwave.

SALMON BISQUE

Barbara Parks, Renton, Washington

Nutrition experts recommend two fish meals per week. This soup recipe is a tempting way to meet this dietary goal and extend expensive fresh salmon. Even though it uses 2% milk, it has a rich mouth feel. Serve with a salad and crusty whole-grain bread.

1 small sweet red pepper
1 salmon fillet (8 ounces)
1/2 cup finely chopped carrot
1 tablespoon chopped shallot
1 tablespoon canola oil
2 garlic cloves, minced
3 tablespoons all-purpose flour
1 can (14-1/2 ounces) chicken broth
2 cups 2% milk
1 teaspoon seafood seasoning
1/4 teaspoon Liquid Smoke, optional

Broil red pepper 4 in. from the heat until skin blis-ters, about 5 minutes. With tongs, rotate pepper a quarter turn. Broil and rotate until all sides are blistered and blackened. Immediately place pep-per in a bowl; cover and let stand for 15-20 min-utes. Peel off and discard charred skin. Remove stems and seeds. Set roasted pepper aside.

Broil salmon 4 in. from the heat for 7-10 min-utes on each side or until fish flakes easily with a fork. Break salmon into small pieces; set aside.

In a large saucepan, saute carrot and shallot in oil until tender. Add garlic; saute 1 minute longer. Stir in flour until blended. Gradually add broth. Bring to a boil; cook and stir for 1-2 minutes or until thickened.

Transfer to a blender; add roasted pepper. Cov-er and puree until smooth. Return to the pan. Stir in the milk, seafood seasoning, Liquid Smoke if de-sired and salmon; heat through. **Yield:** 4 servings.

12-HOUR SALAD
(Pictured above)

Dorothy Bowen, Thomasville, North Carolina

This recipe was Mom's scrumptious scheme to get her kids to eat vegetables. She thought this salad was a real bonus for the cook since it must be made the night before.

8 cups torn salad greens
1-1/2 cups chopped celery
2 medium green peppers, chopped
1 medium red onion, chopped
1 package (10 ounces) frozen peas, thawed
1 cup mayonnaise
1 cup (8 ounces) sour cream
3 tablespoons sugar
1 cup (4 ounces) shredded cheddar cheese
1/2 pound sliced bacon, cooked and crumbled

Place salad greens in a 3-qt. bowl or 13-in. x 9-in. x 2-in. dish. Top with layers of celery, green peppers, onion and peas; do not toss.

In a bowl, combine the mayonnaise, sour cream and sugar; spread over vegetables. Sprin-kle with cheese and bacon. Cover and refrigerate overnight. **Yield:** 12 servings.

CRUNCHY MARINATED VEGETABLES
(Pictured below)

Lynn Blosser, Lynnwood, Washington

I never worry about my kids getting their veggies when this sweet-and-sour salad is on the menu. My mom gave me the recipe for the eye-catching medley that has a way of disappearing in a hurry.

- 1/2 cup fresh broccoli florets
- 1/2 cup fresh cauliflowerets
- 1 small carrot, sliced
- 2 tablespoons chopped peeled kohlrabi
- 2 tablespoons chopped celery
- 2 tablespoons sliced ripe olives
- 1 large radish, sliced
- 1 tablespoon chopped green pepper

MARINADE:
- 1/4 cup sugar
- 4-1/2 teaspoons white vinegar
- 1/4 teaspoon salt
- 1/4 teaspoon ground mustard
- 4-1/2 teaspoons vegetable oil
- 1 tablespoon finely chopped onion
- 1/8 teaspoon celery seed

Dash Italian seasoning

In a small bowl, combine the first eight ingredients; set aside. In a small saucepan, combine the sugar, vinegar, salt and mustard; cook and stir over low heat just until sugar is dissolved. Pour into a bowl; cool slightly.

Add the oil, onion, celery seed and Italian seasoning; whisk until well combined. Pour over vegetables and toss to coat. Cover and refrigerate for 4 hours or overnight. Serve with a slotted spoon. **Yield:** 2 servings.

MIXED GREENS WITH FRENCH DRESSING
(Pictured above)

Thelma Harrison, Califon, New Jersey

You won't miss the oil in this tasty dressing. People have told me it's so good, they wonder why I haven't marketed it!

- 2/3 cup cider vinegar
- 2/3 cup ketchup
- 1/2 cup sugar
- 1/4 cup chopped onion
- 1-1/2 teaspoons celery salt
- 1-1/2 teaspoons paprika
- 1 teaspoon salt
- 1/2 teaspoon celery seed
- 3 cups torn curly endive
- 3 cups chopped escarole *or* torn romaine

For dressing, place the first eight ingredients in a blender or food processor; cover and process until blended. Transfer to a jar with a tight-fitting lid; cover and refrigerate for at least 1 hour.

Just before serving, combine the endive and escarole. Shake dressing and drizzle over greens. Refrigerate leftover dressing. **Yield:** 4-6 servings (about 1-1/2 cups dressing).

CALICO BLACK BEAN SALAD

Linda Holland, Lantana, Florida

This salad reflects the Caribbean culture here in South Florida. The combination of black beans, tomatoes and onions with a vinaigrette is great alongside pork or chicken. It's perfect for picnics and convenient, too, since you can make it a day ahead.

✓ Uses less fat, sugar or salt. Includes Nutrition Facts.

- 2 cans (15 ounces *each*) black beans, rinsed and drained
- 4 green onions, thinly sliced

2 plum tomatoes, chopped
1 medium onion, chopped
1 large sweet red pepper, chopped

DRESSING:
2 tablespoons olive oil
2 tablespoons red wine vinegar
1 tablespoon lemon juice
1/2 teaspoon salt
1/4 teaspoon pepper
3/4 teaspoon minced fresh basil *or*
  1/4 teaspoon dried basil

In a salad bowl, combine the beans, green onions, tomatoes, onion and red pepper. In a jar with a tight-fitting lid, combine the dressing ingredients; shake well. Drizzle over vegetables and toss to coat. Cover and refrigerate for at least 1 hour before serving. **Yield:** 6 servings.

Nutrition Facts: 3/4 cup equals 123 calories, 5 g fat (1 g saturated fat), 0 cholesterol, 336 mg sodium, 16 g carbohydrate, 4 g fiber, 4 g protein.

AMISH CHICKEN CORN SOUP

Beverly Hoffman, Sandy Lake, Pennsylvania

Cream corn and butter add richness to this homey chicken noodle soup. It makes a big batch, but it freezes well for future meals...that is one reason why soups are my favorite thing to make.

 Uses less fat, sugar or salt. Includes Nutrition Facts.

12 cups water
2 pounds boneless skinless chicken breasts, cubed
1 cup chopped onion
1 cup chopped celery
1 cup shredded carrots
3 chicken bouillon cubes
2 cans (14-3/4 ounces *each*) cream-style corn
2 cups uncooked egg noodles
1/4 cup butter
1 teaspoon salt
1/4 teaspoon pepper

In a Dutch oven or soup kettle, combine the water, chicken, onion, celery, carrots and bouillon. Bring to a boil. Reduce heat; simmer, uncovered, for 30 minutes or until chicken is no longer pink and vegetables are tender.

Stir in the corn, noodles and butter; cook 10 minutes longer or until noodles are tender. Season with salt and pepper. **Yield:** 16 servings (about 4 quarts).

Nutrition Facts: 1 cup equals 134 calories, 5 g fat (2 g saturated fat), 44 mg cholesterol, 498 mg sodium, 10 g carbohydrate, 1 g fiber, 13 g protein.

OPEN-FACED SEAFOOD SANDWICHES

(Pictured below)

Arlene Kroll, Vero Beach, Florida

Delicious seafood sandwiches are as close as your cupboard using canned crabmeat and shrimp. I add fresh parsley, lemon juice and Dijon mustard to give these noontime sandwiches a fresh taste.

4 English muffins, split and toasted
3 tablespoons butter, melted
1 can (6 ounces) lump crabmeat, drained
1 can (6 ounces) small shrimp, rinsed and drained
1 cup (4 ounces) shredded cheddar cheese, *divided*
1/2 cup chopped celery
1/2 cup chopped ripe olives
1 tablespoon minced fresh parsley
1/4 cup mayonnaise
1 teaspoon lemon juice
1/2 teaspoon Dijon mustard
1/2 teaspoon Worcestershire sauce

Brush English muffins with butter; set aside. In a bowl, combine the crab, shrimp, 3/4 cup cheese, celery, olives and parsley. Combine the mayonnaise, lemon juice, mustard and Worcestershire sauce; pour over seafood mixture and toss to coat.

Place a rounded 1/4 cupful of the mixture on each muffin half; sprinkle with remaining cheese. Place on a baking sheet. Broil 4-6 in. from the heat for 3-4 minutes or until heated through and cheese is melted. Serve immediately. **Yield:** 4 servings.

Gelatin Specialties Make a Splash

THINK you've tried every sort of gelatin recipe known to man? Well, think again! Each of the change-of-pace delights featured here put a full-flavored spin on the kitchen staple. Prepare one for your next get-together and see how many guests ask for your secrets.

FROSTED CRANBERRY SALAD

Carolyn Sellers, York, Pennsylvania

Here's a terrific gelatin for the holidays. Pineapple lends a tangy twist and pecan halves add a slight crunch. The combination of cherry and cranberry flavors are treated to a mellow hint of vanilla.

- 1 can (20 ounces) crushed pineapple
- 1 envelope unflavored gelatin
- 1 package (3 ounces) cherry gelatin
- 1 cup chilled ginger ale
- 1 can (16 ounces) jellied cranberry sauce
- 1 package (8 ounces) cream cheese, softened
- 1 envelope whipped topping mix
- 1/2 cup milk
- 1 teaspoon vanilla extract
- 8 pecan halves, toasted
- 8 fresh cranberries

Drain pineapple, reserving juice in a 1 cup measure; set pineapple aside. To the juice, add enough water to measure 1 cup. Transfer to a small saucepan; add the unflavored gelatin and let stand for 1 minute. Bring to a boil. Add cherry gelatin; stir until dissolved. Stir in ginger ale. Pour into a bowl. Refrigerate for 30 minutes or until partially set.

Whisk in the pineapple and cranberry sauce. Transfer to an 11-in. x 7-in. x 2-in. dish coated with cooking spray. Refrigerate until set.

In a large mixing bowl, beat cream cheese until smooth. In a small mixing bowl, beat whipped topping mix, milk and vanilla on low speed until blended. Beat on high for 4 minutes or until thickened. Add to cream cheese; beat until blended. Spread over gelatin. Refrigerate overnight. Cut into squares; garnish each with a pecan half and cranberry. **Yield:** 8 servings.

ASIAN VEGGIE GELATIN
(Pictured below)

Janice Scott, Spokane Valley, Washington

While trying the offerings at a salad potluck, I was excited to sample this refreshing dish. It's a nice change from sweeter gelatin salads. Believe it or not, the special ingredient is soy sauce.

☑ Uses less fat, sugar or salt. Includes Nutrition Facts and Diabetic Exchanges.

- 1 package (.3 ounce) sugar-free orange gelatin
- 3/4 cup boiling water
- 1 cup cold water
- 4-1/2 teaspoons reduced-sodium soy sauce
- 1 tablespoon lemon juice
- 1/2 cup canned bean sprouts
- 1/2 cup sliced celery
- 1/2 cup shredded carrots
- 1/4 cup sliced water chestnuts, halved
- 1 tablespoon chopped green onion

In a large bowl, dissolve gelatin in boiling water. Stir in the cold water, soy sauce and lemon juice.

Add the bean sprouts, celery, carrots, water chestnuts and onion; mix well.

Spoon into four 6-oz. bowls coated with cooking spray. Refrigerate for 1 hour or until set. Invert onto salad plates. **Yield:** 4 servings.

Nutrition Facts: 1 serving equals 30 calories, trace fat (trace saturated fat), 0 cholesterol, 307 mg sodium, 5 g carbohydrate, 1 g fiber, 2 g protein. **Diabetic Exchange:** 1 Free Food.

PINA COLADA MOLDED SALAD
(Pictured at right)

Carol Gillespie, Chambersburg, Pennsylvania

An original recipe, my molded gelatin gets a tropical twist from coconut, pineapple, and macadamia nuts. It's a wonderful, anytime treat.

    1 can (20 ounces) unsweetened crushed
      pineapple
    2 envelopes unflavored gelatin
  1/2 cup cold water
    1 cup cream of coconut
    1 cup (8 ounces) sour cream
  3/4 cup lemon-lime soda
  3/4 cup flaked coconut
  1/2 cup chopped macadamia nuts
Pineapple chunks and freshly shredded
  coconut, optional

Drain pineapple, reserving juice; set the pineapple aside. In a large saucepan, sprinkle gelatin over cold water; let stand for 1 minute. Cook and stir over low heat until gelatin is completely dissolved, about 2 minutes.

Remove from the heat; stir in the cream of coconut, sour cream, soda and reserved pineapple juice. Transfer to a large bowl. Cover and refrigerate for 30 minutes or until thickened, stirring occasionally.

Fold in the flaked coconut, nuts and reserved pineapple. Pour into a 6-cup ring mold coated with cooking spray. Cover and refrigerate for 3 hours or until firm.

To serve, unmold salad onto a platter. Fill the center with pineapple chunks and shredded coconut if desired. **Yield:** 8 servings.

PINEAPPLE LIME GELATIN

Wanda Weathermon, Comanche, Texas

This recipe was passed down by my mother. We serve it often, but especially at Christmas and Thanksgiving. Of course, the green color makes it nice for St. Patrick's Day, too. With the marshmallows, pecans and whipped cream, the sweet salad can even be served as a light dessert.

    1 package (3 ounces) lime gelatin
    2 cups boiling water, *divided*
   16 large marshmallows
    1 package (3 ounces) cream cheese, softened
    1 can (8 ounces) unsweetened crushed
      pineapple, undrained
    1 cup heavy whipping cream, whipped
    1 cup chopped pecans
    2 to 3 drops green food coloring, optional

In a large bowl, dissolve gelatin in 1 cup boiling water; set aside. In a small saucepan, combine marshmallows and remaining water. Cook over low heat until marshmallows are melted, stirring occasionally. Stir into gelatin. Refrigerate until partially set.

In a large mixing bowl, beat cream cheese until smooth. Beat in pineapple. Fold in the gelatin mixture, whipped cream, pecans and food coloring if desired. Pour into a 6-cup mold coated with cooking spray. Refrigerate until set. Unmold onto a serving plate. **Yield:** 12 servings.

GRILLED STEAK AND MUSHROOM SALAD

(Pictured above)

Julie Cashion, Sanford, Florida

My husband loves this salad, especially during summertime. He says he feels like he's eating a healthy meal and getting his steak, too! I always serve it with some great homemade bread.

      6 tablespoons olive oil, *divided*
      2 tablespoons Dijon mustard, *divided*
   1/2 teaspoon salt
   1/4 teaspoon pepper
1-1/2 pounds boneless beef sirloin steak (3/4 inch thick)
      1 pound fresh mushrooms, sliced
   1/4 cup red wine vinegar
      1 medium bunch romaine, torn

In a small bowl, combine 1 tablespoon oil, 1 tablespoon mustard, salt and pepper; set aside.

Grill steak, covered, over medium-hot heat for 4 minutes. Turn; spread with mustard mixture. Grill 4 minutes longer or until meat reaches desired doneness (for medium-rare, a meat thermometer should read 145°; medium, 160°; well-done, 170°).

Meanwhile, in a large skillet, cook mushrooms in 1 tablespoon oil until tender. Stir in vinegar and remaining oil and mustard; mix well.

Thinly slice steak across the grain; add to mushroom mixture. Serve over romaine. **Yield:** 6 servings.

SPINACH BROCCOLI SALAD

(Pictured below)

Edna Hoffman, Hebron, Indiana

Are you getting a little tired of steamed broccoli? You may want to try this attractive broccoli-spinach combo salad for a little variation. The dressing is made with avocados, which contain some of the healthier fats.

☑ Uses less fat, sugar or salt. Includes Nutrition Facts and Diabetic Exchanges.

      1 package (10 ounces) fresh spinach, torn
      3 cups fresh broccoli florets
      1 cup shredded carrots
      1 can (8 ounces) sliced water chestnuts, drained
      3 tablespoons sunflower kernels
CUCUMBER AVOCADO DRESSING:
      1 medium cucumber, peeled, seeded and chopped
   1/2 medium ripe avocado, peeled and chopped
   1/4 cup chopped green onions
      4 teaspoons white wine vinegar
      1 tablespoon water
      1 garlic clove, minced
      2 teaspoons honey
      1 teaspoon minced fresh dill
   1/4 teaspoon salt

In a large bowl, combine the spinach, broccoli, carrots, water chestnuts and sunflower kernels. In a blender or food processor, combine the dressing ingredients; cover and process until smooth. Serve with salad. **Yield:** 8 servings (1 cup dressing).

Nutrition Facts: 1 cup equals 87 calories, 4 g fat (1 g saturated fat), 0 cholesterol, 137 mg sodium, 12 g carbohydrate, 4 g fiber, 4 g protein. **Diabetic Exchanges:** 2 vegetable, 1 fat.

boil. Reduce heat; cover and simmer for 1-3/4 to 2 hours or until beans are tender.

Stir in the milk, molasses, salt and bacon. Remove about 2-1/2 cups of soup; cool slightly. Place in a blender or food processor; cover and process until pureed. Return to the pan; heat through. **Yield:** 6 servings.

■.■.■.■.■.■.■.■.■.■.■.■

Swiss Pear Sandwiches
(Pictured below)

Janet Akey, Presque Isle, Wisconsin

Here's a quick recipe for busy retired couples. The sandwiches are microwavable so you don't even need to dirty a pan.

- 4 slices whole wheat bread
- 4 teaspoons honey mustard
- 4 slices (3/4 ounce each) reduced-fat Swiss cheese
- 1 large pear, sliced
- 2 slices red onion
- 2 tablespoons chopped pecans

Spread two slices of bread with mustard. Layer each with cheese, pear and onion slices and pecans; top with remaining cheese and bread.

Place sandwiches on a microwave-safe plate. Cover and microwave on high for 20-30 seconds or until cheese is melted. **Yield:** 2 servings.

■.■.■.■.■.■.■.■.■.■.■.■

Yankee Bean Soup
(Pictured above)

Ann Nace, Perkasie, Pennsylvania

My family really enjoys this hearty soup, which is perfect for a wintry day. Bacon, molasses and onion add great flavor. A friend from Massachusetts gave me the recipe years ago, and I've made it countless times since then.

- 1-1/2 cups dried navy beans
- 1/2 pound sliced bacon, diced
- 3/4 cup chopped onion
- 1/2 cup chopped carrot
- 1/3 cup chopped celery leaves
- 4 cups water
- 2 cups milk
- 2 teaspoons molasses
- 1-1/2 teaspoons salt

Place the beans in a Dutch oven or soup kettle; add water to cover by 2 in. Bring to a boil; boil for 2 minutes. Remove from the heat; cover and let stand for 1 hour.

Drain and rinse beans, discarding liquid. Set beans aside. In the same pan, cook the bacon over medium heat until crisp. Using a slotted spoon, remove to paper towels; drain, reserving 2 tablespoons drippings. In the drippings, saute onion until tender. Stir in carrot and celery leaves. Return beans to the pan. Add water. Bring to a

HOLIDAY TOSSED SALAD
(Pictured above)

Pat Loeffler, Grafton, Wisconsin

With its red and green ingredients, this salad is perfect for Christmas meals. Local cranberries and blue cheese make a great combination with salad greens, apples, walnuts and a simple cranberry vinaigrette.

    8 cups torn mixed salad greens
    2 medium red apples, diced
1/2 cup crumbled blue cheese
1/3 cup dried cranberries
1/3 cup coarsely chopped walnuts, toasted
1/4 cup sliced green onions
    2 tablespoons olive oil
    2 tablespoons cranberry juice concentrate
    1 tablespoon white wine vinegar
Dash salt and pepper

In a large salad bowl, combine the greens, apples, blue cheese, cranberries, walnuts and onions. In a small bowl, whisk the remaining ingredients. Drizzle over salad and toss gently to coat. Serve immediately. **Yield:** 6-8 servings.

TO TOSS OR NOT TO TOSS?

Not sure whether it's time to throw out your favorite bottle of salad dressing? The "shelf lives" of salad dressings vary somewhat. Generally, vinaigrettes can be kept refrigerated for up to 2 weeks. Dairy-based dressings, such as buttermilk, will keep up to 1 week. If you've created your own salad dressing from ingredients, like chopped onion, fresh herbs or even tomato sauce, it will usually keep for up to a week.

TURKEY MEATBALL SOUP
(Pictured below)

Lora Rehm, Endicott, New York

I made up this recipe myself to take advantage of the abundance of fresh vegetables available in our state. It's an economical yet hearty main dish that my husband and three children love year-round.

1/2 cup dry bread crumbs
    3 tablespoons milk
    1 egg, lightly beaten
1/2 teaspoon salt
1-1/4 pounds ground turkey
2-1/2 cups water
    1 can (14-1/2 ounces) stewed tomatoes
    2 medium zucchini, halved and sliced
    2 small carrots, thinly sliced
2/3 cup frozen corn
1/2 cup fresh *or* frozen cut green beans
    2 teaspoons chicken bouillon granules
    1 teaspoon dried basil
1/4 teaspoon pepper

In a large bowl, combine the bread crumbs, milk, egg and salt. Crumble turkey over mixture and mix well. Shape into 1/2-in. balls. In a nonstick skillet over medium heat, brown meatballs in batches; drain if necessary.

In a large saucepan, combine the remaining ingredients. Bring to a boil. Carefully add meatballs. Reduce the heat; cover and simmer for 20-25 minutes or until the vegetables are tender. **Yield:** 6 servings.

SPICY TOMATO SOUP
(Pictured below)

Jaime Hampton, Richmond, Virginia

When you'd rather be playing than cooking, you might want to give this tomato soup a try. Using canned corn and black beans, it goes together fast and is a great accompaniment to sandwiches.

- 8 ounces uncooked elbow macaroni
- 1 can (46 ounces) tomato juice
- 1 can (15-1/4 ounces) whole kernel corn, drained
- 1 can (15 ounces) black beans, rinsed and drained
- 1/4 cup salsa
- 3 teaspoons dried oregano
- 1-1/2 teaspoons garlic powder
- 1 teaspoon dried basil
- 1 teaspoon ground cumin
- 1/2 to 1 teaspoon crushed red pepper flakes, optional

Shredded cheddar *or* Monterey Jack cheese, optional

Cook the macaroni according to package directions. Meanwhile, in a large saucepan, combine the tomato juice, corn, beans, salsa, oregano, garlic powder, basil, cumin and pepper flakes if desired; bring to a boil. Reduce heat; cover and simmer for 8-10 minutes.

Drain macaroni; stir into the soup. Garnish with cheese if desired. **Yield:** 8-10 servings.

GORGONZOLA PEAR SALAD
(Pictured above)

Melinda Singer, Tarzana, California

Tired of tossed salads? Here's an irresistible variation featuring pears that makes an attractive first course. The cheese and pecans are tasty additions.

- 3 medium pears, cored and halved
- 3 tablespoons olive oil
- 1/2 teaspoon salt
- 6 cups spring mix salad greens
- 2 plum tomatoes, seeded and chopped
- 1 cup crumbled Gorgonzola cheese
- 1/2 cup pecan halves, toasted
- 3/4 cup balsamic vinaigrette

Place pears in an ungreased 13-in. x 9-in. x 2-in. baking dish. Drizzle with oil and sprinkle with salt. Bake, uncovered, at 400° for 25-30 minutes, basting occasionally with cooking juices.

In a large salad bowl, combine the greens, tomatoes, cheese and pecans. Drizzle with dressing and toss to coat. Divide among six serving plates; top each with a pear half. **Yield:** 6 servings.

SPICY TWO-BEAN CHILI
(Pictured below)

Lesley Pew, Lynn, Massachusetts

Chili fans will get a kick out of this untraditional recipe. Tomatoes with green chilies, lime juice and kidney and black beans give it an original twist. It's wonderful ladled over steaming rice.

      2 pounds ground beef
      3 large onions, chopped
      6 garlic cloves, minced
      2 cans (16 ounces *each*) kidney beans,
        rinsed and drained
      2 cans (15 ounces *each*) black beans,
        rinsed and drained
      2 cans (10 ounces *each*) diced tomatoes
        and green chilies, undrained
      1 can (14-1/2 ounces) chicken broth
  1/2 cup lime juice
      6 tablespoons cornmeal
  1/4 cup chili powder
      4 teaspoons dried oregano
      3 teaspoons ground cumin
      2 teaspoons salt
      2 teaspoons rubbed sage
  1/2 teaspoon white pepper
  1/2 teaspoon paprika
  1/2 teaspoon pepper
Hot cooked rice
Shredded cheddar cheese

In a Dutch oven, cook the beef, onions and garlic over medium heat until meat is no longer pink; drain. Transfer to a 5-qt. slow cooker. Stir in the beans, tomatoes, broth, lime juice, cornmeal and seasonings.

  Cover and cook on low for 8 hours or until heated through. Serve over rice; sprinkle with cheese. **Yield:** 11 servings.

MARINATED VEGETABLE SALAD
(Pictured above)

Elizabeth Powell, Elizabethton, Tennessee

A bevy of vegetables makes this tangy salad a hit. Jazzing up a bottle of salad dressing means I don't have to spend much time in the kitchen.

      1 cup frozen corn, thawed
      1 cup frozen peas, thawed
  1/3 cup finely chopped celery
  1/3 cup finely chopped green pepper
  1/3 cup finely chopped onion
      1 jar (2 ounces) diced pimientos, drained
      2 tablespoons sugar
      2 tablespoons red wine vinegar
      2 tablespoons vegetable oil
  1-1/2 teaspoons French salad dressing

In a small bowl, combine the first six ingredients. In another bowl, whisk the sugar, vinegar, oil and salad dressing. Pour over vegetable mixture and stir to coat. Cover and refrigerate for 2 hours or overnight. **Yield:** 2-3 servings.

CREAMY CRANBERRY APPLE SALAD
(Pictured below)

Ruth Turpin, Cincinnati, Ohio

For over 30 years, this recipe has been a holiday tradition in my family. With marshmallows, cranberries, apples and grapes, it has a sweet-tart flavor and comforting creaminess that appeals to all ages.

> 1 package (12 ounces) fresh *or* frozen cranberries, thawed
> 3 cups miniature marshmallows
> 1 cup sugar
> 2 medium apples, diced
> 1/2 cup halved seedless red grapes
> 1/2 cup chopped walnuts
> 1/4 teaspoon salt
> 1 carton (8 ounces) frozen whipped topping, thawed

Coarsely chop the cranberries; place in a large bowl. Stir in marshmallows and sugar. Cover and refrigerate for several hours or overnight.

Just before serving, stir in the apples, grapes, walnuts and salt. Fold in whipped topping. **Yield:** 8-10 servings.

TURKEY REUBENS
(Pictured above)

Chris Boshoven, Hebron, Indiana

I've had this recipe in my files for a long time and it's always a lunchtime favorite. I recommend draining the cabbage well before starting.

> 1 tablespoon butter, softened
> 4 slices rye bread
> 2 tablespoons mayonnaise
> 4 ounces thinly sliced deli turkey
> 2/3 cup canned sweet-and-sour red cabbage
> 2 slices (1/2 ounce *each*) Monterey Jack cheese

Spread butter over one side of each slice of bread; spread mayonnaise over the other side. On the mayonnaise side of two slices, layer the turkey, cabbage and cheese; top with remaining bread, buttered side up.

On a griddle or in a large skillet, toast sandwiches over medium heat for 3 minutes on each side or until golden brown. **Yield:** 2 servings.

SURPRISING SANDWICH

For a fun change, cut off the top of a hard roll and "hollow" it out. Fill the roll with tuna or egg salad. Add onion, lettuce and tomato, then replace the "top" for a brown-bag treat.

DIG IN to the comforting goodness of a piping hot dinner. Each of these entrees is loaded with heartwarming appeal.

FAMILY FAVORITE. Creamed Chicken and Mushrooms (p. 45).

Main Dishes

CREAMED CHICKEN AND MUSHROOMS

(Pictured at left)

Dixie Merrill, Newark, Ohio

Stovetop cooking means spending less time in the kitchen, and you just can't go wrong with this comforting main course. It's also a delicious way to use up leftover rice.

    1/2 cup sliced fresh mushrooms
      1 tablespoon butter
      1 tablespoon all-purpose flour
  1-1/2 teaspoons minced fresh parsley
    1/4 teaspoon salt
    1/8 teaspoon paprika
Dash ground nutmeg
    1/2 cup chicken broth
    1/4 cup milk
      1 cup cubed cooked chicken
Hot cooked rice

In a small saucepan, saute mushrooms in butter until tender. Stir in the flour, parsley, salt, paprika and nutmeg until blended. Gradually add broth and milk. Bring to a boil; cook and stir for 2 minutes. Reduce heat; stir in chicken. Cook 2 minutes longer or until heated through. Serve over rice. **Yield:** 2 servings.

BEEF 'N' NOODLE CASSEROLE

Here's a specialty shared by the American Dairy Association, located in Rosemont, Illinois. It comes together in a pinch when you want all the satisfaction of a casserole with only an ounce of the effort.

      1 package (8 ounces) medium noodles
    1/3 cup sliced green onions
    1/3 cup chopped green pepper
      2 tablespoons butter
      1 pound ground beef
      1 can (6 ounces) tomato paste
    1/2 cup sour cream
      1 cup (8 ounces) 4% cottage cheese
      1 can (8 ounces) tomato sauce

Cook noodles according to package directions; drain. In a large skillet, saute onions and green pepper in butter 3 minutes or until tender. Add beef and cook until no longer pink. Drain excess fat.

In a medium bowl, combine tomato paste and sour cream; stir in the noodles and cottage cheese. Layer half the noodle mixture in 2-qt. casserole; top with half the beef mixture. Repeat.

Pour tomato sauce evenly over the top of the casserole. Bake at 350° for 30-35 minutes or until heated through. **Yield:** 6 servings.

SOUTHWESTERN CHICKEN SKILLET

Renee Shepherd, Felton, California

Dress up chicken breasts with lemon juice, peppers and ground cumin, and you'll come to rely on this recipe time and again. Red pepper flakes and garlic add a bit of kick, helping you beat the dinner doldrums.

☑ Uses less fat, sugar or salt. Includes Nutrition Facts.

      1 pound boneless skinless chicken
        breasts, cut into strips
      3 tablespoons lemon juice
      2 garlic cloves, minced
      2 tablespoons vegetable oil
      2 large sweet red peppers, julienned
      2 large sweet yellow peppers, julienned
      1 large onion, halved and thinly sliced
      2 teaspoons minced fresh oregano *or*
        3/4 teaspoon dried oregano
      1 teaspoon ground cumin
    1/4 to 1/2 teaspoon crushed red pepper flakes
    1/2 teaspoon salt
    1/4 teaspoon pepper
      3 tablespoons minced fresh cilantro

Sprinkle chicken with lemon juice; set aside. In a large skillet, saute garlic in oil for 1 minute. Add the peppers, onion, oregano, cumin and pepper flakes. Reduce the heat; cover and simmer for 10 minutes.

Add the chicken, salt and pepper; cover and simmer for 10-15 minutes or until vegetables are tender and chicken is no longer pink. Sprinkle with cilantro. **Yield:** 5 servings.

Nutrition Facts: 1-1/2 cups equals 202 calories, 8 g fat (1 g saturated fat), 50 mg cholesterol, 285 mg sodium, 13 g carbohydrate, 3 g fiber, 20 g protein.

CHICKEN BROCCOLI CREPES
(Pictured below)

Deanna Naivar, Temple, Texas

When I organized food and nutrition training for our county 4-H'ers, we had cooking demonstrations representing different countries. We chose these crepes as a French dish, and everyone really loved them.

    1 cup plus 2 tablespoons milk
    2 eggs
    2 tablespoons butter, melted
    1 cup all-purpose flour
    1/4 teaspoon salt
FILLING:
    1/4 cup butter
    1/4 cup all-purpose flour
    2 cups chicken broth
    2 teaspoons Worcestershire sauce
    3 cups (12 ounces) shredded cheddar
       cheese, *divided*
    2 cups (16 ounces) sour cream
    2 packages (8 ounces *each*) frozen
       broccoli spears, cooked and drained
2-1/2 cups cubed cooked chicken

In a small mixing bowl, beat the milk, eggs and butter. Combine flour and salt; add to egg mixture and beat until smooth. Cover and refrigerate for 1 hour.

Heat a lightly greased 8-in. nonstick skillet. Stir batter; pour 1/4 cup into the center of skillet. Lift and tilt pan to evenly coat bottom. Cook until top appears dry; turn and cook 15-20 seconds longer. Remove to a wire rack. Repeat with remaining batter, greasing skillet as needed. When cool, stack crepes with waxed paper or paper towels in between.

In a large saucepan, melt butter. Stir in flour until smooth. Gradually stir in broth and Worcestershire sauce. Bring to a boil; cook and stir for 2 minutes. Reduce heat; stir in 2 cups of cheese. Cook and stir for 10 minutes or until cheese is melted. Remove from the heat; stir in sour cream until smooth.

Place four broccoli spears and 1/3 cup of chicken down the center of each crepe; top with 1/3 cup cheese sauce.

Roll up and place seam side down in a greased 13-in. x 9-in. x 2-in. baking dish.

Pour remaining cheese sauce over crepes; sprinkle with remaining cheese. Bake, uncovered, at 350° for 20 minutes or until heated through. **Yield:** 8 crepes.

HAMBURGER HOT DISH

Kathleen Larson, Cooperstown, North Dakota

My dad particularly enjoyed this casserole, which has been a family favorite for more than 60 years. It's just a simple, hearty combination of ground beef, potatoes, kidney beans and seasonings.

☑ Uses less fat, sugar or salt. Includes Nutrition Facts.

    1 pound ground beef
    1 small onion, chopped
    5 medium potatoes, peeled and diced
    1 can (16 ounces) kidney beans, rinsed
       and drained
    1 can (10-3/4 ounces) condensed tomato
       soup, undiluted
    2 tablespoons minced fresh parsley
    1 teaspoon chili powder, optional
3/4 teaspoon salt
1/4 to 1/2 teaspoon pepper

In a large skillet, cook the beef and onion over medium heat until meat is no longer pink; drain. Stir in the potatoes, beans, soup, parsley, chili powder if desired, salt and pepper.

Spoon into a greased 2-qt. baking dish. Cover and bake at 350° for 45 minutes. Uncover; bake 5-10 minutes longer or until potatoes are tender. **Yield:** 6 servings.

Nutrition Facts: 1-1/3 cups equals 362 calories, 7 g fat (3 g saturated fat), 37 mg cholesterol, 777 mg sodium, 52 g carbohydrate, 8 g fiber, 23 g protein.

Uses less fat, sugar or salt. Includes
Nutrition Facts.

1-1/2 teaspoons ground coriander
    1 teaspoon ground cumin
  1/2 teaspoon salt
  1/2 teaspoon sugar
  1/2 teaspoon ground chipotle pepper
  1/2 teaspoon smoked Spanish paprika
    2 pork tenderloins (3/4 pound *each*)

MANGO RELISH:
    1 medium mango, peeled and chopped
    2 plum tomatoes, seeded and chopped
  1/3 cup chopped onion
  1/3 cup chopped seeded peeled cucumber
  1/4 cup minced fresh cilantro
    1 jalapeno pepper, seeded and chopped
    3 tablespoons lime juice

In a small bowl, combine the first six ingredients. Set aside 1/2 teaspoon for relish; rub remaining spice mixture over tenderloins. Place in a lightly greased 13-in. x 9-in. x 2-in. baking pan. Bake, uncovered, at 350° for 45-50 minutes or until a meat thermometer reads 160°. Let stand for 5 minutes.

Meanwhile, in a small bowl, combine the mango, tomatoes, onion, cucumber, cilantro and jalapeno. Combine lime juice and reserved spice mixture; add to mango mixture and toss to coat. Slice pork; serve with relish. **Yield:** 6 servings.

Nutrition Facts: 4 ounces equals 106 calories, 2 g fat (1 g saturated fat), 32 mg cholesterol, 223 mg sodium, 10 g carbohydrate, 2 g fiber, 12 g protein.

Editor's Note: When cutting or seeding hot peppers, use rubber or plastic gloves to protect your hands. Avoid touching your face.

TUNA NOODLE SKILLET
(Pictured above)

Ruth Simon, Buffalo, New York

Prepared Alfredo sauce makes my stovetop entree a breeze to whip up. Toss in whatever vegetables your gang prefers.

    2 jars (16 ounces *each*) Alfredo sauce
    1 can (14-1/2 ounces) chicken broth
    1 package (16 ounces) wide egg noodles
    1 package (10 ounces) frozen peas
  1/4 teaspoon pepper
    2 cans (6 ounces *each*) albacore tuna,
       drained and flaked

In a large skillet over medium heat, bring Alfredo sauce and broth to a boil. Add noodles; cover and cook for 8 minutes.

Reduce the heat; stir in the peas and pepper. Cover and cook 4 minutes longer or until noodles are tender. Stir in the tuna; heat through. **Yield:** 6 servings.

PORK TENDERLOIN WITH MANGO RELISH
(Pictured at right)

Gloria Bradley, Naperville, Illinois

Colorful mango relish is a refreshing counterpoint to the "heat" in the rub I use to pep up a number of pork dishes. These roasted tenderloins are sure to turn out juicy every time.

ALMOND PORK CHOPS WITH HONEY MUSTARD

(Pictured at far right)

Lillian Julow, Gainesville, Florida

I love how crunchy almonds and sweet mustard sauce jazz up this tender pork dish. Usually, I double the recipe. One chop is never enough for each of my grown children and grandkids.

- 1/2 cup smoked almonds
- 1/2 cup dry bread crumbs
- 2 eggs
- 1/3 cup all-purpose flour
- 1/4 teaspoon salt
- 1/8 teaspoon pepper
- 4 boneless pork loin chops (1 inch thick and 6 ounces *each*)
- 2 tablespoons olive oil
- 2 tablespoons butter
- 1/2 cup reduced-fat mayonnaise
- 1/4 cup honey
- 2 tablespoons Dijon mustard

In a food processor, process the almonds until finely chopped. Transfer to a shallow bowl; add bread crumbs. In another bowl, beat the eggs. In a large resealable plastic bag, combine flour, salt and pepper. Add pork chops, one at a time, and shake to coat. Dip in eggs, then coat with almond mixture.

In a large skillet over medium heat, cook chops in oil and butter for 5 minutes on each side or until juices run clear. Meanwhile, in a small bowl, combine the mayonnaise, honey and mustard. Serve with pork chops. **Yield:** 4 servings.

COUNTRY STYLE PORK MEDALLIONS

(Pictured above, far right)

Pamela Jessen, Calgary, Alberta

Be prepared to hand out recipes after you pass around this impressive entree. Leftovers would be great in sandwiches…but I've never had any extras to try a sample!

- 2 pork tenderloins (1 pound *each*)
- 6 tablespoons butter, *divided*
- 2 small onions, sliced and separated into rings
- 3/4 pound small fresh mushrooms
- 2 small apples, cored and cut into rings

APPLE CREAM SAUCE:
- 1 cup apple cider or juice
- 1 package (8 ounces) cream cheese, cubed
- 1/4 cup apple brandy *or* additional apple cider
- 1 teaspoon dried basil

Cut pork into 1/2-in. slices; flatten to 1/4-in. thickness. In a large skillet over medium-high heat, cook pork in batches in 3 tablespoons butter until juices run clear. Remove to a serving platter and keep warm.

In the same skillet, saute onions and mushrooms in remaining butter for 4 minutes or until crisp-tender. Add apples; saute for 3-4 minutes or until vegetables and apples are tender. Arrange over pork.

Add cider and cream cheese to the skillet; cook and stir over medium heat for 3 minutes or until cheese is melted and sauce is smooth. Stir in brandy or additional cider and basil; heat through. Serve with pork and vegetables. **Yield:** 6 servings.

HERB-CRUSTED PORK ROAST

(Pictured at right and on front cover)

Mary Ann Lee, Clifton Park, New York

There is nothing like a well-seasoned pork roast, pan-seared and baked to perfection. The moist meat gets a flavor boost from a cheesy, herbal crust and simple reduction sauce.

- 1 teaspoon ground mustard
- 1 teaspoon lemon-herb seasoning
- 1 teaspoon salt
- 1/2 teaspoon pepper
- 1 bone-in pork loin roast (4 pounds)
- 2 tablespoons plus 1/4 cup olive oil, *divided*
- 1 tablespoon Dijon mustard
- 1-1/2 cups soft bread crumbs
- 1/2 cup grated Parmesan cheese
- 1/4 cup minced fresh basil *or* 4 teaspoons dried basil
- 2 teaspoons minced fresh thyme
- 2 teaspoons minced fresh rosemary
- 2 garlic cloves, minced
- 1 cup white wine *or* chicken broth

In a small bowl, combine the ground mustard, herb seasoning, salt and pepper; rub over roast. In a large skillet, brown roast in 2 tablespoons oil. Place roast fat side up on a rack in a shallow roasting pan. Brush top with Dijon mustard. Combine the bread crumbs, Parmesan cheese, basil, thyme, rosemary, garlic and remaining oil; press onto roast.

Bake, uncovered, at 350° for 2 to 2-1/4 hours or until a meat thermometer reads 160°. Place on

a warm serving platter. Let stand for 10-15 minutes before slicing.

Stir wine or broth into roasting pan, scraping to loosen browned bits. Pour into a saucepan. Bring to a boil over medium-high heat; cook until reduced by half. Serve with roast. **Yield:** 12-14 servings.

🏵 SPICE-RUBBED RIBS
(Pictured above)

Cheryl Ewing, Ellwood City, Pennsylvania

For grilling, here's the rub I recommend. It's made with a wonderful blend of spices. If you have some left after making ribs, put it in a shaker and use it another day on pork or beef roasts, tenderloins, steaks and more.

  3 tablespoons paprika
  2 tablespoons plus 1 teaspoon salt
  2 tablespoons plus 1 teaspoon
     garlic powder
  2 tablespoons cayenne pepper
  4 teaspoons onion powder
  4 teaspoons dried oregano
  4 teaspoons dried thyme
  4 teaspoons pepper
 10 pounds pork baby back ribs

In a small bowl, combine the seasonings; rub over the ribs.

Prepare grill for indirect heat, using a drip pan.

Grill ribs, covered, over indirect medium heat for 1 hour or until juices run clear and meat is tender, turning occasionally. **Yield:** 10 servings.

HAMBURGER STROGANOFF

Deb Helmer, Lynden, Washington

Here's a fast take on an old standby. Ground beef and canned cream of mushroom soup make this savory stroganoff an effortless main course on busy weeknights.

 1-1/2 pounds ground beef
   1/2 cup chopped onion
 Dash garlic salt
     2 tablespoons all-purpose flour
 Salt and pepper to taste
     1 can (10-3/4 ounces) condensed cream
        of mushroom soup, undiluted
     1 can (4-1/2 ounces) mushrooms, drained
     1 cup (8 ounces) sour cream
 Cooked noodles *or* rice
 Chopped fresh parsley

In a skillet, brown meat. Add onion and garlic salt; continue to cook until onion is soft. Stir in the flour; add salt and pepper to taste. Simmer 5 minutes. Add soup and mushrooms and continue to simmer 15 minutes.

Fold in sour cream and heat only until warm. Serve over noodles or rice and garnish with parsley. **Yield:** 4-6 servings.

One-Dish Breakfasts

GREET THE DAY with a smile when a meal-in-one specialty graces your breakfast table. Whip up any of these egg bakes, pour some orange juice and watch the family race to the table!

VEGETABLE FRITTATA
(Pictured below)

Janet Eckhoff, Woodland, California

Red potatoes, green pepper and zucchini make this mouth-watering frittata so colorful. It's a special breakfast or a great change-of-pace dinner.

> 1/2 cup chopped onion
> 1/2 cup chopped green pepper
> 1/2 cup chopped sweet red pepper
> 1 garlic clove, minced
> 3 tablespoons olive oil, *divided*
> 2 medium red potatoes, cooked and cubed
> 1 small zucchini, cubed
> 6 eggs
> 1/2 teaspoon salt
> Pinch pepper

In a 10-in. cast-iron or ovenproof skillet, saute onion, peppers and garlic in 2 tablespoons of oil until the vegetables are tender. Remove vegetables with a slotted spoon; set aside.

In the same skillet over medium heat, lightly brown potatoes in remaining oil. Add vegetable mixture and zucchini; simmer for 4 minutes.

In a bowl, beat eggs, salt and pepper; pour over vegetables. Cover and cook for 8-10 minutes or until eggs are nearly set. Broil 6 in. from the heat for 2 minutes or until eggs are set on top. Cut into wedges. **Yield:** 4-6 servings.

SUNDAY BRUNCH CASSEROLE

Roy Lyon, Coupeville, Washington

My father was a chef, and this was one of his best-loved recipes. He served it in the hotels where he worked as well as at home. Whenever I prepare it, I'm flooded with fond memories of a table laden with food and encircled with family and friends.

> 6 slices sourdough bread
> 3 to 4 tablespoons butter, softened
> 2 cups (8 ounces) shredded cheddar cheese
> 1 pound bulk pork sausage, cooked and drained
> 1/2 medium sweet red pepper, cut into thin strips
> 1/4 cup sliced green onion tops
> 3 eggs
> 1 can (10-3/4 ounces) condensed cream of asparagus soup, undiluted
> 2 cups milk
> 1/4 cup white wine *or* chicken broth
> 1/2 teaspoon Dijon mustard
> 1/4 teaspoon pepper

Remove and discard crust from bread if desired. Butter bread; cube and place in a greased 13-in. x 9-in. x 2-in. baking dish. Sprinkle with the cheese, sausage, red pepper and onions in order given.

In a large bowl, beat eggs. Add the soup, milk, wine, mustard and pepper. Pour over bread mixture; cover and refrigerate overnight.

Remove from the refrigerator 30 minutes before baking. Bake, uncovered, at 300° for 1 hour or until a knife comes out clean. Let stand for 5 minutes before cutting. **Yield:** 8-10 servings.

SAGE ONION QUICHE

(Pictured above)

Shelley Johnson, Indianapolis, Indiana

I reach for this recipe often because it's so versatile—you can serve it for brunch, as a side dish or as a meatless entree. The fresh sage adds great flavor to the onions.

- 2 large onions, thinly sliced
- 2 tablespoons butter
- 2 tablespoons minced fresh sage
- 1 teaspoon minced fresh thyme *or* 1/4 teaspoon dried thyme
- 1 unbaked pastry shell (9 inches)
- 1 cup (4 ounces) shredded cheddar cheese
- 4 eggs
- 1 can (12 ounces) evaporated milk
- 1/2 teaspoon salt
- 1/8 teaspoon pepper
- 1/8 teaspoon ground nutmeg

In a large skillet, saute onions in butter until tender; drain. Stir in sage and thyme. Spoon into pastry shell. Sprinkle with cheese. In a bowl, whisk the eggs, milk, salt, pepper and nutmeg. Pour over cheese.

Bake at 425° for 15 minutes. Reduce heat to 375°; bake 20-25 minutes longer or until a knife inserted near the center comes out clean. Let the quiche stand for 10 minutes before cutting. **Yield:** 6-8 servings.

SCRAMBLED EGG CASSEROLE

(Pictured below)

Mary Anne McWhirter, Pearland, Texas

This recipe combines flavors of hearty, old-time country breakfasts with the ease of a modern, make-ahead dish.

CHEESE SAUCE:
- 2 tablespoons butter
- 2-1/2 tablespoons flour
- 2 cups milk
- 1/2 teaspoon salt
- 1/8 teaspoon ground pepper
- 1 cup process cheese (Velveeta), shredded
- 1 cup cubed ham
- 1/4 cup chopped green onion
- 3 tablespoons melted butter
- 12 eggs, beaten
- 1 can (4 ounces) sliced mushrooms, drained

TOPPING:
- 1/4 cup melted butter
- 2-1/4 cups soft bread crumbs

To make cheese sauce, melt butter, blend in flour and cook for 1 minutes. Gradually stir in milk; cook until thick. Add salt, pepper and cheese; stir until cheese melts. Set aside.

Saute ham and green onion in 3 tablespoons butter until onion is tender. Add eggs and cook over medium heat until eggs are set; stir in the mushrooms and cheese sauce.

Spoon eggs into greased 13-in. x 9-in. x 2-in. baking pan. Combine topping ingredients; spread evenly over egg mixture. Cover; chill overnight. Uncover; bake at 350° for 30 minutes. **Yield:** 10-12 servings.

PEANUTTY CHICKEN
(Pictured below)

Brenda Branum, Bay Minette, Alabama

Peanut butter makes a tasty sauce for tender chicken. Don't let the unique combination of ingredients—tomato sauce, chili powder, garlic, onion and peanut butter—keep you from trying it. My family loves it!

- 1/4 cup all-purpose flour
- 1-1/2 teaspoons salt
- 1/8 teaspoon pepper
- 1 broiler/fryer chicken (3 pounds), cut up
- 1/2 cup vegetable oil
- 1 medium onion, chopped
- 1 garlic clove, minced
- 1 can (8 ounces) tomato sauce
- 1 cup water
- 1/3 cup creamy peanut butter
- 1 tablespoon sugar
- 1 tablespoon cider vinegar
- 1 teaspoon chili powder
- 2 teaspoons cornstarch
- 2 teaspoons cold water

In a large resealable plastic bag, combine the flour, salt and pepper. Add chicken, a few pieces at a time, and shake to coat.

In a large skillet, brown chicken in oil on all sides; remove to paper towels. Drain, reserving 2 tablespoons drippings.

In the drippings, saute onion and garlic until tender. Add the tomato sauce, water, peanut butter, sugar, vinegar and chili powder. Bring to a boil; reduce heat. Return chicken to the pan; cover and simmer for 30 minutes or until juices run clear.

Remove chicken and keep warm. In a small bowl, combine cornstarch and cold water until smooth; stir into pan juices. Bring to a boil over medium heat; cook and stir for 2 minutes or until thickened. Serve with chicken. **Yield:** 6-8 servings.

TANGY STUFFED PEPPERS
(Pictured above)

Rosie Wendel, Bay City, Texas

My parents were farmers, so I've always liked to cook with fresh vegetables. This recipe represents our part of the country, since both green peppers and rice are grown here. It's one of my family's favorites…the Worcestershire sauce is what makes the filling so tangy.

- 4 large green peppers
- 1 pound ground beef
- 1 small onion, chopped
- 1-1/2 cups cooked long grain rice
- 1/4 cup grated Parmesan cheese
- 6 teaspoons Worcestershire sauce, *divided*
- 1/2 teaspoon salt
- 1 can (15 ounces) tomato sauce
- 1/3 cup water

Additional Parmesan cheese, optional

Cut tops off peppers and remove seeds. Finely chop pepper tops; set aside. In a large saucepan, cook whole peppers in boiling water for 3-5 minutes. Drain and rinse in cold water; set aside.

In a large skillet, cook the beef, onion and chopped peppers over medium heat until meat is no longer pink and vegetables are tender; drain. Remove from the heat. Stir in the rice, Parmesan cheese, 4 teaspoons Worcestershire sauce and salt. Spoon into peppers.

Place in a greased 2-qt. baking dish. Combine the tomato sauce, water and remaining Worcestershire sauce; drizzle over peppers. Cover and bake at 350° for 25-30 minutes or until peppers are tender. Sprinkle with additional Parmesan cheese if desired. **Yield:** 4 servings.

PORK CHILI VERDE
(Pictured above)

Kimberly Burke, Chico, California

Pork slowly stews with jalapenos, onion, green enchilada sauce and spices in this flavor-packed Mexican dish. It's great on its own or stuffed in a warm tortilla with sour cream, grated cheese or olives on the side.

✓ Uses less fat, sugar or salt. Includes Nutrition Facts.

- 1 boneless pork sirloin roast (3 pounds), cut into 1-inch cubes
- 4 medium carrots, sliced
- 1 medium onion, thinly sliced
- 1 cup minced fresh cilantro
- 4 garlic cloves, minced
- 3 tablespoons vegetable oil
- 1 can (28 ounces) green enchilada sauce
- 2 jalapeno peppers, seeded and chopped
- 1 tablespoon cornstarch
- 1/4 cup cold water
- Hot cooked rice
- Flour tortillas, warmed

In a large skillet, saute the pork, carrots, onion, cilantro and garlic in oil in batches until pork is browned. Transfer to a 5-qt. slow cooker. Add the enchilada sauce and jalapenos. Cover and cook on low for 6 hours or until meat is tender.

In a small bowl, combine cornstarch and water until smooth; stir into pork mixture. Cover and cook on high for 30 minutes or until thickened. Serve with rice and tortillas. **Yield:** 8 servings.

Nutrition Facts: 1 cup pork mixture (calculated without rice and tortillas) equals 312 calories, 12 g fat (4 g saturated fat), 102 mg cholesterol, 616 mg sodium, 11 g carbohydrate, 1 g fiber, 37 g protein.

Editor's Note: When cutting or seeding hot peppers, use rubber or plastic gloves to protect your hands. Avoid touching your face.

SOUTHERN BARBECUED BRISKET
(Pictured below)

Lorraine Hodge, McLean, Virginia

Ever since a former neighbor shared this recipe with me, it has been a staple in my home. Since it makes a lot, it's good for a company dinner or buffet.

- 1 fresh beef brisket (5 pounds)
- 1 large onion, chopped
- 1 cup ketchup
- 1/4 cup water
- 3 tablespoons brown sugar
- 1 tablespoon Liquid Smoke, optional
- 2 teaspoons celery seed
- 1 teaspoon salt
- 1 teaspoon ground mustard
- 1/8 teaspoon cayenne pepper

Place brisket on a large sheet of heavy-duty foil; seal tightly. Place in a greased shallow roasting pan. Bake at 325° for 2 to 2-1/2 hours or until meat is tender.

Meanwhile, in a small saucepan, combine the remaining ingredients. Bring to a boil. Reduce heat; cover and simmer for 20 minutes, stirring occasionally. Remove from the heat.

Carefully open foil to allow steam to escape. Remove brisket from foil; let stand for 20 minutes. Thinly slice meat across the grain. Place in an ungreased 13-in. x 9-in. x 2-in. baking dish. Spoon sauce over meat. Cover and bake for 1 hour or until heated through. **Yield:** 12 servings.

Editor's Note: This is a fresh beef brisket, not corned beef. The meat comes from the first cut of the brisket.

CRAWFISH FETTUCCINE
(Pictured below)

Carolyn Lejeune, Welsh, Louisiana

Along with a green salad and garlic bread, this dish is great for family gatherings. The recipe can easily be doubled to serve a larger group, and if you'd like it less spicy, remove the seeds from the jalapeno before chopping it.

- 1 large onion, chopped
- 1 medium sweet red pepper, chopped
- 2/3 cup sliced green onions
- 1 celery rib, chopped
- 1 garlic clove, minced
- 1-1/4 cups butter, cubed
- 1/4 cup all-purpose flour
- 8 ounces process cheese (Velveeta), cubed
- 1 cup half-and-half cream
- 1 tablespoon chopped jalapeno pepper
- 1/2 teaspoon salt
- 8 ounces uncooked fettuccine
- 1-1/2 pounds frozen cooked crawfish tails, thawed *or* cooked medium shrimp, peeled and deveined

In a Dutch oven, saute the onion, red pepper, green onions, celery and garlic in butter for 5 minutes or until vegetables are crisp-tender. Stir in flour until blended; cook and stir for 2 minutes. Add the cheese, cream, jalapeno and salt; cook and stir for 10 minutes or until mixture is thickened and cheese is melted.

Meanwhile, cook fettuccine according to package directions; drain. Stir fettuccine and crawfish into the vegetable mixture. Cook, uncovered, over medium heat for 10 minutes or until heated through, stirring occasionally. **Yield:** 8 servings.

Editor's Note: When cutting or seeding hot peppers, use rubber or plastic gloves to protect your hands. Avoid touching your face.

EASY OVEN STEW

Carol Smith, Stuart, Florida

Because I've never entered a recipe contest before, I hesitated before sending in my stew. I knew, however, that it was as tasty as it was easy. You just throw the ingredients into a pot and stir.

☑ Uses less fat, sugar or salt. Includes Nutrition Facts and Diabetic Exchanges.

- 2 pounds lean beef stew meat, cut into 1-inch cubes
- 4 large carrots, cut into 1-inch pieces
- 2 medium onions, cut into 1-inch pieces
- 2 celery ribs, cut into 1-inch pieces
- 2 medium parsnips, cut into 1-inch pieces
- 1 garlic clove, minced
- 1 can (14-1/2 ounces) Italian stewed tomatoes
- 1-1/2 cups beef broth
- 1 can (8 ounces) tomato sauce
- 1/2 cup quick-cooking tapioca
- 1 teaspoon instant coffee granules
- 1/2 teaspoon dried thyme
- 1/2 teaspoon dried oregano
- 1/2 teaspoon salt, optional

In a 5-qt. Dutch oven, combine all ingredients. Cover and bake at 300° for 2-1/2 to 3 hours, stirring every hour, or until the meat and vegetables are tender. **Yield:** 8 servings.

Nutrition Facts: 1-1/3 cups (prepared with low-sodium beef broth and tomato sauce; calculated without added salt) equals 230 calories, 6 g fat (0 saturated fat), 53 mg cholesterol, 401 mg sodium, 27 g carbohydrate, 0 fiber, 23 g protein. **Diabetic Exchanges:** 2 meat, 2 vegetable, 1 starch.

PEAR 'N' PROSCIUTTO PORK LOIN
(Pictured above right)

Anthony Guaetta, Peabody, Massachusetts

This pork is magnificent served on a bed of mesclun with fresh goat cheese and roasted veggies. If prosciutto is unavailable, use thin deli ham in the stuffing.

- 1 bottle (750 milliliters) sweet white wine
- 2 cups water

2 cups sugar
2 tablespoons ground ginger
2 cinnamon sticks (3 inches)
3 whole cloves
4 medium Bosc pears, peeled and quartered
1 boneless whole pork loin roast (3 to 4 pounds)
3/4 teaspoon salt, *divided*
1/2 teaspoon pepper, *divided*
8 thin slices prosciutto (about 4 ounces)
1/4 cup butter, cubed

In a large saucepan, combine the wine, water, sugar, ginger, cinnamon sticks and cloves; bring to a boil. Reduce heat; simmer, uncovered, for 10 minutes. Add pears; cover and simmer for 15-20 minutes or until tender.

Using a slotted spoon, carefully remove pears and cool to room temperature. Continue to simmer poaching liquid, uncovered, for 15-25 minutes or until reduced to 2 cups. Remove and discard cinnamon sticks and cloves. Cover and refrigerate liquid.

Cut a lengthwise slit down center of roast to within 1/2 in. of bottom. Open roast so it lies flat; cover with plastic wrap. Flatten to 3/4-in. thickness. Remove plastic; sprinkle meat with 1/2 teaspoon salt and 1/4 teaspoon pepper. Top with prosciutto and pears. Roll up jelly-roll style, starting with a long side; tie several times with kitchen string.

Place in a shallow roasting pan lined with heavy-duty foil. Bake, uncovered, at 350° for 1-1/2 to 2 hours or until a meat thermometer reads 160°. Cover and let stand 10-15 minutes before slicing.

Pour poaching liquid into a small saucepan. Add remaining salt and pepper. Bring to a boil. Reduce heat; simmer, uncovered, for 5 minutes. Stir in butter until melted. Serve with meat. **Yield:** 12 servings.

VEGETARIAN PASTA SHELLS
(Pictured below)
Helen Phillips, Horseheads, New York

This colorful entree has a lot going for it. It has a fresh-from-the-garden flavor, it's filling but not overly high in calories and you can make it ahead of time. It's special enough for company, too.

1/2 cup chopped green onions
1/2 cup shredded carrot
1/2 cup diced yellow summer squash
1 teaspoon olive oil
1 garlic clove, minced
2 cups reduced-fat ricotta cheese
1/2 cup shredded part-skim mozzarella cheese
2 egg whites
2 tablespoons minced fresh basil *or* 2 teaspoons dried basil
3/4 teaspoon salt
1/8 teaspoon pepper
1-1/2 cups meatless spaghetti sauce, *divided*
15 jumbo pasta shells, cooked and drained
1/2 cup shredded Parmesan cheese

In a nonstick skillet, saute the onions, carrot and squash in oil until tender. Add garlic; saute 1 minute longer. Stir in the ricotta, mozzarella, egg whites, basil, salt and pepper.

Spread 1 cup of spaghetti sauce into a 3-qt. baking dish coated with cooking spray. Stuff pasta shells with cheese mixture; arrange in prepared dish. Top with the remaining spaghetti sauce; sprinkle with Parmesan cheese.

Cover and bake at 350° for 40-45 minutes or until heated through. **Yield:** 5 servings.

roast and cover with plastic wrap. Flatten to 3/4-in. thickness. Remove plastic wrap.

In a small bowl, combine the ripe pears, dried pears, walnuts, cilantro, honey, garlic and pepper flakes; spread over roast to within 1 in. of edges. Roll up from a long side; tie with kitchen string at 2-in. intervals. Place in a shallow roasting pan lined with heavy-duty foil.

Combine the glaze ingredients; spoon over roast. Bake, uncovered, at 350° for 1-1/4 to 1-1/2 hours or until a meat thermometer reads 160°, basting occasionally with pan drippings. Let stand for 10-15 minutes before slicing. **Yield:** 12 servings.

Nutrition Facts: 4 ounces equals 246 calories, 8 g fat (2 g saturated fat), 56 mg cholesterol, 100 mg sodium, 20 g carbohydrate, 2 g fiber, 24 g protein.

Editor's Note: When cutting or seeding hot peppers, use rubber or plastic gloves to protect your hands. Avoid touching your face.

PEAR-STUFFED PORK LOIN

(Pictured above)

Mary Shivers, Ada, Oklahoma

From just two trees, we get an abundance of pears, so I'm always looking for new ideas on how to use them. This elegant roast offers a delicious way to incorporate pears into a main dish and its glaze.

✓ Uses less fat, sugar or salt. Includes Nutrition Facts.

- 1 boneless whole pork loin roast (3 to 4 pounds)
- 1/2 cup chopped peeled ripe pears
- 1/2 cup chopped dried pears
- 1/2 cup chopped walnuts
- 1/4 cup minced fresh cilantro
- 3 tablespoons honey
- 2 garlic cloves, minced
- 1/4 teaspoon crushed red pepper flakes

GLAZE:
- 1 cup finely chopped peeled ripe pears
- 1/2 cup finely chopped onion
- 1/4 cup maple syrup
- 2 tablespoons Worcestershire sauce
- 2 tablespoons chili sauce
- 1 jalapeno pepper, seeded and finely chopped
- 1/8 teaspoon cayenne pepper

Cut a lengthwise slit down the center of roast to within 1/2 in. of bottom. Open roast so it lies flat. On each half, make another lengthwise slit down the center to within 1/2 in. of bottom; open

MEAT SAUCE FOR SPAGHETTI

Mary Tallman, Arbor Vitae, Wisconsin

Here's a thick, hearty sauce that turns ordinary spaghetti and garlic bread into a filling feast. When I'm in a hurry, I make this slow cooker recipe in an electric frying pan instead.

- 1 pound ground beef
- 1 pound bulk Italian sausage
- 1 can (28 ounces) crushed tomatoes, undrained
- 1 medium green pepper, chopped
- 1 medium onion, chopped
- 1 cup finely chopped carrots
- 1 cup water
- 1 can (8 ounces) tomato sauce
- 1 can (6 ounces) tomato paste
- 1 tablespoon brown sugar
- 1 tablespoon Italian seasoning
- 2 garlic cloves, minced
- 1/2 teaspoon salt
- 1/4 teaspoon pepper

Hot cooked spaghetti

In a large skillet, cook beef and sausage over medium heat until no longer pink; drain. Transfer to a 5-qt. slow cooker. Stir in the tomatoes, green pepper, onion, carrots, water, tomato sauce, tomato paste, brown sugar, Italian seasoning, garlic, salt and pepper. Cover and cook on low for 8-10 hours or until bubbly. Serve over the spaghetti. **Yield:** 9 servings.

PARMESAN-PORK ZUCCHINI BOATS

(Pictured below)

Michelle Masciarelli, Torrington, Connecticut

My father-in-law grows zucchini, so we try as many different recipes as we can. Stuffed with a sausage-cheese filling, these zucchini boats are hearty enough to be a main dish. We usually serve them with rice.

    4 medium zucchini
    1 pound bulk pork sausage
    1 small onion, chopped
    1 garlic clove, minced
    2/3 cup seasoned bread crumbs
    1/2 cup plus 2 tablespoons shredded
        Parmesan cheese, *divided*
    1 egg, beaten
    1/4 teaspoon salt
    1/2 cup water

Cut each zucchini in half lengthwise. Scoop out seeds and pulp, leaving a 1/4-in. shell; set aside. Chop pulp; set aside.

In a large skillet, cook the sausage and onion over medium heat until meat is no longer pink; drain. Add garlic and zucchini pulp; saute for 3-5 minutes or until pulp is tender. Remove from the heat. Stir in the bread crumbs, 1/2 cup Parmesan cheese and egg.

Sprinkle salt inside zucchini shells. Fill each with 3 tablespoons meat mixture. Sprinkle with remaining Parmesan cheese.

Place in an ungreased 13-in. x 9-in. x 2-in. baking dish. Pour water into dish. Cover and bake at 350° for 15 minutes. Uncover; bake 15 minutes longer or until zucchini is tender and filling is heated through. **Yield:** 4 servings.

SWEET 'N' SOUR CURRY CHICKEN

(Pictured above)

Carol Conrad, Edmonton, Alberta

Mango chutney is a wonderful ingredient for dressing up everyday meals. Here, I use it to jazz up a slow-cooked chicken dish. Curry powder further enhances the flavor.

☑ Uses less fat, sugar or salt. Includes Nutrition Facts.

    1 pound boneless skinless chicken
        breasts, cut into 1-inch pieces
    1 can (14-1/2 ounces) stewed tomatoes,
        cut up
    1 large green pepper, cut into 1-inch
        pieces
    1 large onion, sliced
    1/2 cup mango chutney
    2 tablespoons cornstarch
    1-1/2 teaspoons curry powder
    1/4 cup water

In a 3-qt. slow cooker, combine the chicken, tomatoes, green pepper, onion and chutney. In a small bowl, combine the cornstarch, curry powder and water until smooth; stir into chicken mixture.

Cover and cook on low for 4 hours or until chicken juices run clear. **Yield:** 4 servings.

Nutrition Facts: 1-1/2 cups equals 314 calories, 3 g fat (1 g saturated fat), 63 mg cholesterol, 583 mg sodium, 46 g carbohydrate, 3 g fiber, 25 g protein.

CORSICAN CHICKEN
(Pictured below)

Mary Bergfeld, Eugene, Oregon

Moist and tender chicken thighs make a delicious hot entree for winter months. I set the table with warm, sunny Mediterranean shades and patterns that look gorgeous with the colorful meal.

- 3 tablespoons butter, softened
- 2 tablespoons herbes de Provence
- 1 teaspoon salt
- 2 garlic cloves, minced
- 1/2 teaspoon coarsely ground pepper
- 2 pounds boneless skinless chicken thighs
- 1 large onion, chopped
- 1/2 cup oil-packed sun-dried tomatoes, julienned
- 1 can (10-1/2 ounces) condensed beef consomme, undiluted
- 1/2 cup dry vermouth *or* orange juice
- 1/2 cup pitted Greek olives, quartered
- 1 teaspoon grated orange peel
- 2 teaspoons cornstarch
- 1 tablespoon cold water
- 2 tablespoons minced fresh basil
- 2 tablespoons diced pimientos
- 2 tablespoons minced fresh parsley

In a small bowl, combine the butter, herbes de Provence, salt, garlic and pepper; rub over chicken. Place in a 5-qt. slow cooker. Add the onion, tomatoes, consomme and vermouth or orange juice. Cover and cook on low for 4-5 hours or until the chicken juices run clear.

Add the olives and orange peel. Cover and cook on high for 30 minutes.

Remove chicken and keep warm. Pour cooking juices into a small saucepan; skim fat. Combine cornstarch and water until smooth; gradually stir into cooking juices. Bring to a boil; cook and stir for 2 minutes or until smooth. Pour over chicken. Sprinkle with basil, pimientos and parsley. **Yield:** 6-8 servings.

Editor's Note: Look for herbes de Provence in the spice aisle of your grocery store.

SEAFOOD STUFFED RAINBOW TROUT

Myroniuk Tracy, Edmonton, Alberta

This is a special way to serve fresh rainbow trout, stuffed with a mixture of scallops, shrimp, rice, bacon and vegetables. But don't wait for a special occasion to serve it—it's easy to put together and set in the oven.

- 4 tablespoons butter, melted, *divided*
- 1 tablespoon lemon juice
- 2 pan-dressed trout (about 12 ounces *each*)
- 1/4 teaspoon pepper
- 1/4 cup cooked long grain rice
- 2 bacon strips, cooked and crumbled
- 2 tablespoons chopped onion
- 2 tablespoons diced sweet red pepper
- 15 frozen cooked salad shrimp, thawed
- 4 sea scallops, diced
- 1 tablespoon vegetable oil
- 2 medium lemons, thinly sliced

Combine 2 tablespoons butter and the lemon juice; brush over trout cavities. Sprinkle with pepper; set aside.

In a small skillet, saute the rice, bacon, onion, red pepper, shrimp and scallops in oil for 5 minutes or until scallops are firm and opaque. Spoon into fish cavities. Top with lemon slices.

Brush remaining butter over a sheet of heavy-duty foil; wrap fish in foil and seal tightly. Place on a baking sheet. Bake at 425° for 25-28 minutes or until fish flakes easily with a fork. **Yield:** 4 servings.

CHUNKY PASTA SAUCE
(Pictured above right)

Edythe Hawkinson, Tumwater, Washington

A cousin of mine in Minnesota was the first one in our family to make this meatless spaghetti sauce, and it has become a mainstay in my family. With its veggies and great garlic and herb flavor, you don't miss the meat at all.

✓ Uses less fat, sugar or salt. Includes Nutrition Facts.

1 large onion, chopped
2 celery ribs, chopped
6 garlic cloves, minced
2 tablespoons olive oil
1 large green pepper, chopped
1 can (6 ounces) pitted ripe olives, drained and sliced
4 beef bouillon cubes
1 cup hot water
2 cans (15 ounces *each*) tomato sauce
1 can (28 ounces) diced tomatoes, undrained
1 can (6 ounces) tomato paste
1 jar (6 ounces) sliced mushrooms, drained
2 teaspoons dried basil
2 teaspoons dried oregano
1/2 teaspoon salt, optional
1/2 teaspoon pepper
Hot cooked pasta

In a Dutch oven, saute the onion, celery and garlic in oil until tender. Add green pepper and olives; saute 2-3 minutes longer. Dissolve bouillon in hot water; add to vegetable mixture. Stir in the tomato sauce, tomatoes, tomato paste, mushrooms, basil, oregano, salt if desired and pepper.

Bring to a boil. Reduce heat; cover and simmer for 1 hour, stirring occasionally. Serve over pasta. **Yield:** 12-14 servings.

Nutrition Facts: 3/4 cup sauce equals 77 calories, 3 g fat (trace saturated fat), trace cholesterol, 631 mg sodium, 11 g carbohydrate, 3 g fiber, 2 g protein.

CHIPOTLE-TERIYAKI PORK CHOPS

(Pictured below)

Kathleen Boulanger, Williston, Vermont

These flavorful pork chops have both Southwestern and Asian flair. In addition, they're topped with queso fresco—a white, fresh Mexican cheese that has a fine-grained texture and mild flavor.

1/4 cup lime juice
1/4 cup orange juice
2 tablespoons soy sauce
2 tablespoons grated onion
1 tablespoon teriyaki sauce
1 chipotle pepper in adobo sauce, drained
1 garlic clove, peeled
1/8 teaspoon ground ginger
2 tablespoons ground ancho pepper
2 tablespoons olive oil
1 teaspoon salt
1/2 teaspoon dried oregano
1/2 teaspoon coarsely ground pepper
1/4 teaspoon ground cumin
4 boneless pork loin chops (8 ounces *each*)
1/2 cup queso fresco *or* shredded Monterey Jack cheese

For sauce, combine the first eight ingredients in a blender or food processor; cover and process until smooth. Transfer to a small bowl; set aside. Combine the ancho pepper, oil, salt, oregano, pepper and cumin; gently rub over both sides of pork chops.

Grill chops, covered, over medium-hot heat for 5-7 minutes on each side or until juices run clear, basting occasionally with 1/3 cup of the sauce. Sprinkle with queso fresco; grill 2-3 minutes longer or until cheese is softened. Serve with remaining sauce. **Yield:** 4 servings.

Easily Impress with Poultry

WHETHER you need a fast weeknight fix or a fancy entree for the weekend, no-fuss chicken and turkey are classic dinner lifesavers.

COMPANY TURKEY POTPIE

(Pictured at right)

You'll want to make this posh potpie from our home economists. It features a crust of no-fuss phyllo dough.

1/2 pound sliced baby portobello mushrooms
2 shallots, chopped
2 teaspoons olive oil
2 cups cubed peeled butternut squash
1 cup chopped sweet red pepper
1/2 cup sliced fennel bulb
2 cups reduced-sodium chicken broth, *divided*
1/3 cup all-purpose flour
1/2 cup 2% milk
3 cups cubed cooked turkey breast
2 tablespoons sherry *or* additional reduced-sodium chicken broth
1 teaspoon rubbed sage
1/2 teaspoon salt
1/2 teaspoon dried thyme
1/4 teaspoon pepper
10 sheets phyllo dough (14 inches x 9 inches)
Refrigerated butter-flavored spray

In a large skillet, saute mushrooms and shallots in oil until tender. Add the squash, red pepper and fennel; saute 5 minutes longer. Add 1/4 cup broth. Cover and cook over medium-low heat until vegetables are tender, about 15 minutes.

Sprinkle flour over vegetables; cook and stir for 1 minute. Gradually add milk and remaining broth. Bring to a boil; cook and stir for 1-2 minutes or until thickened. Stir in the turkey, sherry or additional broth, sage, salt, thyme and pepper. Transfer to a 2-qt. baking dish coated with cooking spray.

Stack all 10 phyllo sheets. Roll up, starting with a long side; cut into 1/2-in. strips. Place strips in a large bowl and toss to separate; spritz with butter-flavored spray. Arrange over turkey mixture; spritz again. Bake, uncovered, at 425° for 10-15 minutes or until golden brown. **Yield:** 6 servings.

Editor's Note: This recipe was tested with I Can't Believe It's Not Butter Spray.

CORNISH HENS WITH WILD RICE

(Pictured above)

Our Test Kitchen staff saved time here by using pre-cooked wild rice, sold in pouches in the rice section.

2-1/4 cups reduced-sodium chicken broth
2/3 cup uncooked wild rice
1/4 cup chopped onion
1/4 cup chopped celery
1 teaspoon olive oil
1 garlic clove, minced
1/2 cup chopped dried apricots
2 tablespoons chopped almonds
1 cup apricot nectar, *divided*
1/2 cup sweet white wine *or* apple juice, *divided*
1/4 teaspoon plus 1/8 teaspoon salt, *divided*
1/4 teaspoon poultry seasoning
1/4 teaspoon pepper, *divided*
2 Cornish game hens (20 ounces *each*), split lengthwise
1 teaspoon white balsamic vinegar
Dash ground cinnamon

In a small saucepan, bring broth and rice to a boil. Reduce heat; cover and simmer for 60-70 minutes or until rice is tender and liquid is absorbed.

Meanwhile, in a nonstick skillet, saute onion and celery in oil until tender. Add garlic; saute 1 minute longer. Stir in the apricots, almonds, 1/3 cup apricot nectar, 1/4 cup wine or apple juice, 1/4 teaspoon salt, poultry seasoning and 1/8 teaspoon pepper. Stir into cooked rice.

Spoon mixture into four mounds in a shallow roasting pan coated with cooking spray; top each with a Cornish hen half. Cover and bake at 375° for 45 minutes. Uncover; bake 15-20 minutes longer or until juices run clear.

In a saucepan, combine the remaining nectar and wine or juice. Bring to a boil; cook for 5-7 minutes or until reduced to 1/2 cup. Add the vinegar, cinnamon and remaining salt and pepper. Reduce heat; cook and stir over medium-low heat for 1 minute. Serve with hens and rice. **Yield:** 4 servings.

HERBED-RUBBED TURKEY

(Pictured below right)

Ruby Bergschneider, Jacksonville, Illinois

Here is a new twist on turkey. I put a salt-free rub under the turkey skin before baking it.

    1 turkey (14 pounds)
    2 tablespoons all-purpose flour
    1 turkey-size oven roasting bag
    2 celery ribs, chopped
    2 small carrots, chopped
    1 small onion, chopped
    1 small potato, sliced
    6 garlic cloves, minced
    2 tablespoons plus 2 teaspoons rubbed sage
    1 tablespoon minced fresh thyme *or*
      1 teaspoon dried thyme
    2 teaspoons pepper
  1/2 teaspoon *each* ground allspice, ginger
      and mustard
  1/4 teaspoon cayenne pepper
    1 tablespoon cornstarch
    2 tablespoons cold water

Pat turkey dry. Place flour in oven bag and shake to coat. Place the bag in a roasting pan; add the celery, carrots, onion and potato. Combine the garlic, the sage, thyme, pepper, allspice, ginger, mustard and cayenne; sprinkle 5 teaspoons over vegetables.

Carefully loosen skin of turkey. Rub half of the remaining seasoning mixture under the skin; rub remaining mixture inside cavity. Skewer turkey openings; tie drumsticks together.

Place turkey, breast side up, over vegetables; close bag with nylon tie. Cut six 1/2-in. slits in top of bag. Bake at 325° for 2-1/4 to 2-3/4 hours or until a meat thermometer inserted in the thigh reads 180°.

Remove turkey to a serving platter and keep warm. Let stand for 15 minutes before carving. Strain contents of oven bag into a small saucepan; skim fat. Discard vegetables. In a small bowl,

combine cornstarch and water until smooth. Gradually stir into cooking juices. Bring to a boil; cook and stir for 2 minutes or until thickened. Serve with turkey. **Yield:** 14 servings.

THYME CHICKEN MARSALA

(Pictured below)

Dorothy Smith, El Dorado, Arkansas

Here's a quick little recipe with restaurant presentation and flavor, perfect for impromptu entertaining.

    2 boneless skinless chicken breast halves
      (4 ounces *each*)
    1 tablespoon all-purpose flour
  1/8 teaspoon plus 1/4 teaspoon salt, *divided*
  1/8 teaspoon plus 1/4 teaspoon pepper,
      divided
    1 medium carrot, julienned
    1 small sweet yellow *or* red pepper, julienned
    3 teaspoons olive oil, *divided*
    2 garlic cloves, minced
  1/3 cup marsala wine *or* reduced-sodium
      chicken broth
    1 tablespoon minced fresh thyme *or*
      1 teaspoon dried thyme

Place chicken in a large resealable plastic bag; flatten to 1/4-in. thickness. Add flour and 1/8 teaspoon each salt and pepper; shake to coat. Set aside.

In a large skillet, saute carrot and yellow pepper in 1-1/2 teaspoons oil for 3 minutes. Add garlic and remaining salt and pepper; cook and stir until vegetables are crisp-tender. Transfer to two serving plates; keep warm.

In the same skillet, heat remaining oil over medium heat. Cook chicken for 2-3 minutes on each side or until juices run clear; place over vegetables. Add wine or broth and thyme to the pan; cook for 1 minute, stirring to loosen browned bits. Pour over chicken. **Yield:** 2 servings.

★★★★★★★★★★★★★

BEEF PINWHEELS

(Pictured above)

Ruthmarie Hosler, Endwell, New York

Our summer season in Upstate New York is not very long, so we try to cook outdoors often. This recipe is one of my most popular requests. I really don't know where it originated, but it's been handed down for many years.

  3/4 cup vegetable oil
  2/3 cup water
  1/4 cup soy sauce
    1 tablespoon lemon-pepper seasoning
    2 teaspoons Worcestershire sauce
    4 drops hot pepper sauce
    1 flank steak (2 to 2-1/2 pounds), trimmed

In a bowl, combine oil, water, soy sauce, lemon-pepper, Worcestershire sauce and hot pepper sauce; set aside.

Pound flank steak on each side. Cut into 1/2-in. strips on the diagonally; add to marinade. Cover and refrigerate for 4 hours or overnight.

Divide meat strips into eight portions. Roll and shape strips, using larger strips around edges, into pinwheels. Secure each with a skewer.

Grill over hot heat for 5-6 minutes per side or until done. **Yield:** 8 servings.

★★★★★★★★★★★★★

LEMON-HERB TURKEY BREAST

(Pictured at right)

Joy Luster, Mt. Vernon, Missouri

The first time I tried this recipe, and told my kids I'd prepared the turkey differently, they threw a fit...un-til they tasted it! Now they prepare it in their own homes. The marinade makes the turkey moist and flavorful. Using a turkey breast is a nice change from roasting a whole turkey.

    1 cup lemon juice
  1/2 cup olive oil
  1/4 cup soy sauce
  1/2 cup packed fresh parsley sprigs
    4 green onions, chopped
    2 garlic cloves, peeled
  1/2 teaspoon Dijon mustard
  1/2 teaspoon *each* dried oregano and sage leaves
  1/2 teaspoon salt
  1/2 teaspoon pepper
    1 bone-in turkey breast (6 to 7 pounds)

In a blender, combine the lemon juice, oil, soy sauce, parsley, onions, garlic, mustard and seasonings; cover and process until smooth. Pour 1 cup marinade into a 2-gal. resealable plastic bag; add turkey. Seal bag and turn to coat; refrigerate for up to 24 hours. Cover and refrigerate remaining marinade for basting.

Line the bottom of a large shallow roasting pan with foil. Drain and discard marinade; place turkey on a rack in prepared pan.

Bake, uncovered, at 325° for 2 to 2-1/2 hours or until a meat thermometer reads 170°, basting every 30 minutes with reserved marinade. (Cover loosely with foil if turkey browns too quickly.) Cover and let stand for 15 minutes before carving. **Yield:** 12-14 servings.

Main Dishes

AUTUMN SAUSAGE CASSEROLE
(Pictured below)

Diane Brunell, Washington, Massachusetts

Apple, raisins and spices give this tasty casserole plenty of autumnal flair. We enjoy it with a green salad on a cold fall day. It would be a nice potluck dish, too—just double the recipe.

    1 pound bulk pork sausage
    1 medium apple, peeled and chopped
    1 medium onion, chopped
  1/2 cup chopped celery
    3 cups cooked long grain rice
  1/2 cup raisins
  1/3 cup minced fresh parsley
    1 tablespoon brown sugar
  1/2 teaspoon salt
  1/4 teaspoon ground allspice
  1/4 teaspoon ground cinnamon
  1/8 teaspoon pepper

In a large skillet, cook the sausage, apple, onion and celery over medium heat until meat is no longer pink; drain. Stir in the remaining ingredients. Transfer to a greased 2-qt. baking dish. Cover and bake at 350° for 25-30 minutes or until heated through. **Yield:** 4-6 servings.

BRATS WITH SAUERKRAUT
(Pictured above)

Darlene Dixon, Hanover, Minnesota

I've made many variations of this excellent main dish. The bratwurst can be plain, smoked or cheese-flavored, served whole or cut in slices, with a bun or without. It would be popular at a party.

    8 uncooked bratwurst
    1 can (14 ounces) sauerkraut, rinsed and
      well drained
    2 medium apples, peeled and finely
      chopped
    3 bacon strips, cooked and crumbled
  1/4 cup packed brown sugar
  1/4 cup finely chopped onion
    1 teaspoon ground mustard
    8 brat buns, split

Place the bratwurst in a 5-qt. slow cooker. In a large bowl, combine the sauerkraut, apples, bacon, brown sugar, onion and mustard; spoon over bratwurst.

Cover and cook on low for 6-7 hours or until sausage is no longer pink. Place brats in buns; using a slotted spoon, top with sauerkraut mixture. **Yield:** 8 servings.

SLOW COOKERS VS. CROCK-POTS

A "Crock-Pot" is a trademarked term for a slow cooker that has a crockery insert encased in a lining where heat coils surround the food. Most of these slow cookers feature two heat settings: low and high. All of the slow-cooked recipes in this book were tested with a crockery-type of slow cooker. Other slow cookers involve thin, metal pots that sit on electric heating bases.

Asian Barbecued Short Ribs

(Pictured below)

Connie McDowell, Lincoln, Nebraska

Here in beef country, we find all sorts of different ways to serve beef. A former boss of mine, who owned a Midwestern meat plant, gave me this recipe. It was an immediate hit with my family! The soy sauce, ketchup, brown sugar, ginger and other seasonings make a great barbecue sauce for the ribs.

        4 pounds bone-in beef short ribs
        1 tablespoon vegetable oil
        1 medium onion, sliced
      3/4 cup ketchup
      3/4 cup water, *divided*
      1/4 cup soy sauce
        2 tablespoons lemon juice
        1 tablespoon brown sugar
        1 teaspoon ground mustard
      1/2 teaspoon ground ginger
      1/4 teaspoon salt
      1/8 teaspoon pepper
        1 bay leaf
        2 tablespoons all-purpose flour

In a Dutch oven, brown the ribs in oil on all sides in batches. Remove ribs; discard pan drippings. In the same pan, saute the onion for 2 minutes or until tender. Return ribs to the pan.

Combine the ketchup, 1/2 cup water, soy sauce, lemon juice, brown sugar, mustard, ginger, salt, pepper and bay leaf; pour over ribs. Cover and bake at 325° for 1-3/4 to 2 hours or until meat is tender.

Remove ribs and keep warm. Discard bay leaf. Skim fat from pan drippings. In a small bowl, combine flour and remaining water until smooth; gradually stir into drippings. Bring to a boil; cook and stir for 2 minutes or until thickened. Serve with ribs. **Yield:** 6 servings.

Herb-Rubbed Pork Tenderloin

(Pictured above)

If you want a quick recipe using lean pork tenderloin, try this idea from our Test Kitchen. In minutes, you can create a great-tasting rub using spices you likely already have in your cupboard. This rub has a nice little kick to it so you won't miss the salt, either.

        1 tablespoon garlic powder
        2 teaspoons brown sugar
        2 teaspoons rubbed sage
    1-1/2 teaspoons dried thyme
        1 teaspoon ground mustard
      1/2 teaspoon cayenne pepper
      1/2 teaspoon pepper
        2 pork tenderloins (1 pound *each*)

In a small bowl, combine the first seven ingredients; rub over pork. Place in a large ungreased shallow glass dish. Cover and refrigerate for up to 8 hours.

Place tenderloins on a rack in a shallow roasting pan. Bake at 400° for 35-40 minutes or until a meat thermometer reads 160°. Let stand for 5 minutes before slicing. **Yield:** 8 servings.

OVEN-BAKED FRIED CHICKEN

Esther Hylden, Park River, North Dakota

This recipe reminds me of the wonderful, crispy fried chicken my mother used to make for Sunday dinner. Flaxseed, olive oil and skinless chicken make it a healthier version of her old specialty.

1/2 cup canola oil
1/2 cup grated Parmesan cheese
1/2 cup crushed cornflakes
1/2 cup ground flaxseed
  2 teaspoons seasoned salt
1/2 teaspoon pepper
  1 broiler/fryer chicken (3 to 4 pounds),
    skin removed

Place olive oil in a shallow bowl. In another shallow bowl, combine the Parmesan cheese, cornflake crumbs, flaxseed, seasoned salt and pepper. Dip chicken into oil, then coat with crumb mixture.

Arrange chicken in a greased 15-in. x 10-in. x 1-in. baking pan. Bake, uncovered, at 375° for 40-45 minutes or until chicken juices run clear. **Yield:** 4 servings.

CAJUN-STYLE CATFISH

Irene Cliett, Cedar Bluff, Mississippi

This dish features the green pepper, onion and celery combination common to Cajun dishes, but it's not too spicy. It's a colorful and flavorful way to serve our locally raised catfish.

1/2 cup chopped onion
1/2 cup chopped celery
1/2 cup chopped green pepper
  1 tablespoon olive oil
  1 can (14-1/2 ounces) diced tomatoes and
    green chilies, undrained
1/2 cup sliced fresh mushrooms
  1 can (2-1/4 ounces) sliced ripe olives,
    drained
1/2 teaspoon garlic powder
  4 catfish fillets (6 ounces *each*)
1/4 cup grated Parmesan cheese

In a large skillet, saute the onion, celery and green pepper in oil until tender. Add the tomatoes, mushrooms, olives and garlic powder. Bring to a boil. Reduce heat; simmer, uncovered, for 10 minutes or until heated through.

Place the catfish in an ungreased 13-in. x 9-in. x 2-in. baking dish. Top with vegetable mixture; sprinkle with Parmesan cheese. Bake, uncovered, at 400° for 15-20 minutes or until fish flakes easily with a fork. **Yield:** 4 servings.

BEEFY NOODLE CASSEROLE

(Pictured above)

Grace Lema, Winton, California

This casserole is perfect when there's a busy day coming up, because you can prepare it ahead of time. It's ideal for a potluck, too. The flavors blend together to create a delicious combination.

    2 pounds ground beef
    1 large onion, chopped
    1 medium green pepper, chopped
    1 can (14-3/4 ounces) cream-style corn
    1 can (10-3/4 ounces) condensed tomato
      soup, undiluted
    1 can (8 ounces) tomato sauce
    1 jar (2 ounces) sliced pimientos, drained
    2 tablespoons chopped jalapeno pepper
1-1/2 teaspoons salt
  1/2 teaspoon chili powder
  1/4 teaspoon ground mustard
  1/4 teaspoon pepper
    1 package (8 ounces) medium egg
      noodles, cooked and drained
    1 jar (4-1/2 ounces) sliced mushrooms,
      drained
1-1/2 cups (6 ounces) shredded cheddar cheese

In a large skillet, cook beef, onion and green pepper until the meat is no longer pink and vegetables are tender; drain. Add the next nine ingredients. Stir in noodles and mushrooms.

Transfer to a greased 13-in. x 9-in. x 2-in. baking dish. Sprinkle with cheese. Bake, uncovered, at 350° for 45 minutes or until heated through. **Yield:** 8-10 servings.

Editor's Note: When cutting or seeding hot peppers, use rubber or plastic gloves to protect your hands. Avoid touching your face.

Asian Pork Kabobs

(Pictured below)

Trisha Kruse, Eagle, Idaho

Sweet and tangy, these kabobs have a delicious kick thanks to the hot pepper sauce. My recipe can be adapted to add your favorite vegetables. It's great with rice and a fresh salad.

  1/4 cup teriyaki sauce
    2 tablespoons balsamic vinegar
    2 tablespoons sesame oil
    2 tablespoons honey
    2 teaspoons sriracha Asian hot chili sauce
    or 1 teaspoon hot pepper sauce
    1 pound pork tenderloin, cut into 1-inch cubes
    1 medium onion, quartered
    1 medium sweet red pepper, cut into 2-inch pieces

In a bowl, combine the teriyaki sauce, vinegar, oil, honey and hot pepper sauce. Pour 1/3 cup marinade into a large resealable plastic bag; add pork. Seal bag and turn to coat; refrigerate for at least 2 hours. Cover and refrigerate remaining marinade for basting.

Drain and discard marinade. On four metal or soaked wooden skewers, alternately thread the pork, onion and red pepper.

Grill kabobs, covered, over medium heat for 10-15 minutes or until vegetables are tender and meat is no longer pink, turning occasionally and basting frequently with reserved marinade. **Yield:** 4 servings.

Easy Chicken Fajitas

(Pictured above)

Shannon Mills, El Paso, Texas

Here's a simple recipe for a colorful, wrapped sandwich that everybody enjoys. The chicken cooks up nice and tender, and the onion, tomato, cilantro and Italian dressing add a finger-licking blend of flavors.

    1 medium tomato, seeded and chopped
    2 tablespoons chopped onion
    2 tablespoons minced fresh cilantro
4-1/2 teaspoons olive oil
Dash salt
FAJITAS:
  1/2 pound boneless skinless chicken breasts, cut into 1/4-inch strips
  1/3 cup Italian salad dressing
  1/2 cup sliced onion
    1 tablespoon vegetable oil
    4 flour tortillas (6 inches), warmed
Shredded Monterey Jack cheese, shredded lettuce and sour cream

In a small bowl, combine the first five ingredients; set aside. Place the chicken in a large resealable plastic bag; add salad dressing. Seal bag and turn to coat; refrigerate for 15 minutes. Drain and discard marinade.

In a large skillet, saute onion in oil for 3 minutes; remove and set aside. In the same skillet, saute chicken until no longer pink. Return onion to the pan; cook and stir until onion is tender.

Spoon chicken mixture onto one side of each tortilla. Top with tomato mixture, as well as the cheese, lettuce and sour cream; fold tortilla over filling. **Yield:** 4 fajitas.

from the heat; add the stuffing cubes, corn bread, broth and egg. Mix well. Spoon over chicken mixture. Cover and bake at 350° for 35-40 minutes or until a thermometer inserted near the center reads 160°.

For gravy, melt butter in a small saucepan. Stir in flour until smooth; gradually add broth and milk. Bring to a boil; cook and stir for 2 minutes or until thickened. Serve with chicken and dressing. **Yield:** 8 servings.

★★★★★★★★★★★★

GRILLED LEMON PORK CHOPS

(Pictured below)

Angela Oelschlaeger, Tonganoxie, Kansas

These melt-in-your-mouth pork chops are always a hit with my family and with company, too. Lemonade concentrate is what gives them their tangy lemon flavor. They're so easy to make that we have them often.

  1 can (12 ounces) frozen lemonade
    concentrate, thawed
2/3 cup soy sauce
  2 teaspoons seasoned salt
  1 teaspoon celery salt
1/4 teaspoon garlic powder
  6 boneless butterflied pork chops
    (1/2-inch thick and 6 ounces *each*)

In a bowl, combine the lemonade concentrate, soy sauce, seasoned salt, celery salt and garlic powder. Pour 1-1/2 cups into a large resealable plastic bag; add pork chops. Seal bag and turn to coat; refrigerate for at least 4 hours. Cover and refrigerate remaining marinade for basting.

Coat grill rack with cooking spray before starting the grill. Drain and discard marinade. Grill pork chops, uncovered, over medium heat for 4 minutes. Turn; brush with reserved marinade. Grill 4-6 minutes longer or until meat juices run clear. **Yield:** 6 servings.

★★★★★★★★★★★★

CHICKEN 'N' DRESSING CASSEROLE

(Pictured above)

Billie Blanton, Kingsport, Tennessee

This casserole is a real favorite in our area and with my family as well. It's a great way to use leftover chicken or turkey, and so easy that even beginner cooks will have success making it.

  4 cups cubed cooked chicken
  2 tablespoons all-purpose flour
1/2 cup chicken broth
1/2 cup milk
Salt and pepper to taste
DRESSING:
  2 celery ribs, chopped
  1 small onion, finely chopped
  1 tablespoon butter
  1 teaspoon rubbed sage
1/2 teaspoon poultry seasoning
1/4 teaspoon salt
1/8 teaspoon pepper
  2 cups unseasoned stuffing cubes,
    crushed
  2 cups coarsely crumbled corn bread
1/2 cup chicken broth
  1 egg, beaten
GRAVY:
1/4 cup butter
  6 tablespoons all-purpose flour
  2 cups chicken broth
1/2 cup milk

Place chicken in a greased 2-qt. baking dish; set aside. In a small saucepan, combine the flour, broth and milk until smooth. Bring to a boil; cook and stir for 2 minutes. Season with salt and pepper. Spoon over chicken.

In a large skillet, saute the celery and onion in butter until tender. Stir in seasonings. Remove

Mustard-Herb Chicken Breasts

(Pictured at far right)

Terri Weme, Smithers, British Columbia

Even though I learned to cook when I was young, and helped make supper for our family, I didn't really enjoy it until I discovered incredible recipes such as this.

☑ Uses less fat, sugar or salt. Includes Nutrition Facts.

- 1/4 cup chopped green onions
- 1/4 cup Dijon-mayonnaise blend
- 2 tablespoons lemon juice
- 1 garlic clove, minced
- 1/2 teaspoon salt
- 1/2 teaspoon dried thyme
- 1/4 teaspoon pepper
- 4 boneless skinless chicken breast halves

In a large resealable plastic bag, combine the first seven ingredients; add chicken. Seal bag and turn to coat. Refrigerate for 2 hours, turning once.

Grill chicken, covered, over medium heat for 6-8 minutes on each side or until juices run clear. **Yield:** 4 servings.

Nutrition Facts: 1 chicken breast half equals 163 calories, 3 g fat (1 g saturated fat), 73 mg cholesterol, 720 mg sodium, 2 g carbohydrate, trace fiber, 27 g protein.

Glazed Corned Beef and Cabbage

Byrnadine Lawson, Columbus, Ohio

This unique dish features a Dijon mustard glaze on corned beef, and a tangy horseradish sauce with the cabbage and red potatoes.

- 1 corned beef brisket with spice packet (2-1/2 pounds)
- 1 medium head cabbage, cut into wedges
- 1 pound small red potatoes, halved

DIJON GLAZE:
- 2 tablespoons honey
- 1 tablespoon orange juice concentrate
- 2 teaspoons Dijon mustard

HORSERADISH SAUCE:
- 1/4 cup butter, cubed
- 2 to 3 tablespoons prepared horseradish
- 2 tablespoons chopped green onion
- 1/8 teaspoon salt
- 1/8 teaspoon pepper

Place brisket and contents of spice packet in a Dutch oven; cover with water. Bring to a boil. Reduce the heat; cover and simmer for 2-1/2 hours

or until the meat is tender.

Place cabbage and potatoes in a steamer basket; place in a large saucepan over 1 in. of water. Bring to a boil; cover and steam for 25-30 minutes or until tender, adding more water to pan if necessary.

Transfer the brisket to a broiler pan. Combine glaze ingredients; brush over beef. Broil 4-6 in. from the heat for 3-4 minutes or until beef is glazed. Thinly slice across the grain.

In a small microwave-safe bowl, combine the sauce ingredients. Cover and microwave on high for 30-45 seconds or until butter is melted. Drizzle over cabbage and potatoes. **Yield:** 6-8 servings.

Chile Rellenos Quiche

Linda Miritello, Mesa, Arizona

This is a quick and easy recipe, and I usually have the ingredients on hand.

- Pastry for single-crust pie (9 inches)
- 2 tablespoons cornmeal
- 1-1/2 cups (6 ounces) shredded Monterey Jack cheese
- 1 cup (4 ounces) shredded cheddar cheese
- 1 can (4 ounces) chopped green chilies
- 3 eggs
- 3/4 cup sour cream
- 1 tablespoon minced fresh cilantro
- 2 to 4 drops hot pepper sauce, optional

Line unpricked pastry shell with a double thickness of heavy-duty foil. Bake at 450° for 8 minutes. Remove foil; bake 5 minutes longer. Cool on a wire rack. Reduce heat to 350°.

Sprinkle cornmeal over bottom of pastry shell. In a bowl, combine the cheeses; set aside 1/2 cup for topping. Add chilies to the remaining cheese mixture; sprinkle into crust.

In a small bowl, beat the eggs, sour cream, cilantro and hot pepper sauce if desired. Pour into crust; sprinkle with reserved cheese mixture. Bake for 35-40 minutes or until a knife inserted near the center comes out clean. Let stand for 5 minutes before cutting. **Yield:** 6 servings.

Quick Quiche Test

To avoid overbaking a quiche, do the "knife test" when the quiche appears to have set around the edges but still seems a little soft in the very center. The quiche is done if the knife inserted near the center comes out clean.

BISCUIT HAM SPIRALS

(Pictured below)

Peggy Zgonc, Chisholm, Minnesota

This is a great way to use leftover ham...in fact, a friend thinks it's one of the best ham dishes she has ever tried.

      2 cups all-purpose flour
3-1/2 teaspoons baking powder
      2 teaspoons sugar
      1 teaspoon salt
   1/2 cup shortening
      1 egg
   3/4 cup milk
FILLING:
2-1/2 cups ground fully cooked ham
      1 small onion, finely chopped
      1 egg
      2 tablespoons prepared mustard
      2 tablespoons minced fresh parsley *or*
         2 teaspoons dried parsley flakes
      1 tablespoon prepared horseradish
   1/4 teaspoon pepper
CHEESE SAUCE:
      3 tablespoons butter
      3 tablespoons all-purpose flour
   1/2 teaspoon salt
   1/4 teaspoon white pepper
      2 cups milk
      1 cup (4 ounces) shredded cheddar
         cheese

In a bowl, combine the flour, baking powder, sugar and salt. Cut in shortening until mixture resembles coarse crumbs. Combine egg and milk; stir into crumb mixture just until moistened. Turn onto a floured surface; knead 12 times. Roll into a 12-in. x 10-in. rectangle.

Combine the filling ingredients; spread over dough to within 1/2 in. of edges. Roll up jelly-roll style, starting with a long side; pinch seam to seal. Cut into 1-in. slices. Place cut side down on a greased baking sheet. Bake at 425° for 15-18 minutes or until golden brown.

Meanwhile, in a small saucepan, melt butter. Stir in flour, salt and white pepper until smooth. Gradually add milk. Bring to a boil; cook and stir for 2 minutes or until thickened. Remove from the heat; stir in cheese until melted. Serve with ham slices. **Yield:** 12 slices.

FAVORITE BARBECUED CHICKEN

Bobbie Morgan, Woodstock, Georgia

What better place to find a fantastic barbecue sauce than Texas, and that's where this one is from—it's my father-in-law's own recipe. We've served it at many family reunions and think it's the best!

      1 broiler/fryer chicken (3 pounds), cut up
Salt and pepper to taste
BARBECUE SAUCE:
      1 small onion, finely chopped
      1 tablespoon vegetable oil
      1 cup ketchup
      2 tablespoons lemon juice
      1 tablespoon brown sugar
      1 tablespoon water
   1/2 teaspoon ground mustard
   1/4 teaspoon garlic powder
   1/8 teaspoon pepper
Dash salt
Dash hot pepper sauce

Sprinkle chicken with salt and pepper. Grill chicken, skin side down, uncovered, over medium heat for 20 minutes.

Meanwhile, in a small saucepan, saute the onion in oil until tender. Stir in the remaining sauce ingredients. Bring to a boil. Reduce heat; simmer, uncovered, for 10 minutes.

Turn chicken; grill 15-25 minutes longer or until no longer pink, brushing often with barbecue sauce. **Yield:** 6 servings.

DELICIOUS MEAL IDEAS

Round out the barbecued chicken easily with deli coleslaw or pick up a bag of spinach leaves from the produce department for a fast salad. Freshly baked corn bread adds a hearty addition to the meal, and angel food cake topped with berries ends supper on a sweet note.

GERMAN-STYLE SHORT RIBS

(Pictured above)

Bregitte Rugman, Shanty Bay, Ontario

Our whole family gets excited when I plug in the slow cooker to make these fall-off-the-bone-tender ribs. We like them served over rice or egg noodles.

✓ Uses less fat, sugar or salt. Includes Nutrition Facts.

3/4 cup dry red wine *or* beef broth
1/2 cup mango chutney
3 tablespoons quick-cooking tapioca
1/4 cup water
3 tablespoons brown sugar
3 tablespoons cider vinegar
1 tablespoon Worcestershire sauce
1/2 teaspoon salt
1/2 teaspoon ground mustard
1/2 teaspoon chili powder
1/2 teaspoon pepper
4 pounds bone-in beef short ribs
2 medium onions, sliced
Hot cooked egg noodles

In a 5-qt. slow cooker, combine the first 11 ingredients. Add ribs and turn to coat. Top with onions. Cover and cook on low for 8-10 hours or until meat is tender. Remove ribs from slow cooker. Skim fat from cooking juices; serve over ribs and noodles. **Yield:** 8 servings.

Nutrition Facts: 8 ounces equals 302 calories, 11g fat (5 g saturated fat), 55 mg cholesterol, 378 mg sodium, 28 g carbohydrate, 1 g fiber, 19 g protein.

GRILLED FAJITAS WITH PICO DE GALLO

(Pictured at right)

Christine Yost, Copeland, Kansas

This is a good recipe when you're pressed for time. The beef doesn't need to marinate very long before grilling, and the accompanying vegetable relish is easy to stir up with just a few ingredients.

3 tablespoons lime juice, *divided*
2 tablespoons vegetable oil
2 garlic cloves, minced
1 boneless beef sirloin steak (3/4 inch thick and 1 pound)
3/4 cup diced zucchini
3/4 cup chopped tomato
1/3 cup picante sauce *or* salsa
8 flour tortillas (8 inches), warmed

In a large resealable plastic bag, combine 2 tablespoons lime juice, oil and garlic; add steak. Seal bag and turn to coat; refrigerate for 30 minutes.

For pico de gallo, in a small bowl, combine the zucchini, tomato, picante sauce and remaining lime juice; set aside.

Drain and discard marinade. Grill steak, covered, over medium heat for 6-8 minutes on each side or until meat reaches desired doneness (for medium-rare, a meat thermometer should read 145°; medium, 160°; well-done, 170°).

Thinly slice steak across the grain; place on tortillas. Top with pico de gallo; roll up and serve immediately. **Yield:** 4 servings.

CILANTRO CHICKEN
(Pictured below)

Mary Pipkin, Melba, Idaho

If you like cilantro, you will definitely enjoy this dish. The herb adds great flavor to chicken along with the tangy lemon juice and caramelized onions. From the first time we tried it, my husband and I loved it.

- 1 pound boneless skinless chicken breasts, cut into 1-inch cubes
- 1/2 teaspoon salt
- 1/2 teaspoon ground cumin
- 1/4 teaspoon pepper
- 4 tablespoons butter, *divided*
- 2 large onions, sliced
- 1/2 cup lemon juice
- 1/4 cup minced fresh cilantro

Hot cooked rice

Sprinkle chicken with salt, cumin and pepper. In a large skillet over medium heat, cook and stir the chicken in 2 tablespoons butter until no longer pink. Remove and keep warm.

In the same skillet, saute onions in remaining butter until tender and golden brown. Return chicken to the pan. Stir in lemon juice and cilantro; bring to a boil. Serve with rice. **Yield:** 4 servings.

ITALIAN SHRIMP AND PASTA
(Pictured above)

Frank Fader, Payson, Arizona

We like pasta with Italian tomato sauces, and this recipe is one we make often. It's heavy on the shrimp and light on the pasta, and that's the way we like it.

- 1 garlic clove, minced
- 2 tablespoons olive oil
- 2 cans (14-1/2 ounces *each*) diced tomatoes, undrained
- 1/2 cup chicken broth
- 1/2 teaspoon dried basil
- 1/2 teaspoon dried oregano
- 1/4 teaspoon pepper
- 6 ounces uncooked angel hair pasta
- 1 pound uncooked medium shrimp, peeled and deveined

In a large skillet, saute garlic in oil. Add the tomatoes, broth, basil, oregano and pepper. Bring to a boil over medium heat. Reduce heat; simmer, uncovered, for 15 minutes.

Meanwhile, cook pasta according to package directions. Add the shrimp to the tomato mixture; cook for 5-6 minutes or until shrimp turn pink. Drain pasta; toss with shrimp mixture. **Yield:** 4 servings.

SAUSAGE POTATO SUPPER

Nancy Russell, Englewood, Colorado

One Saturday night a few years ago, I came up with this dish on the spur of the moment. It was dinnertime, and I had to use what I had on hand. It's been popular with my family ever since.

Main Dishes

2 small red potatoes, cubed
1 small zucchini, cut into 1/4-inch slices
1/4 to 1/2 teaspoon garlic salt
1 tablespoon butter
1/2 pound smoked sausage, cut into
  1/2-inch slices
4 tablespoons grated Parmesan cheese,
  divided
1/8 to 1/4 teaspoon pepper

Place potatoes in a small saucepan and cover with water. Bring to a boil. Reduce heat; cover and cook for 15-20 minutes or until tender.

Meanwhile, sprinkle zucchini with garlic salt. In a small skillet, stir-fry zucchini in butter until crisp-tender. Add sausage; cook until browned.

Drain potatoes; add to skillet. Sprinkle with 2 tablespoons Parmesan cheese and pepper; heat through. Sprinkle with remaining cheese. **Yield:** 2 servings.

PIEROGI SKILLET

Bernice Rembisz, Housatonic, Massachusetts

With sauerkraut, cabbage, onion and egg noodles, this dish has all the flavor of traditional pierogies but without all the work of making the dumplings. Just combine the ingredients in a skillet and let it simmer. I call it "Lazy Man's Pierogi."

1/2 pound sliced bacon, diced
1 large onion, chopped
1 can (27 ounces) sauerkraut, rinsed and
  squeezed dry
1 small head cabbage, shredded
1/2 teaspoon pepper
5 cups uncooked egg noodles
6 tablespoons butter
1-1/2 teaspoons salt

In a large skillet or Dutch oven, cook the bacon until almost crisp. Add onion; cook and stir until bacon is crisp and onion is tender. Drain. Add the sauerkraut, cabbage and pepper; mix well. Cover and simmer for 45 minutes.

Meanwhile, cook the noodles according to package directions; drain. Stir the noodles, butter and salt into cabbage mixture. Cover and simmer 30 minutes longer. **Yield:** 12 servings.

HONEY ORANGE CHICKEN

(Pictured at right)

Marie Hannah, Hemet, California

This dish is elegant enough for company and tastes like you spent all day in the kitchen. With five children to keep up with, I look for recipes that are easy to prepare. They love this chicken and pasta meal, with its honey-orange sauce. I use citrus fruits and juices often in cooking since citrus is always plentiful here in Southern California.

1 pound boneless skinless chicken
  breasts, cut into 1/2-inch strips
3 tablespoons butter, *divided*
1 teaspoon salt
1/2 teaspoon paprika
1/4 teaspoon pepper
1 medium onion, sliced
1 tablespoon cornstarch
1/2 teaspoon ground ginger
1/4 teaspoon ground nutmeg
1 cup orange juice
1/4 cup honey
1/2 cup pitted ripe olives, halved
Hot cooked linguine

In a large skillet, saute chicken in 2 tablespoons butter until juices run clear. Sprinkle with salt, paprika and pepper. Remove and keep warm. In the same pan, saute the onion in remaining butter until tender.

In a small bowl, combine the cornstarch, ginger, nutmeg, orange juice and honey. Pour over onion. Bring to a boil; cook and stir for 2 minutes or until thickened. Add olives and chicken. Simmer, uncovered, for 5 minutes or until chicken is heated through. Serve over the linguine. **Yield:** 4 servings.

ROUND OUT dinners with the tasty accompaniments found here. In addition to vegetables dishes and dressings, you'll find cranberry sauces, chutneys and more!

ATTRACTIVE ADDITION. Sauteed Baby Carrot Medley (p. 75).

Sauteed Baby Carrot Medley

(Pictured at left)

Lisa McNeece, Bakersfield, California

Convenient baby-cut carrots star in this colorful, quick-to-fix side dish. I'm on the staff of a top grower and processor of baby-cut carrots, and this recipe is a favorite.

☑ Uses less fat, sugar or salt. Includes Nutrition Facts.

- 3 cups fresh baby carrots
- 2 tablespoons olive oil
- 1 small yellow summer squash, thinly sliced
- 1 small sweet red pepper, julienned
- 1-1/2 cups fresh sugar snap peas
- 2 garlic cloves, minced
- 1/2 cup water
- 2 tablespoons sun-dried tomatoes (not packed in oil), finely chopped
- 1 tablespoon capers, drained
- 1/2 teaspoon salt
- 1/4 teaspoon pepper

In a large skillet, saute carrots in oil for 1 minute. Add squash; saute 1 minute longer. Stir in the red pepper, peas and garlic; saute 1 minute more.

Add water. Reduce heat to medium. Cook and stir until liquid is evaporated and vegetables are crisp-tender. Stir in the tomatoes, capers, salt and pepper. **Yield:** 8 servings.

Nutrition Facts: 2/3 cup equals 71 calories, 4 g fat (trace saturated fat), 0 cholesterol, 240 mg sodium, 9 g carbohydrate, 2 g fiber, 2 g protein.

Cajun Sweet Potatoes

Stacy Cox, Palestine, Texas

If you like a sweet and spicy flavor combo, you'll get a kick out of these sweet potatoes. I use Cajun seasoning and cayenne pepper to bring unexpected flavor to the dinner accompaniment.

☑ Uses less fat, sugar or salt. Includes Nutrition Facts.

- 3 pounds sweet potatoes, peeled and cubed
- 2 tablespoons olive oil
- 3 tablespoons brown sugar
- 1 teaspoon Cajun seasoning
- 1/2 teaspoon salt
- 1/8 to 1/4 teaspoon cayenne pepper

In a large bowl, toss the sweet potatoes and oil. Arrange potatoes in a single layer in two 15-in. x 10-in. x 1-in. baking pans coated with cooking spray. Bake, uncovered, at 450° for 20 minutes.

Combine brown sugar, Cajun seasoning, salt and cayenne; sprinkle over potatoes. Bake 5-6 minutes longer or until tender. **Yield:** 6 servings.

Nutrition Facts: 3/4 cup equals 208 calories, 5 g fat (1 g saturated fat), 0 cholesterol, 324 mg sodium, 40 g carbohydrate, 4 g fiber, 2 g protein.

Feta Zucchini Pancakes

Lisa Kivirist, Browntown, Wisconsin

Guests at our farmhouse bed and breakfast see zucchini in our garden one day and savor it in these moist and flavorful pancakes the next. The patties make a refreshing side dish and a unique use for the popular vegetable.

- 4 eggs, *separated*
- 4 cups shredded zucchini
- 1 cup (4 ounces) crumbled feta cheese
- 1/2 cup finely chopped green onions
- 1/2 cup all-purpose flour
- 1 tablespoon chopped fresh mint *or* 1 teaspoon dried mint
- 1/2 teaspoon salt
- 1/4 teaspoon pepper
- 6 teaspoons vegetable oil, *divided*

In a small mixing bowl, beat egg whites until stiff peaks form; set aside. In a large bowl, combine the egg yolks, zucchini, feta cheese, onions, flour, mint, salt and pepper; fold in egg whites.

In a large skillet, heat 2 teaspoons of oil over medium heat; drop four 1/3 cupfuls of batter into skillet. Fry for 2 minutes on each side or until golden brown. Repeat, making two more batches with remaining oil and batter. **Yield:** 1 dozen.

In a small saucepan, whisk the brown sugar, flour, salt, ginger, vinegar, soy sauce and reserved pineapple juice until smooth. Bring to a boil; cook and stir for 2 minutes or until thickened. Pour over potato mixture and toss to coat.

Cover and bake at 350° for 65-70 minutes or until potatoes are tender. Sprinkle with remaining coconut. Bake, uncovered, for 10 minutes or until lightly browned. **Yield:** 4-6 servings.

Nutrition Facts: 3/4 cup equals 221 calories, 6 g fat (5 g saturated fat), 0 cholesterol, 406 mg sodium, 42 g carbohydrate, 3 g fiber, 2 g protein.

▪▪▪▪▪▪▪▪▪▪▪▪▪▪▪

RICE AND GREEN PEA SIDE DISH
(Pictured below)

Kathie Landmann, Lexington Park, Maryland

This recipe combines two of my family's favorite foods—peas and rice. The ingredients may be simple, but the colorful combination is unbeatable.

>   1 cup uncooked long grain rice
>   2 cups water
>   1 medium onion, chopped
>   2 cups frozen peas, defrosted
>   1 carrot, peeled and shredded
>   1 teaspoon chicken bouillon granules
>   1 teaspoon salt-free herb seasoning
> Salt and pepper to taste

Place all ingredients in a 3-qt. saucepan. Cover and bring to a boil. Reduce heat to simmer and continue to cook 15 minutes or until rice is tender. **Yield:** 6 servings.

▪▪▪▪▪▪▪▪▪▪▪▪▪▪▪

PINEAPPLE COCONUT POTATOES
(Pictured above)

Paula Pelis, Lenhartsville, Pennsylvania

There's nothing like potatoes…and this recipe gives them a bit of tropical flair with pineapple, coconut, soy sauce and ginger. My family thinks they're out of this world.

☑ Uses less fat, sugar or salt. Includes Nutrition Facts.

>   1 can (20 ounces) unsweetened pineapple chunks
>   2 cups diced peeled potatoes
>   1 cup flaked coconut, *divided*
>   1 medium onion, sliced
> 1/4 cup packed brown sugar
>   2 tablespoons all-purpose flour
> 1/2 teaspoon salt
> 1/2 teaspoon ground ginger
> 1/4 cup cider vinegar
>   1 tablespoon soy sauce

Drain pineapple, reserving juice. In a large bowl, combine the pineapple, potatoes, 3/4 cup coconut and onion. Transfer to a greased 1-qt. baking dish; set aside.

🎀 SPICE CRANBERRY SAUCE

(Pictured above)

Allison Thompson, Lansing, Michigan

While this cranberry sauce is simmering, the wonderful fragrance of the spices brings back happy memories of when my mother made it for the holidays. My husband and three sons are glad I carry on her tradition.

    1 package (12 ounces) fresh *or* frozen
      cranberries
1-3/4 cups sugar
  1/2 cup water
  1/2 teaspoon ground cinnamon
  1/2 teaspoon ground allspice
  1/8 teaspoon salt
  1/8 teaspoon ground ginger
  1/8 teaspoon ground cloves

In a large saucepan, combine all ingredients. Bring to a boil. Reduce heat; simmer, uncovered, until the berries pop and mixture is thickened, about 30 minutes. Cool. Transfer to a serving bowl; cover and refrigerate until chilled. **Yield:** 2 cups.

FREEZER COLESLAW

Connie Wilkinson, Napanee, Ontario

It's great to prepare this coleslaw early in the summer, then freeze it for whenever you need a quick side dish. No one will guess the fresh-tasting slaw has been stored in the freezer.

    1 medium head cabbage (3 pounds),
      shredded
  1/2 green pepper, chopped
  1/2 cup shredded carrot
    1 small onion, chopped
    1 teaspoon salt
DRESSING:
    1 cup sugar
    1 cup white vinegar

  1/4 cup water
    1 teaspoon salt
  1/2 teaspoon celery seed
  1/2 teaspoon mustard seed

In a large bowl, combine the first five ingredients. Let stand 1 hour. Drain.

Bring all dressing ingredients to a boil; simmer 2-3 minutes. Cool. Pour over cabbage. Pack in freezer containers; freeze. **Yield:** about 4 pints.

STIR-FRIED BROCCOLI

(Pictured below)

Sara Farley, Brielle, New Jersey

Here's a stovetop side dish that only takes a few moments to toss together. You can serve the brightly colored broccoli with just about anything.

1-1/2 teaspoons cornstarch
    1 teaspoon sugar
  1/3 cup chicken broth
    2 tablespoons reduced-sodium soy sauce
    2 cups fresh broccoli florets
    1 garlic clove, minced
    2 tablespoons vegetable oil

In a small bowl, whisk the cornstarch, sugar, broth and soy sauce until smooth; set aside. In a small skillet, stir-fry the broccoli and garlic in oil for 2 minutes. Stir broth mixture and add to broccoli mixture. Bring to a boil; cook and stir for 1-2 minutes or until broccoli is tender and sauce is thickened. **Yield:** 2 servings.

SWEET-AND-SOUR BEETS

Elnora Willhite, Ontario, California

My family thinks these beets are as good on the holiday table as they are at summer picnics. If you're cooking for two, don't shy away from this recipe—the beets keep well and actually taste better the second and third day.

    2 cans (15 ounces *each*) sliced beets,
        drained
    1 tablespoon chopped green pepper
    1 tablespoon chopped onion
  1/2 cup sugar
  1/2 cup vegetable oil
  1/2 cup white vinegar
    1 teaspoon salt

In a salad bowl, combine the beets, green pepper and onion. In a small bowl, whisk the sugar, oil, vinegar and salt until sugar is dissolved. Pour over beet mixture and toss to coat. Cover and refrigerate overnight. **Yield:** 8 servings.

CRANBERRY SAUCE WITH WALNUTS

(Pictured below)

Dee Buckley, Salado, Texas

You'll be the most popular person at Thanksgiving dinner when you bring this sauce to the table. All the women in my family serve it.

    2 cups sugar
    1 cup water
    1 package (12 ounces) fresh or frozen
        cranberries

  1/2 cup apricot preserves
  1/4 cup lemon juice
  1/2 cup chopped walnuts, toasted

In a large saucepan over medium heat, bring sugar and water to a boil. Simmer, uncovered, for 10 minutes. Stir in the cranberries. Cook until berries pop, about 15 minutes.

Remove from the heat. Stir in preserves and lemon juice. Transfer to a bowl. Serve warm, at room temperature or chilled. Stir in walnuts just before serving. **Yield:** 3-1/2 cups.

PORTUGUESE DRESSING

(Pictured above)

Jean Repose, North Kingstown, Rhode Island

With beef and smoked sausage, this meaty dressing is a change from many other dressing and stuffing recipes. It's delicious alongside roasted chicken or turkey for holidays or any occasion. I like to use chourico, a Portuguese specialty sausage that's popular in our area.

    1 pound ground beef
    1 medium onion, chopped
  1/2 pound smoked sausage, chopped
    2 teaspoons poultry seasoning
  1/2 teaspoon garlic powder
  1/8 teaspoon ground allspice
    1 package (12 ounces) unseasoned
        stuffing cubes
    1 can (14-1/2 ounces) chicken broth
    1 egg, lightly beaten
  1/4 cup minced fresh parsley
    2 tablespoons butter, melted

In a large skillet, cook beef and onion over medium heat until meat is no longer pink; drain. Set beef mixture aside. In the same skillet, saute the sausage, poultry seasoning, garlic powder and allspice for 2 minutes.

In a large bowl, toss the beef mixture, sausage mixture and stuffing cubes. Add the broth, egg and parsley; mix well. Transfer to a greased 2-1/2-qt. baking dish. Drizzle with butter.

Cover and bake at 325° for 45 minutes. Uncover; bake 10-15 minutes longer or until lightly browned and a thermometer reads 160°. **Yield:** 8 servings.

SAUSAGE-PECAN TURKEY STUFFING

(Pictured below)

Sharon Miller, Millet, Alberta

Since I first tried this, I haven't made another stuffing. The sausage and pecans really give it a savory flavor.

    9 cups soft bread crumbs
    1 pound bulk pork sausage
    2 cups chopped onion
  1/4 cup butter, cubed
    3 unpeeled tart apples, coarsely chopped
    1 cup chopped pecans
  1/2 cup minced fresh parsley
1-1/2 teaspoons dried thyme
    1 teaspoon rubbed sage
  1/4 teaspoon salt
  1/4 teaspoon pepper
  1/4 cup apple juice
Chicken broth
    1 turkey (14 to 16 pounds)

Place bread crumbs in a large bowl; set aside. In a large skillet, cook sausage and onion in butter until sausage is no longer pink and onion is tender; do not drain. Add to bread crumbs. Stir in apples, pecans, parsley, thyme, sage, salt and pepper; stir in apple juice and enough broth to moisten.

Just before baking, stuff the turkey. Skewer openings; tie drumsticks together. Place on rack in a roasting pan. Bake at 325° for 5 to 5-1/2 hours or until a meat thermometer reads 185°. When the turkey begins to brown, cover lightly

with a tent of aluminum foil and baste if needed. Remove all stuffing. **Yield:** 12-14 servings.

Editor's Note: Stuffing may be baked in a greased 3-qt. covered baking dish at 325° for 70 minutes (uncover for the last 10 minutes). Stuffing yields about 12 cups.

BAKED CAULIFLOWER

(Pictured above)

Viola Cirillo, Mohawk, New York

I created this recipe myself. The cheddar cheese and bread crumb topping make it a pretty casserole for a special dinner. You can easily double the amounts if you're having a large group.

    1 medium onion, chopped
    1 garlic clove, minced
    4 tablespoons butter, *divided*
    2 tablespoons olive oil
    1 package (16 ounces) frozen cauliflower, thawed
  1/2 teaspoon salt
  1/8 teaspoon pepper
  1/8 teaspoon ground nutmeg
  1/4 cup dry bread crumbs
  1/4 cup shredded cheddar cheese

In a large skillet, saute onion and garlic in 2 tablespoons butter and oil until onion is tender. Add the cauliflower, salt, pepper and nutmeg; saute for 2 minutes.

Transfer to a greased 1-qt. baking dish. Melt remaining butter; toss with bread crumbs. Sprinkle over cauliflower mixture.

Cover and bake at 350° for 15 minutes. Uncover; bake for 10 minutes or until heated through. Sprinkle with cheese; bake 3-5 minutes longer or until cheese is melted. **Yield:** 4-6 servings.

1/4 teaspoon ground allspice
1/8 teaspoon ground ginger
1/8 teaspoon ground cloves

In a small saucepan, combine all ingredients. Bring to a boil. Reduce heat; simmer, uncovered, for 30-35 minutes, stirring every 3-4 minutes. Remove from the heat; cool. Store in airtight containers in the refrigerator. **Yield:** 1-1/2 cups.

CHUNKY RHUBARB APPLESAUCE
(Pictured below)

Cheryl Miller, Fort Collins, Colorado

Our backyard was filled with rhubarb when I was growing up in Illinois, and my mom would always add some to her applesauce. We liked ours tart, but you can adjust the sugar to your taste.

✓ Uses less fat, sugar or salt. Includes Nutrition Facts.

    1 pound rhubarb, trimmed and cut into
      1/2-inch chunks
    2 pounds tart cooking apples, peeled and
      cut into 1/2-inch chunks
1/2 to 1 cup sugar
1/4 teaspoon ground cinnamon
1/8 teaspoon ground nutmeg

Place rhubarb, apples and sugar to taste in a large saucepan. Cover and simmer until fruit is soft, about 40-45 minutes. Stir in cinnamon and nutmeg. Serve warm or cold. **Yield:** 4 cups.

Nutrition Facts: 1/4 cup equals 58 calories, trace fat (trace saturated fat), 0 cholesterol, 1 mg sodium, 15 g carbohydrate, 1 g fiber, trace protein.

CANDIED ACORN SQUASH RINGS
(Pictured above)

Rita Addicks, Weimar, Texas

Brown sugar sweetens acorn squash nicely in this effortless side dish. I think it's wonderful during the fall with poultry.

    2 acorn squash, cut into 1-inch rings and
      seeded
2/3 cup packed brown sugar
1/2 cup butter, softened

Arrange squash in a shallow baking pan; cover with foil. Bake at 350° for 35-40 minutes or until squash is tender.

Combine sugar and butter; spread over squash. Bake uncovered, for 15-20 minutes, basting occasionally. **Yield:** 6 servings.

SPEEDY APPLE BUTTER

Florence Reiss, Floral Park, New York

This shortcut version of an old standby only takes about a half hour to prepare. I make my own sauce from the Golden Delicious apple tree in my yard. It's great for anyone who wants the taste of homemade apple butter, but only needs a small amount.

    2 cups unsweetened applesauce
1/4 to 1/2 cup sugar
    1 teaspoon ground cinnamon

GERMAN POTATO SALAD
(Pictured above)

Violette Klevorn, Jennings, Missouri

I used to eat lunch at the same diner almost every day and always ordered the potato salad. When the owner learned I was getting married, he gave me the recipe as a wedding gift!

3 pounds medium red potatoes
5 bacon strips, diced
1 medium onion, chopped
1/4 cup all-purpose flour
2 teaspoons salt
1/4 teaspoon celery seed
1/4 teaspoon pepper
1-1/4 cups sugar
1 cup cider vinegar
3/4 cup water
3 tablespoons minced fresh parsley

Place the potatoes in a Dutch oven or large saucepan; cover with water. Bring to a boil. Reduce heat; cover and simmer for 25-30 minutes or until tender. Drain and rinse in cold water. Refrigerate until cooled; cut potatoes into 1/4-in. slices.

In a large skillet, cook bacon over medium heat until crisp; remove to paper towels. Drain, reserving 4 tablespoons drippings. In the drippings, saute the onion until tender. Stir in the flour, salt, celery seed and pepper until blended. Gradually add the sugar, vinegar and water. Bring to a boil over medium-high heat; cook and stir for 2 minutes or until thickened.

Reduce heat to low. Add the potatoes and bacon; stir gently. Sprinkle with parsley. Serve warm. **Yield:** 8 servings.

BACON CHEESE POTATOES
(Pictured below)

Bertha Jensen, Mooresville, Indiana

I received this recipe from a friend who's a wonderful cook. This goes great with any main course, but it's especially good with ham.

8 to 10 medium potatoes (2-1/2 to 3 pounds)
1/2 cup finely chopped onion
1 pound process cheese (Velveeta)
1 cup mayonnaise
1/2 pound sliced bacon, cooked and crumbled
3/4 cup sliced ripe olives
Chopped fresh parsley, optional
Paprika, optional

Peel the potatoes; place in a saucepan and cover with water. Cook until tender but firm; drain and cube. In a bowl, mix potatoes with onion, cheese and mayonnaise.

Transfer to an ungreased 13-in. x 9-in. x 2-in. baking dish. Sprinkle with bacon and olives. Cover and bake at 350° for 30 minutes or until heated through. If desired, sprinkle with parsley and paprika. **Yield:** 8-10 servings.

Tart 'n' Tangy Vegetables
(Pictured below)

Susan Thoms, Spartanburg, South Carolina

We have a long growing season here, so we find many ways to use fresh vegetables from our garden. This is a Southern favorite in my family that is both easy and flavorful.

☑ Uses less fat, sugar or salt. Includes Nutrition Facts.

1-1/2 cups white vinegar
   1 cup water
  1/2 cup sugar
  1/2 teaspoon pepper
  1/4 teaspoon salt
   2 tablespoons mixed pickling spices
   4 small cucumbers, sliced
   2 large tomatoes, cubed
   2 medium carrots, thinly sliced

In a 1-1/2-qt. bowl, combine the vinegar, water, sugar, pepper and salt. Place pickling spices on a double thickness of cheesecloth; bring up corners of cloth and tie with string to form a bag. Add to vinegar mixture.

Stir in the cucumbers, tomatoes and carrots. Cover and refrigerate for at least 4 hours or overnight. Discard spice bag before serving. **Yield:** 4 cups.

Nutrition Facts: 1/2 cup equals 76 calories, trace fat (trace saturated fat), 0 cholesterol, 85 mg sodium, 19 g carbohydrate, 2 g fiber, 1 g protein.

Green Bean Bundles
(Pictured above)

Virginia Stadler, Nokesville, Virginia

I found this recipe in a rural newspaper years ago and have made it often. The bean bundles are excellent with chicken or beef. Sometimes I'll arrange them around a mound of wild rice to make an attractive presentation.

   1 pound fresh green beans, trimmed
   8 bacon strips, partially cooked
   1 tablespoon finely chopped onion
   3 tablespoons butter
   1 tablespoon white wine vinegar
   1 tablespoon sugar
  1/4 teaspoon salt

Cook the beans until crisp-tender. Wrap about 15 beans in each bacon strip; secure with a toothpick. Place on a foil-covered baking sheet. Bake at 400° for 10-15 minutes or until bacon is done.

In a skillet, saute onion in butter until tender. Add vinegar, sugar and salt; heat through. Remove bundles to a serving bowl or platter; pour sauce over and serve immediately. **Yield:** 8 servings.

Almond Pear Chutney

Michaela Rosenthal, Woodland Hills, California

My sweet, chunky chutney…flavored with orange, almond and ginger…is great with chicken, turkey or pork. You can prepare it a couple of days in advance and use it to dress up a plain weekday supper.

   4 cups chopped peeled ripe pears
   1 small unpeeled navel orange, halved and thinly sliced
  1/2 cup water

2 teaspoons lemon juice
1-1/2 cups sugar
1/4 teaspoon ground cinnamon
1/3 cup coarsely chopped unblanched
   almonds, toasted
2 tablespoons candied ginger, chopped

In a large saucepan, combine the pears, orange, water and lemon juice. Bring to a boil, stirring constantly. Reduce heat; simmer, uncovered, for 10 minutes. Stir in sugar and cinnamon. Bring to a boil. Reduce heat; simmer, uncovered, for 15-20 minutes or until thickened, stirring occasionally.

Remove from the heat; stir in almonds and ginger. Serve warm or cold. May be refrigerated for up to 1 week. **Yield:** 3 cups.

DILLY CUCUMBERS
(Pictured below)

Linda Graber, Archbold, Ohio

Summer just isn't complete without a few servings of Dilly Cucumbers. Try them with grilled foods.

✓ Uses less fat, sugar or salt. Includes Nutrition Facts.

1/4 cup white vinegar
2 tablespoons vegetable oil
1/4 minced fresh dill *or* 1 tablespoon dill weed
1 teaspoon sugar
3 to 4 small cucumbers, peeled and sliced

In a bowl, combine vinegar, oil, dill and sugar. Add cucumbers and stir well. Refrigerate until serving. **Yield:** 6 servings.

Nutrition Facts: 1 cup equals 52 calories, 5 g fat (1 g saturated fat), 0 cholesterol, 2 mg sodium, 3 g carbohydrate, 1 g fiber, trace protein.

KENTUCKY SPOON BREAD
(Pictured above)

Caroline Brown, Lexington, Kentucky

This is a traditional Kentucky recipe. It's a popular side dish served all year long. If you've never tried spoon bread before, I think you'll find it's tasty and comforting.

4 cups milk, *divided*
1 cup cornmeal
3 teaspoons sugar
1 teaspoon salt
1/2 teaspoon baking powder
2 tablespoons butter
3 eggs, *separated*

In a large saucepan, heat 3 cups milk over medium heat until bubbles form around sides of pan.

Meanwhile, in a bowl, combine the cornmeal, sugar, salt and remaining milk until smooth. Slowly whisk cornmeal mixture into hot milk. Cook and stir until mixture comes to a boil. Reduce heat; simmer for 5 minutes, stirring constantly.

Remove from the heat. Sprinkle baking powder over the cornmeal mixture, then stir it in with the butter. In a small bowl, beat egg yolks; stir in a small amount of hot cornmeal mixture. Return all to the pan and mix well.

In a small mixing bowl, beat egg whites until stiff peaks form. Fold a fourth of the egg whites into the cornmeal mixture. Fold in remaining egg whites until blended.

Transfer to a greased 2-1/2-qt. baking dish. Bake, uncovered, at 350° for 40-45 minutes or until puffed and golden brown. Serve immediately. **Yield:** 8 servings.

Warm Up to Side Dish Casseroles

COMFORTING goodness is sure to abound when a bubbling casserole's on the menu. Not only do these oven-fresh side dishes offer hearty appeal, but they leave time for busy cooks to tend to other things as they bake on their own.

⬛⬛⬛⬛⬛⬛⬛⬛⬛⬛⬛⬛

POTATO STUFFING CASSEROLE

(Pictured below)

Elsa Kerschner, Kunkletown, Pennsylvania

I adapted this recipe from a Pennsylvania Dutch cookbook, and it's indicative of the fine German cooking found in this area.

    1/4 cup chopped celery
    1   onion, chopped
    4   tablespoons butter, *divided*
    3   slices bread, cubed
    4 to 5 large potatoes, peeled, cooked and
        mashed
    1/4 cup chopped fresh parsley
    1/2 teaspoon salt
    1/4 teaspoon pepper

    1   cup hot milk
    1   egg, beaten
    Additional parsley

In a medium skillet, saute celery and onion in 2 tablespoons of butter until tender. Add bread cubes and stir until lightly browned. Stir in potatoes, parsley, salt, pepper, milk and egg; mix well.

Spoon into a greased 1-1/2-qt. baking dish. Dot with remaining butter. Bake at 350°, uncovered, for 30-40 minutes or until lightly browned. Garnish with additional parsley. **Yield:** 6-8 servings.

⬛⬛⬛⬛⬛⬛⬛⬛⬛⬛⬛⬛

GREEN BEAN 'N' CORN BAKE

Christy Hughes, Sunset Beach, North Carolina

I serve this side dish for many occasions and holidays because it goes so well with different entrees. The creamy casserole includes green beans, corn, pimientos and cheddar cheese with a buttery cracker topping. If your family is like mine, there won't be any left.

    1   can (14-1/2 ounces) French-style green
        beans, drained
    1   can (11 ounces) shoepeg corn, drained
    1   can (10-3/4 ounces) condensed cream
        of celery soup, undiluted
    1/2 cup sliced celery
    1/2 cup chopped onion
    1/2 cup sour cream
    1/2 cup shredded cheddar cheese
    1   jar (2 ounces) diced pimientos, drained
    1/2 teaspoon salt
    1/2 teaspoon pepper
    1/2 cup crushed butter-flavored crackers
        (about 13 crackers)
    2   tablespoons butter, melted

In a large bowl, combine the first 10 ingredients. Transfer to a greased 1-1/2-qt. baking dish. Combine the cracker crumbs and butter; sprinkle over vegetable mixture.

Bake, uncovered, at 350° for 30-35 minutes or until topping is golden brown. **Yield:** 6 servings.

CRANBERRY BAKED BEANS

Creacle Baxter, Yuma, Arizona

A little cranberry sauce lends change-of-pace flair to baked beans in this easy hot dish. It's great when you have to feed a crowd or are attending a potluck.

☑ Uses less fat, sugar or salt. Includes Nutrition Facts.

- 1 can (16 ounces) jellied cranberry sauce
- 1 can (8 ounces) tomato sauce
- 2 cans (31 ounces *each*) pork and beans, undrained
- 1 tablespoon prepared mustard
- 1/2 cup chopped onion
- 6 strips bacon, halved
- 3 tablespoons brown sugar

In a large bowl, combine the cranberry sauce, tomato sauce, beans, mustard and onion. Place in a greased 13-in. x 9-in. x 2-in. baking dish. Lay bacon on top. Sprinkle with brown sugar. Bake at 350° for 1 hour. **Yield:** 12-16 servings.

Nutrition Facts: 3/4 cup equals 150 calories, 5 g fat (2 g saturated fat), 6 mg cholesterol, 322 mg sodium, 24 g carbohydrate, 3 g fiber, 4 g protein.

GREEK SPINACH BAKE

Sharon Olney, Galt, California

"Spanakopita" is the Greek name for this traditional recipe featuring spinach and feta cheese. My dad and I used to argue over the last piece!

- 2 cups (16 ounces) 4% cottage cheese
- 1 package (10 ounces) frozen chopped spinach, thawed and squeezed dry
- 8 ounces crumbled feta cheese
- 6 tablespoons all-purpose flour
- 1/2 teaspoon pepper
- 1/4 teaspoon salt
- 4 eggs, lightly beaten

In a large mixing bowl, combine the cottage cheese, spinach and feta cheese. Add the flour, pepper and salt; mix well. Stir in eggs.

Spoon into a greased 9-in. square baking dish. Bake, uncovered, at 350° for 1 hour or until set. **Yield:** 6 servings.

CREAMY BRUSSELS SPROUTS BAKE

(Pictured above)

Elizabeth Metz, Albuquerque, New Mexico

Eating brussels sprouts was a ho-hum experience at our house…until I put together this cheesy bake. After one taste, my husband declared it a "keeper." It's ideal alongside ham, pork or beef roasts.

- 1 package (8 ounces) cream cheese, softened
- 1 cup (8 ounces) sour cream
- 1/2 pound sliced fresh mushrooms
- 1 medium onion, chopped
- 2 tablespoons butter
- 2 packages (10 ounces *each*) frozen brussels sprouts, thawed and drained
- 3/4 cup shredded cheddar cheese

In a small mixing bowl, beat cream cheese and sour cream until smooth; set aside. In a large skillet, saute mushrooms and onion in butter until tender. Stir in brussels sprouts. Remove from the heat; stir in cream cheese mixture.

Spoon into a greased shallow 2-qt. baking dish. Cover and bake at 350° for 25-30 minutes or until bubbly. Uncover; sprinkle with cheddar cheese. Bake 5 minutes longer or until cheese is melted. **Yield:** 6-8 servings.

SUGAR SNAP PEA STIR-FRY
(Pictured above and on front cover)

Fresh ginger, balsamic vinegar, soy sauce and sesame oil provide a nice blend of flavors in this Asian-inspired recipe for fresh sugar snap peas. Our home economists think the quick-to-cook recipe complements most any spring entree.

> 1 pound fresh sugar snap peas
> 2 teaspoons canola oil
> 1 garlic clove, minced
> 2 teaspoons minced fresh gingerroot
> 1-1/2 teaspoons balsamic vinegar
> 1-1/2 teaspoons reduced-sodium soy sauce
> 1 teaspoon sesame oil
> Dash cayenne pepper
> 1 tablespoon minced fresh basil *or* 1 teaspoon dried basil
> 2 teaspoons sesame seeds, toasted

In a large nonstick skillet or wok, saute the peas in canola oil until crisp-tender. Add the garlic, ginger, vinegar, soy sauce, sesame oil and cayenne; saute 1 minute longer. Add basil; toss to combine. Sprinkle with sesame seeds. **Yield:** 6 servings.

QUICK BAKED BEANS

Connie Tiesenausen, Demmitt, Alberta

It's a cinch to dress up canned pork and beans with bacon, barbecue sauce and a few other kitchen staples. Remember this idea when you're short on time, but have several mouths to feed.

> 1 pound bacon, diced
> 1 large onion, chopped
> 3 cans (28 ounces *each*) pork and beans, undrained
> 1/2 cup packed brown sugar
> 1/3 cup prepared mustard
> 1 cup barbecue sauce

In a large saucepan, cook bacon and onion until bacon is crisp and onion is tender. Drain drippings. Add all remaining ingredients; simmer 10 minutes. **Yield:** 10-12 servings.

BASIL BAKED TOMATOES
(Pictured below)

Mary Detzi, Wind Gap, Pennsylvania

This recipe has been in our family for many years. My mother brought it with her when she came to the United States from Italy. When fresh tomatoes are plentiful, this is a great way to serve them.

☑ Uses less fat, sugar or salt. Includes Nutrition Facts.

> 1 garlic clove, minced
> 1 tablespoon olive oil
> 1/2 cup soft bread crumbs
> 2 large tomatoes
> 4 fresh basil leaves, chopped
> 1/8 teaspoon coarsely ground pepper

In a small skillet, saute garlic in oil for 1 minute. Add bread crumbs; cook and stir until lightly browned. Remove from the heat.

IOWA CORN CASSEROLE

(Pictured below)

Dorothy Morgan, Cedar Falls, Iowa

I only wish I knew how many times I've made this casserole for get-togethers during the past 40 years. No matter how much I make, there are never leftovers.

  1 pound bacon, diced
  2 cups soft bread crumbs
1/4 cup minced onion
1/2 cup chopped green pepper
  2 cans (16-1/2 ounces *each*) cream-style corn

In a skillet, fry the bacon until lightly browned. Remove and set aside. Pour 1/8 to 1/4 cup of bacon drippings over bread crumbs; set aside. Discard all but 2 tablespoons of remaining drippings; saute onion and green pepper until tender. Stir in corn, bacon and half of the bread crumbs.

Spoon into a 1-qt. baking dish; sprinkle with remaining crumbs. Bake at 350° for 20-25 minutes or until heated through. **Yield:** 6-8 servings.

CASSEROLES FOR TWO

It's easy to pare down a casserole. If the recipe calls for a 13-in. x 9-in. baking dish, reduce the ingredients by half and divide the mixture into two 1-quart dishes. You can then bake and serve one casserole for the two of you, and freeze the other for future use.

Cut tomatoes in half widthwise. Place cut side up in an 8-in. square baking dish. Sprinkle with basil and pepper; top with bread crumb mixture. Bake at 325° for 15-20 minutes or until tomatoes are slightly softened. **Yield:** 4 servings.

Nutrition Facts: 1 serving equals 65 calories, 4 g fat (1 g saturated fat), trace cholesterol, 39 mg sodium, 7 g carbohydrate, 1 g fiber, 1 g protein.

STEWED OKRA

(Pictured above)

Suzanne Runtz, Mt. Pleasant, South Carolina

I came up with this recipe one summer when I had lots of okra and tomatoes. Everyone really enjoyed it and said how delicious it was. Friends always ask when I'm going to cook my tomato and okra dish. Sometimes I'll serve it over rice.

  3 cups chopped fresh tomatoes
  1 cup sliced fresh *or* frozen okra
1/4 cup chopped onion
  1 tablespoon sugar
  1 tablespoon butter
1/2 teaspoon salt

In a large saucepan, combine all ingredients. Bring to a boil. Reduce heat; simmer, uncovered, for 25 minutes. **Yield:** 6 servings.

BUTTERY GRILLED ONIONS
(Pictured above)

Penny Mays, Memphis, Tennessee

Cooking on the grill is a year-round treat in the South, and we even use our grill for side dishes such as these onions. This recipe usually doesn't require a trip to the grocery store, and you can even prepare the onions ahead of time.

- 6 medium onions, peeled
- 6 tablespoons butter, softened
- 6 teaspoons beef bouillon granules
- 1/8 teaspoon garlic powder
- 1/8 teaspoon coarsely ground pepper
- 6 teaspoons sherry, optional

Shredded Parmesan cheese

Carefully remove a 1-in. x 1-in. core from the center of each onion (save removed onion for another use). Place each onion on a double thickness of heavy-duty foil (about 12 in. square).

Combine the butter, bouillon, garlic powder and pepper; spoon into onions. Sprinkle with sherry if desired. Fold foil around onions and seal tightly.

Grill, covered, over medium heat for 30-40 minutes or until tender. Carefully unwrap foil to allow steam to escape. Sprinkle onions with Parmesan cheese. **Yield:** 6 servings.

SELECTING SIDE DISHES

Entrees and side dishes should complement one another. If your entree has intense flavor, pair it with a mild-flavored item. If your main course has lots of garlic, onion or nuts, for instance, stay away from a side dish that's loaded with any of those same ingredients.

TURNIP PUFF
(Pictured below)

Helen Hackwood, Meaford, Ontario

This recipe has been in our family for years. We like turnips with turkey, so my mother used to serve this side dish with our turkey dinner at Christmas. Then I served this dish, and now my daughter, who has taken over as hostess of our Christmas dinners, is carrying on the tradition.

- 3 medium turnips, peeled and cubed
- 4 tablespoons butter, *divided*
- 2 eggs
- 3 tablespoons all-purpose flour
- 1 tablespoon brown sugar
- 3 teaspoons baking powder
- 3/4 teaspoon salt
- 1/4 teaspoon pepper

Dash ground nutmeg
- 1/2 cup dry bread crumbs

Place turnips in a small saucepan and cover with water. Bring to a boil. Reduce heat; cover and simmer for 10-12 minutes or until tender. Drain.

In a small mixing bowl, combine the turnips, 2 tablespoons butter and eggs. Combine the flour, brown sugar, baking powder, salt, pepper and nutmeg; add to turnip mixture and mix well. Transfer to a greased 8-in. square baking dish.

Melt remaining butter; toss with bread crumbs. Sprinkle over the top. Bake, uncovered, at 375° for 25-30 minutes or until a knife inserted near the center comes out clean. Serve immediately. **Yield:** 8 servings.

Editor's Note: Carrots, parsnips or rutabagas may be substituted for the turnips.

Baked Shredded Carrots

(Pictured above)

Carole Hartwig, Horicon, Wisconsin

Everyone who samples these crisp and tender carrots loves them. I make them often when we have fresh produce from our garden. The bright orange color looks so pretty on our Thanksgiving table.

☑ Uses less fat, sugar or salt. Includes Nutrition Facts.

  6 cups shredded carrots (about 2 pounds)
  3/4 cup chopped green onions
  2 tablespoons sugar
  1/2 teaspoon salt
  1/2 teaspoon celery salt
  1/4 cup butter

In a large bowl, combine the carrots, onions, sugar, salt and celery salt. Transfer to an ungreased 1-1/2-qt. baking dish. Dot with butter.

Cover and bake at 325° for 45-50 minutes or until carrots are crisp-tender. **Yield:** 6 servings.

Nutrition Facts: 3/4 cup equals 135 calories, 8 g fat (5 g saturated fat), 20 mg cholesterol, 438 mg sodium, 16 g carbohydrate, 4 g fiber, 1 g protein.

Mushroom Barley Casserole

Melba Cleveland, Groveland, California

My family enjoys this with meat entrees as a substitute for potatoes. It's great to take to a potluck for a dish to pass, but be prepared to also pass the recipe!

  1 cup medium pearl barley
  1 small onion, chopped
  1/4 cup butter
1-1/2 cups sliced fresh mushrooms
  1 cup slivered almonds, toasted
  1 envelope onion soup mix
  2 tablespoons minced fresh parsley *or*
    2 teaspoons dried parsley flakes
  3 to 3-1/2 cups chicken broth

In a skillet, saute barley and onion in butter for 5 minutes or until onion is tender. Transfer to an ungreased 2-qt. baking dish. Stir in the mushrooms, almonds, soup mix and parsley. Add 3 cups broth; mix well.

Bake, uncovered, at 350° for 1-1/4 hours or until barley is tender, adding more broth if needed. **Yield:** 8-10 servings.

BROCCOLI TOMATO CUPS

(Pictured below)

Beatrice Gallo, Richfield Springs, New York

I had an abundance of tomatoes and broccoli one year, so I began experimenting to see how best I could use both of them. Now this recipe is a staple.

1-1/2 cups soft bread crumbs, *divided*
    1 cup grated Parmesan cheese, *divided*
    6 to 8 medium tomatoes
    2 cups chopped broccoli
    1 cup (4 ounces) shredded cheddar cheese
  3/4 cup mayonnaise
Salt and pepper to taste

Combine 1/2 cup of bread crumbs and 1/4 cup Parmesan cheese; set aside. Cut a thin slice off the top of each tomato; scoop out pulp and place in a strainer to drain. Place tomatoes upside down on paper towels.

Cook broccoli until crisp-tender; drain. Chop tomato pulp and place in a bowl. Add broccoli, cheddar cheese, mayonnaise, salt, pepper and remaining crumbs and Parmesan; mix gently.

Stuff tomatoes; place in a greased 11-in. x 7-in. x 2-in. baking dish. Sprinkle with reserved crumb mixture. Bake, uncovered, at 375° for 30-40 minutes. **Yield:** 6-8 servings.

CREAMY CORN CASSEROLE

(Pictured above)

Brenda Wood, Egbert, Ontario

If you're looking for a different way to serve vegetables, give this idea a try. The hot bake is one of my family's favorites. It just might become a favorite at your house, too.

✓ Uses less fat, sugar or salt. Includes Nutrition Facts.

    1 cup finely chopped celery
  1/4 cup finely chopped onion
  1/4 cup finely chopped sweet red pepper
    3 tablespoons butter, *divided*
    1 can (10-3/4 ounces) condensed cream of chicken soup, undiluted
    3 cups fresh, frozen *or* drained canned corn
    1 can (8 ounces) sliced water chestnuts, drained
  1/3 cup slivered almonds, optional
  1/2 cup soft bread crumbs

In a medium skillet, saute celery, onion and red pepper in 2 tablespoons of butter for 2-3 minutes or until vegetables are tender. Remove from the heat; stir in soup, corn, water chestnuts and almonds if desired.

Transfer to a 2-qt. baking dish. Melt remaining butter; toss with bread crumbs. Sprinkle on top of casserole. Bake, uncovered, at 350° for 25-30 minutes or until bubbly. **Yield:** 8 servings.

Nutrition Facts: 1 serving equals 148 calories, 7 g fat (3 g saturated fat), 15 mg cholesterol, 372 mg sodium, 20 g carbohydrate, 3 g fiber, 4 g protein.

CRANBERRY SWEET POTATO BAKE
(Pictured below)

Isabell Burrows, Livermore, California

With its combination of sweet potatoes, cranberries and apples, this colorful casserole is the perfect side dish for Thanksgiving. I find it convenient to cook the potatoes in the morning and assemble the dish, then bake it later in the day.

☑ Uses less fat, sugar or salt. Includes Nutrition Facts.

    2 large sweet potatoes
    3 tablespoons butter
1/2 cup packed brown sugar
    2 medium apples, peeled and cubed
1/2 cup dried cranberries
1/2 teaspoon ground cinnamon
1/2 teaspoon ground nutmeg

Place sweet potatoes in a large saucepan and cover with water. Bring to a boil. Reduce heat; cover and cook for 30-45 minutes or just until tender. Drain; cool slightly. Peel potatoes and cut into 1/2-in. slices; set aside.

In a large skillet, melt butter and brown sugar over medium heat. Add apples; cook and stir until crisp-tender. Stir in the cranberries, cinnamon and nutmeg.

In a greased 1-1/2-qt. baking dish, layer half of the sweet potatoes and half of the apple mixture; repeat layers. Cover and bake at 375° for 30-35 minutes or until bubbly. **Yield:** 8 servings.

Nutrition Facts: 3/4 cup equals 175 calories, 4 g fat (3 g saturated fat), 11 mg cholesterol, 53 mg sodium, 35 g carbohydrate, 2 g fiber, 1 g protein.

SAUCY POTATOES WITH HAM
(Pictured above)

Patricia Tjugum, Tomahawk, Wisconsin

Being a potato fan, I make this old-fashioned specialty when I'm in the mood for real comfort food. It's always a hit on a buffet table. Add more ham, and you can serve it as an entree.

    1 can (10-3/4 ounces) condensed cream of potato soup, undiluted
1/2 cup heavy whipping cream
1/2 teaspoon salt
1/4 teaspoon pepper
    4 large red potatoes, thinly sliced
    1 cup cubed fully cooked ham
1/2 cup thinly sliced green onions with tops
1/2 cup salad croutons, crushed

In a large bowl, combine the soup, cream, salt and pepper. Fold in the potatoes, ham and onions. Transfer to a greased 2-qt. baking dish.

Cover and bake at 350° for 50 minutes. Uncover; sprinkle with croutons. Bake 15-20 minutes longer or until potatoes are tender and topping is golden brown. **Yield:** 6-8 servings.

TRAVEL MADE EASY

To transport a casserole, slide the dish into an oven bag and seal it. The bag will trap any spills that may occur on the drive and easily slips out of the bag when it's time to set the buffet.

WHOLESOME *goodness is what you'll find with every recipe in this chapter. Let the welcoming aroma of freshly baked breads, biscuits, muffins and more greet your family at the door after a long day.*

SIMPLY SCRUMPTIOUS. Maple Butter Twists (p. 93).

RECIPE FOR: MAPLE BUTTER
1 PACKAGE (¼ OZ.) ACTIVE DR
¼ CUP WARM WATER (110° T
¼ CUP WARM MILK (110° T
3 T SUGAR
2 EGGS
¼ C SALT
3¼-3½ CUP

Breads & Rolls

MAPLE BUTTER TWISTS
(Pictured at left)

Marna Krause, Las Vegas, Nevada

Back almost 30 years ago, when I was an Indiana farmer's daughter and a 4-H'er, this won me champion honors at the county fair—then a blue ribbon at the state fair!

    1 package (1/4 ounce) active dry yeast
    1/4 cup warm water (110° to 115°)
    1/2 cup warm milk (110° to 115°)
    1/4 cup butter, melted
      2 eggs, beaten
      3 tablespoons sugar
  1-1/2 teaspoons salt
  3-1/4 to 3-1/2 cups all-purpose flour
  FILLING:
    1/2 cup packed brown sugar
    1/2 cup chopped walnuts
    1/3 cup sugar
    1/4 cup maple syrup
    1/4 cup butter, softened
      2 tablespoons all-purpose flour
    1/2 teaspoon ground cinnamon
    1/2 teaspoon maple flavoring

In a large mixing bowl, dissolve yeast in water. Add the milk, butter, eggs, sugar, salt and 2 cups flour; beat until smooth. Stir in enough remaining flour to form a soft dough.

Turn onto a floured surface and knead until it's smooth and elastic, about 6-8 minutes. Place in a greased bowl, turning once to grease top. Cover and let rise in a warm place until doubled, about 1 hour.

Punch dough down. Turn onto a lightly floured surface; divide in half. Roll each portion into a 14-in. x 8-in. rectangle. Combine filling ingredients; spread over each rectangle to within 1/2 in. of edges.

Roll up jelly-roll style, starting with a long side; pinch seam to seal. Place seam side down on greased baking sheets. With a sharp knife, cut each roll in half lengthwise; carefully turn cut sides up. Loosely twist strips around each other, keeping cut sides up. Shape into a ring and pinch ends together. Cover and let rise for 30 minutes.

Bake the rings at 350° for 25-30 minutes or until browned. Remove from pans to wire racks to cool. **Yield:** 2 coffee cakes.

QUICK HOMEMADE BREAD

Virginia Scott, Destin, Florida

Instant potato flakes and quick-rise yeast make this delightful recipe one you'll turn to time and again.

☑ Uses less fat, sugar or salt. Includes Nutrition Facts.

  2-1/2 cups water
    1/2 cup butter
    1/3 cup sugar
      3 tablespoons instant potato flakes
      2 packages (1/4 ounce *each*) quick-rise yeast
      1 teaspoon salt
      6 cups all-purpose flour or bread flour
  Vegetable oil

Heat water and butter to 125°-130°. In a large mixing bowl, combine with remaining ingredients except oil to form a stiff batter. Place in a greased bowl; oil top of dough. Cover and let rise in a warm place until doubled, about 30-45 minutes.

Punch dough down. On a lightly floured surface, knead dough until smooth and elastic, about 4-6 minutes. Divide dough into three portions. Shape into loaves and place in greased 8-1/2-in. x 4-1/2-in. x 2-in. loaf pans; oil tops of loaves. Cover and let rise until doubled, about 30 minutes.

Bake at 350° until bread sounds hollow when tapped, about 30-35 minutes. Remove from pans and cool on wire racks. **Yield:** 3 loaves.

Nutrition Facts: 1 slice equals 80 calories, 2 g fat (1 g saturated fat), 5 mg cholesterol, 69 mg sodium, 14 g carbohydrate, trace fiber, 2 g protein.

EASY ADVANTAGES
Quick-rise yeast has two time-saving advantages over active dry yeast: It does not need to be dissolved in water before mixing, and it requires only one rise after shaping. The dry yeast is added to the flour mixture which is combined with warm liquid. In place of the first rise, quick-rise yeast only needs to rest for a short period of time before shaping.

WHITE CASSEROLE BREAD

Lona Sage, Belvidere, Illinois

This bread won a blue ribbon when I entered it in a competition at a local fair. No matter how many times I prepare it, my friends and family always proclaim it a real winner!

☑ Uses less fat, sugar or salt. Includes Nutrition Facts.

  1 package (1/4 ounce) active dry yeast
1-1/4 cups warm water (110° to 115°)
  1 tablespoon sugar
1/2 teaspoon salt
2-1/2 to 3 cups all-purpose flour

In a large mixing bowl, dissolve yeast in water. Add sugar, salt and 1-1/2 cups flour; beat until smooth. Add enough remaining flour to form a soft dough.

Turn dough onto a floured surface; knead until smooth and elastic, about 6-8 minutes. Place in a greased bowl, turning once to grease top. Cover and let rise in a warm place until doubled, about 1 hour.

Punch dough down. Shape into a round loaf and place in a greased 1-qt. baking dish. Cover and let rise until doubled, about 30 minutes.

Using a sharp knife, make three slashes across the top. Bake at 350° for 40-45 minutes. Remove from dish to cool on a wire rack. **Yield:** 1 loaf.

Nutrition Facts: 1 slice equals 90 calories, trace fat (0 saturated fat), 0 cholesterol, 73 mg sodium, 21 g carbohydrate, 0 fiber, 3 g protein. **Diabetic Exchange:** 1 starch.

DILL-ONION BATTER BREAD

(Pictured above)

Gloria Huey, Port Allegany, Pennsylvania

Since the dough doesn't require kneading, this is a very easy bread to make. The tender loaf has a pleasant dill flavor. I serve it with soups, salads and all sorts of main courses.

☑ Uses less fat, sugar or salt. Includes Nutrition Facts.

  1 package (1/4 ounce) active dry yeast
1/4 cup warm water (110° to 115°)
  1 cup warm milk (110° to 115°)
  2 tablespoons butter, softened
  2 tablespoons sugar
  1 egg
  2 teaspoons dill seed
  2 teaspoons dried minced onion
1/2 teaspoon salt
  3 cups all-purpose flour

In a large mixing bowl, dissolve yeast in warm water. Add the milk, butter, sugar, egg, dill seed, onion, salt and 1-1/2 cups flour. Beat on low speed for 30 seconds; beat on high for 3 minutes. Stir in remaining flour (batter will be sticky). Do not knead. Cover and let rise in a warm place until doubled, about 1 hour.

Stir batter down. Spoon into a greased 9-in. x 5-in. x 3-in. loaf pan. Cover and let rise until nearly doubled, about 45 minutes.

Bake at 350° for 30-35 minutes or until golden brown (cover loosely with foil if top browns too quickly). Cool for 10 minutes before removing from pan to a wire rack. **Yield:** 1 loaf.

BEST-EVER BREADSTICKS

Carol Wolfer, Lebanon, Oregon

After just one bite of these delightful treats, you'll understand why we call them the "best ever."

☑ Uses less fat, sugar or salt. Includes Nutrition Facts.

  3 to 3-1/4 cups all-purpose flour, *divided*
  1 tablespoon sugar
  1 package (1/4 ounce) quick-rise yeast
  1 teaspoon salt
3/4 cup milk
1/4 cup warm water (110° to 115°)

1 tablespoon butter
1 egg white
1 tablespoon cold water
Coarse salt

In a large mixing bowl, combine 1-1/2 cups flour, sugar, yeast and salt. In a saucepan, heat the milk, water and butter to 120°-130°. Add to dry ingredients; beat just until moistened. Stir in enough remaining flour to form a stiff dough. Turn onto a lightly floured surface; knead until smooth and elastic, about 6-8 minutes. Place in a greased bowl, turning once to grease top. Cover dough and let rise in a warm place until doubled, about 30 minutes.

Punch the dough down. Pinch off golf ball-size pieces. On a lightly floured surface, roll into pencil-size strips. Place on greased baking sheets 1 in. apart. Cover and let rise for 15 minutes.

Beat egg white and cold water; brush over breadsticks. Sprinkle with coarse salt. Bake at 400° for 10 minutes or until golden. Remove breadsticks from pans to wire racks. **Yield:** about 18 breadsticks.

Nutrition Facts: 1 breadstick equals 185 calories, 2 g fat (1 g saturated fat), 6 mg cholesterol, 292 mg sodium, 34 g carbohydrate, 1 g fiber, 6 g protein.

GREEN ONION CORNMEAL MUFFINS

Naomi Rogers, Essex, Connecticut

This muffin recipe has a tasty twist with green onions and sour cream. The aroma while they are baking is just wonderful! I like to serve the bites with soups, stews and chowders.

✓ Uses less fat, sugar or salt. Includes Nutrition Facts.

1 cup all-purpose flour
3/4 cup yellow cornmeal
3 tablespoons brown sugar
3 teaspoons baking powder
1/4 teaspoon salt
1 egg, lightly beaten
1 cup (8 ounces) sour cream
1/3 cup milk
2 tablespoons butter, melted
1/4 cup chopped green onions

In a large bowl, combine the flour, cornmeal, brown sugar, baking powder and salt. In a small bowl, combine the egg, sour cream, milk, butter and onions; stir the mixture into dry ingredients just until moistened.

Fill greased or paper-lined muffin cups three-fourths full. Bake at 400° for 18-20 minutes or until a toothpick comes out clean. Cool for 5 minutes before removing from pan to a wire rack. Serve warm. **Yield:** 1 dozen.

Nutrition Facts: 1 muffin equals 150 calories, 6 g fat (4 g saturated fat), 37 mg cholesterol, 189 mg sodium, 19 g carbohydrate, 1 g fiber, 3 g protein.

HERBED BREAD SLICES
(Pictured below)

Margaret Wampler, Butler, Pennsylvania

It's a snap to jazz up a loaf of French bread with some salad dressing and a sprinkling of herbs.

✓ Uses less fat, sugar or salt. Includes Nutrition Facts.

3 tablespoons prepared Italian salad dressing
1 loaf (8 ounces) French bread, halved lengthwise
1 teaspoon dried rosemary, crushed
1/2 teaspoon dried oregano

Brush salad dressing over cut sides of bread. Sprinkle with rosemary and oregano. Place on an ungreased baking sheet. Broil 6 in. from the heat for 2-3 minutes or until lightly browned. Cut into 2-in. slices. **Yield:** 8 servings.

Nutrition Facts: 2 slices equals 99 calories, 3 g fat (trace saturated fat), 0 cholesterol, 268 mg sodium, 15 g carbohydrate, 1 g fiber, 3 g protein.

ball. Cover and let rise in a warm place until doubled, about 30 minutes.

Bake at 350° for 12-15 minutes or until golden brown. Remove buns from pans to wire racks to cool.

In a small heavy-duty resealable plastic bag, combine glaze ingredients until smooth. Cut a small hole in a corner of bag; pipe a cross on each bun. **Yield:** 22 buns.

ORANGE HOT CROSS BUNS
(Pictured above)

Ruth Hastings, Louisville, Illinois

For a traditional Easter recipe with a twist, try these yummy, sweet yeast buns. Grated orange peel gives them a mild citrus flavor. You'll end up making them year-round.

        2 packages (1/4 ounce *each*) active dry
          yeast
 1-1/4 cups warm orange juice (110° to 115°),
          divided
    1/2 cup butter, softened
    1/2 cup sugar
      3 eggs
      3 to 4 teaspoons grated orange peel
    1/2 teaspoon salt
    1/2 teaspoon ground cinnamon
      1 cup raisins
      6 to 6-1/2 cups all-purpose flour
GLAZE:
      1 cup confectioners' sugar
      2 to 3 teaspoons water

In a large mixing bowl, dissolve yeast in 3/4 cup warm orange juice. Add the butter, sugar, eggs, orange peel, salt, cinnamon, raisins, remaining orange juice and 3 cups flour. Beat until smooth. Stir in enough remaining flour to form a soft dough.

Turn onto a lightly floured surface; knead until smooth and elastic, about 6-8 minutes. Place in a greased bowl, turning once to grease top. Cover and let rise in a warm place until doubled, about 1 hour.

Punch dough down; turn onto a lightly floured surface. Divide into 22 pieces; shape each into a ball. Place 2 in. apart on greased baking sheets. Using a sharp knife, cut a cross on the top of each

FRUITY CARROT MUFFINS

Joyce Smith Williams, San Antonio, Texas

When it comes to whole grains, these muffins pack a triple-whammy of All-Bran cereal, ground flaxseed and oats. If you have a small household, simply freeze the extras.

      1 cup All-Bran
    3/4 cup ground flaxseed
    3/4 cup quick-cooking oats
    3/4 cup packed brown sugar
    1/2 cup all-purpose flour
      1 teaspoon baking soda
      1 teaspoon baking powder
      1 teaspoon ground cinnamon
    1/4 teaspoon salt
      2 eggs
    3/4 cup buttermilk
    1/2 cup unsweetened applesauce
    1/4 cup canola oil
    3/4 cup grated peeled apple
    3/4 cup shredded carrots
    3/4 cup raisins
    1/3 cup chopped pecans

In a large bowl, combine the first nine ingredients. In another bowl, beat the eggs, buttermilk, applesauce and oil until blended. Stir into dry ingredients just until moistened. Fold in the apple, carrots, raisins and pecans.

Coat muffin cups with cooking spray or use paper liners; fill two-thirds full with batter. Bake at 400° for 10-15 minutes or until a toothpick inserted near the center of the muffin comes out clean. Cool for 5 minutes before removing from pans to wire racks. **Yield:** 1-1/2 dozen.

BANANA CRUNCH MUFFINS

Chelsea Ferguson, Holdrege, Nebraska

Loaded with the old-fashioned banana flavor folks love, these muffins offer a surprising crunch from banana nut cereal.

3 cups all-purpose flour
1 cup packed brown sugar
1 tablespoon baking powder
1 teaspoon baking soda
1 teaspoon salt
1/4 teaspoon ground nutmeg
4 ripe bananas
3/4 cup egg substitute
1/3 cup vegetable oil
1 cup (8 ounces) reduced-fat strawberry yogurt
1-1/2 cups banana nut cereal, slightly crushed

In a bowl, combine flour, brown sugar, baking powder, baking soda, salt and nutmeg; set aside. In a small bowl, mash three of the bananas; stir in egg substitute, oil and yogurt. Coarsely chop the remaining banana; fold into yogurt mixture. Stir into dry ingredients just until moistened.

Fill greased or paper-lined muffin cups one-third full. Spoon 1-1/2 teaspoons cereal on each. Top with remaining batter until the cups are three-fourths full. Sprinkle with remaining cereal. Bake at 375° for 15-18 minutes or until the muffins test done. **Yield:** 2 dozen.

Nutrition Facts: 1 muffin equals 161 calories, 4 g fat (0 saturated fat), 1 mg cholesterol, 244 mg sodium, 27 g carbohydrate, 0 fiber, 3 g protein.

BLENDER YEAST ROLLS

Regena Newton, Oktaha, Oklahoma

If you're looking for a quick and easy homemade roll, you'll want to try my recipe. I use a blender to combine the wet ingredients. Best of all, no kneading is required!

1 cup warm milk (110° to 115°)
1 package (1/4 ounce) active dry yeast
1/4 cup sugar
2 eggs
1/4 cup vegetable oil
3-1/4 cups all-purpose flour
1 teaspoon salt

In a blender, combine the warm milk, yeast, sugar, eggs and oil; cover and process on low speed for 30 seconds or until blended.

In a large bowl, combine the flour and the salt. Add yeast mixture; stir with a spoon until combined (do not knead). Cover and let rise in a warm place until doubled, about 30 minutes.

Stir down dough. Fill greased muffin cups half full. Cover and let rise until doubled, about 30 minutes.

Bake at 350° for 18-20 minutes or until golden brown. Remove from pans to wire racks. Serve warm. **Yield:** about 1 dozen.

APPALACHIAN CORN BREAD

(Pictured below)

Anne Wiehler, Farmington, Pennsylvania

On this westernmost ridge of the Appalachians, we get abundant rain and sunshine, which allows our children to grow a super-sweet corn crop. This corn bread is just one way we use some of the bounty!

2 tablespoons chopped onion
4 tablespoons vegetable oil, *divided*
1 cup all-purpose flour
1 cup cornmeal
2 tablespoons sugar
4 teaspoons baking powder
1/2 teaspoon salt
2 eggs
1 cup milk
1/2 cup fresh *or* frozen corn, thawed
1/3 cup shredded cheddar cheese
1/4 cup salsa
2 tablespoons minced chives

In a small saucepan, saute the onion in 1 tablespoon oil until tender; set aside.

In a large bowl, combine the flour, cornmeal, sugar, baking powder and salt. In another bowl, whisk the eggs, milk and remaining oil. Stir in the corn, cheese, salsa, chives and reserved onion. Stir into the dry ingredients just until combined.

Transfer to a greased 9-in. square baking pan. Bake at 425° for 20-25 minutes or until a toothpick inserted near the center comes out clean and top is lightly browned. Cut into squares; serve warm. **Yield:** 9 servings.

BUTTERMILK BISCUITS
(Pictured at left)

Jean Parsons, Sarver, Pennsylvania

These biscuits are made from a recipe that's been in our family for years. They're simple to make and smell so good when baking! The wonderful aroma takes me back to those days when Mom made this meal—it's as if I'm in our family kitchen again, with her busy at the stove.

✓ Uses less fat, sugar or salt. Includes Nutrition Facts.

    2 cups all-purpose flour
    1 tablespoon sugar
    1 teaspoon baking powder
    1/2 teaspoon salt
    1/2 teaspoon baking soda
    1/4 cup cold shortening
    3/4 cup buttermilk

In a large bowl, combine the flour, sugar, baking powder, salt and baking soda. Cut in shortening until mixture resembles coarse crumbs. Add buttermilk; stir just until the dough clings together.

Turn onto a lightly floured surface; knead gently, about 10-12 times. Roll to 1/2-in. thickness; cut with a floured 2-in. round biscuit cutter. Place 1 in. apart on a greased baking sheet. Bake at 450° for 11-12 minutes or until lightly browned. Serve warm. **Yield:** about 1-1/2 dozen.

Nutrition Facts: 1 biscuit equals 74 calories, 3 g fat (1 g saturated fat), trace cholesterol, 120 mg sodium, 11 g carbohydrate, trace fiber, 2 g protein.

MAPLE-PECAN CORN BREAD
(Pictured at right)

Shirley Brownell, Amsterdam, New York

Corn bread, or johnnycake as it's called here in scenic Mohawk Valley, was a staple of the men fighting in the Revolutionary War. The volunteers, who were known as "Johnnys," carried their rations with them, and the johnnycakes held up well for days.

✓ Uses less fat, sugar or salt. Includes Nutrition Facts.

    1 cup all-purpose flour
    1 cup yellow cornmeal
    1 teaspoon baking powder
    1 teaspoon baking soda
    1 teaspoon salt
    3 tablespoons butter, softened

    2 tablespoons brown sugar
    2 eggs
    1/3 cup pure maple syrup
    3/4 cup buttermilk
    1/2 cup chopped pecans
Additional maple syrup, optional

Combine flour, cornmeal, baking powder, baking soda and salt; set aside. In a mixing bowl, combine butter, sugar and eggs; mix well. Add syrup and buttermilk. Stir in dry ingredients just until moistened. Stir in pecans.

Pour into a greased 8-1/2-in. x 4-1/2-in. x 2-1/2-in. loaf pan. Bake at 350° for 35-40 minutes or until bread tests done. Cool for 10 minutes in pan. Serve warm with syrup if desired or allow to cool. **Yield:** 1 loaf.

Nutrition Facts: 1 slice equals 142 calories, 6 g fat (2 g saturated fat), 33 mg cholesterol, 294 mg sodium, 20 g carbohydrate, 1 g fiber, 3 g protein.

SECRET TO BAKING SUCCESS

The shelf life for baking powder and baking soda is 6 months. To test for freshness, place 1 teaspoon baking powder in a cup and add 1/3 cup hot tap water. For baking soda, place 1/4 teaspoon in a cup and add 2 teaspoons vinegar. If active bubbling occurs, the products are fine to use. If not, they should be replaced.

IRISH SODA BREAD MUFFINS
(Pictured below)

Lorraine Ballsieper, Deep River, Connecticut

Irish soda bread is traditionally made in a loaf shape, but these muffins have the same terrific flavor with buttermilk, caraway seeds and currants. I think they're best when served warm.

✓ Uses less fat, sugar or salt. Includes Nutrition Facts.

2-1/4 cups all-purpose flour
1/2 cup plus 1 tablespoon sugar, *divided*
2 teaspoons baking powder
1/2 teaspoon salt
1/4 teaspoon baking soda
1 teaspoon caraway seeds
1 egg
1 cup buttermilk
1/4 cup butter, melted
1/4 cup vegetable oil
3/4 cup dried currants *or* raisins

In a large bowl, combine the flour, 1/2 cup sugar, baking powder, salt, baking soda and caraway seeds. In another bowl, beat the egg, buttermilk, butter and oil. Stir into dry ingredients just until moistened. Fold in currants.

Fill greased muffin cups three-fourths full. Sprinkle with remaining sugar. Bake at 400° for 15 minutes or until a toothpick comes out clean. Cool for 5 minutes before removing from pan to wire rack. Serve warm. **Yield:** 1 dozen.

Nutrition Facts: 1 muffin equals 235 calories, 9 g fat (3 g saturated fat), 28 mg cholesterol, 247 mg sodium, 35 g carbohydrate, 1 g fiber, 4 g protein.

CRANBERRY NUT BREAD

Marilyn Ellis, Canyon Lake, Pennsylvania

"Wholesome" is one word that comes to mind with every bite of this lovely sweet bread. Featuring cranberries, nuts and just a hint of orange flavor, it's perfect for the holidays.

✓ Uses less fat, sugar or salt. Includes Nutrition Facts.

2 cups all-purpose flour
1/4 teaspoon salt
1-1/2 teaspoons baking powder
1/2 teaspoon baking soda
1 cup sugar
1 egg, beaten
2 tablespoons melted butter
1/2 cup orange juice
2 tablespoons hot water
1/2 pound cranberries, cut in half
1/2 cup whole pecans
Peel of an orange, grated

In a mixing bowl, combine all dry ingredients. Make a well and add the egg, butter, juice and water. Stir until dry ingredients are moistened. Fold in cranberries, nuts and orange peel.

Bake in a greased 9-in. x 5-in. x 3-in. loaf pan at 325° for about 1 hour or until the bread tests done. Cool 10 minutes before removing from the pan to a wire rack. **Yield:** 1 loaf.

Nutrition Facts: 1 slice equals 157 calories, 4 g fat (1 g saturated fat), 17 mg cholesterol, 133 mg sodium, 28 g carbohydrate, 1 g fiber, 2 g protein.

PEASANT BREAD

Sue Ann Chapman, Tulsa, Oklahoma

If you are looking for an easy bread recipe, this is it! A neighbor gave me the delicious recipe years ago. Because there's no kneading involved, the bread is very simple to make.

✓ Uses less fat, sugar or salt. Includes Nutrition Facts.

1 package (1/4 ounce) active dry yeast
2 cups warm water (110° to 115°), *divided*
4 cups all-purpose flour
2 teaspoons salt

1 tablespoon sugar
1 tablespoon butter, melted
1 tablespoon poppy seeds

Dissolve yeast in 1 cup warm water. In a large bowl, combine flour, salt and sugar. Add the yeast mixture and remaining water; stir until combined. Cover and let rise in a warm place until doubled, about 1 hour.

Stir dough down. Divide in half. Place each half in a greased 1-qt. round casserole or oven-proof bowl. Brush tops with butter and sprinkle with poppy seeds. Let rise in a warm place until doubled, about 45 minutes.

Bake at 350° for 45 minutes. Remove from pans; serve warm if desired. **Yield:** 2 loaves.

Nutrition Facts: 1 slice equals 64 calories, 1 g fat (trace saturated fat), 1 mg cholesterol, 152 mg sodium, 12 g carbohydrate, trace fiber, 2 g protein.

▪▪▪▪▪▪▪▪▪▪▪▪▪▪▪

SAVORY PULL APART BREAD
(Pictured above)

Janne Rowe, Wichita, Kansas

Who doesn't like pull apart bread? This version is made with frozen dough, so it couldn't be easier.

1/4 cup grated Parmesan cheese
3 tablespoons sesame seeds
1/2 teaspoon dried basil

1 package (30 ounces) frozen roll dough
    (24 rolls)
1/4 cup butter, melted
2 tablespoons bacon bits, optional

Combine Parmesan cheese, sesame seeds and basil; sprinkle one-third in the bottom and up the sides of a greased 12-cup fluted tube pan. Place half of the unthawed rolls in pan; drizzle with half of the butter. Sprinkle with half of the remaining cheese mixture and bacon bits if desired. Arrange remaining rolls on top; drizzle with remaining butter. Sprinkle with remaining cheese mixture. Cover and refrigerate overnight.

Remove from the refrigerator 30 minutes before baking. Bake at 350° for 20 minutes. Cover loosely with foil; bake 10-15 minutes longer. **Yield:** 10-12 servings.

READY-WHEN-YOU-ARE ROLLS

Frozen bread dough is quite a time-saver for busy cooks. If you take it out of the freezer at lunchtime, set it on the counter and cover it with plastic wrap coated with cooking spray, it should be ready to pop in the oven when you come home before dinner. You also can break off small portions, roll them into balls and have fresh-baked rolls in no time.

GOT MILK? *You'll want to fix yourself a cold glass when these sweet treats come out of the oven. Chocolate sensations, oatmeal bites and cinnamon specialties are just some of the goodies you'll find here.*

SCRUMPTIOUS SNACKING. Double Frosted Brownies (p. 103).

Cookies, Bars & Brownies

DOUBLE FROSTED BROWNIES
(Pictured at left)

Edith Amburn, Mount Airy, North Carolina

I grew up on a farm and always liked to help my mother in the kitchen—especially when it came to making desserts. I'm often asked to bring these brownies when refreshments are served at social meetings.

> 4 eggs
> 1 cup vegetable oil
> 1-1/2 cups sugar
> 1/2 cup packed brown sugar
> 1/4 cup water
> 2 teaspoons vanilla extract
> 1-1/2 cups all-purpose flour
> 1/2 cup baking cocoa
> 1 teaspoon salt
> 1/2 cup chopped walnuts

FROSTING:
> 1 can (16 ounces) vanilla frosting
> 1 tablespoon rum extract

GLAZE:
> 1 cup (6 ounces) semisweet chocolate chips
> 1 tablespoon vegetable oil

In a large mixing bowl, beat the eggs, oil, sugars, water and vanilla. Combine the flour, cocoa, salt and walnuts; stir into egg mixture until blended.

Pour into a greased 15-in. x 10-in. x 1-in. baking pan. Bake at 350° for 20-25 minutes or until center is set. Cool on a wire rack.

Combine frosting and extract; spread over brownies. Chill for 30 minutes. In a microwave or heavy saucepan, melt chocolate chips and oil; stir until smooth. Drizzle over frosting. Let stand until set before cutting. **Yield:** 3 dozen.

ORANGE-DATE BARS

Sue Yaeger, Brookings, South Dakota

If you're looking to serve a lighter, more nutritious dessert, you'll appreciate this recipe. It's an appealing, old-fashioned dessert that's full-flavored.

 Uses less fat, sugar or salt. Includes Nutrition Facts and Diabetic Exchanges.

> 1 cup chopped dates
> 1/3 cup sugar
> 1/3 cup vegetable oil
> 1/2 cup orange juice
> 1 egg, beaten
> 1 cup all-purpose flour
> 1-1/2 teaspoons baking powder
> 1 tablespoon grated orange rind
> 1/2 cup chopped pecans

In a saucepan, combine dates, sugar, oil and juice. Cook for 5 minutes to soften dates. Cool. Add egg; mix well. Combine all remaining ingredients and stir into date mixture.

Spread into a greased 8-in. square baking pan. Bake at 350° for 25-30 minutes. Cool before cutting. **Yield:** 36 servings.

Nutrition Facts: 1 bar equals 56 calories, 3 g fat (0 saturated fat), 8 mg cholesterol, 12 mg sodium, 6 g carbohydrate, 0 fiber, 1 g protein. **Diabetic Exchanges:** 1/2 starch, 1/2 fat.

TWO-MINUTE COOKIES

Kerry Bouchard, Shawmut, Montana

My mom used to pack these no-bake cookies into our lunches. They're inexpensive and easy to prepare, so all seven of us children learned to make them.

✓ Uses less fat, sugar or salt. Includes Nutrition Facts.

> 1/2 cup butter
> 1/2 cup milk
> 2 cups sugar
> 3 cups quick-cooking oats *or* old-fashioned oats
> 5 tablespoons unsweetened cocoa
> 1/2 cup raisins, chopped nuts *or* coconut

In a large saucepan, heat butter, milk and sugar. Bring to a boil, stirring occasionally. Boil for 1 minute. Remove from the heat. Stir in oats, cocoa, raisins, nuts or coconut. Drop by tablespoonsful onto waxed paper. Cool. **Yield:** about 3 dozen cookies.

Nutrition Facts: 2 cookies equals 203 calories, 6 g fat (3 g saturated fat), 15 mg cholesterol, 56 mg sodium, 35 g carbohydrate, 2 g fiber, 3 g protein.

🔳🔳🔳🔳🔳🔳🔳🔳🔳🔳🔳

SNOWMAN TREATS

(Pictured above)

Lori Daniels, Beverly, West Virginia

My daughter, Hannah, and I came up with this recipe on Christmas Eve when she wanted to make treats for Santa. Building a snowman is lots of fun, but coating one in candy is even cooler!

- 1/2 to 3/4 cup creamy peanut butter
- 34 round butter-flavored crackers
- 12 ounces white candy coating, coarsely chopped
- 34 miniature chocolate chips
- 9 pieces candy corn, cut lengthwise in half
- 34 milk chocolate M&M's
- Assorted colors of decorating gel

Spread peanut butter over half of the crackers; top with remaining crackers to make sandwiches.

In a heavy saucepan, melt candy coating; stir until smooth. Dip sandwiches until coated; place on waxed paper.

Immediately position chocolate chips for eyes and mouths and add a candy corn half for nose. For earmuffs, place an M&M on either side of face, connected with a strip of decorating gel. Let the treats stand for 30 minutes or until set. **Yield:** 17 servings.

🔳🔳🔳🔳🔳🔳🔳🔳🔳🔳🔳

HOLLY WREATH COOKIES

Phyllis Rewey, Englewood, Florida

My mom passed along the recipe for these crunchy, wreath-shaped cookies. They look festive dressed up with green and red gumdrops resembling holly leaves and berries.

✓ Uses less fat, sugar or salt. Includes Nutrition Facts.

- 1 cup butter, softened
- 1 cup sugar
- 1 egg
- 2 cups all-purpose flour
- 2 teaspoons cream of tartar
- 1 teaspoon baking soda
- 2 cups ground almonds

ICING:
- 2 cups confectioners' sugar
- 3 tablespoons milk
- 24 green spice gumdrops
- 16 red spice gumdrops

In a large mixing bowl, cream butter and sugar. Beat in egg. Combine the flour, cream of tartar and baking soda; gradually add to creamed mixture and mix well. Stir in almonds. Divide in half. Cover and refrigerate for 2 hours or until dough is easy to handle.

On a lightly floured surface, roll out one portion of dough to 3/8-in. thickness. Cut with a floured 2-1/2-in. round cookie cutter. Place on ungreased baking sheets; cut out centers using a floured 1-in. round cookie cutter.

Bake at 375° for 8-9 minutes or until lightly browned. Cool for 2 minutes before removing to wire racks to cool completely. Repeat with remaining dough. Chill and reroll scraps if desired.

In a bowl, whisk confectioners' sugar and milk until smooth; gently spread over cookies. For holly trim, roll out gumdrops to 1/16-in. thickness; cut two holly leaves from each green gumdrop and nine berries from each red gumdrop. Arrange one leaf and three berries on each cookie. **Yield:** 4 dozen.

Nutrition Facts: 1 cookie equals 127 calories, 6 g fat (3 g saturated fat), 15 mg cholesterol, 68 mg sodium, 17 g carbohydrate, 1 g fiber, 2 g protein.

🔳🔳🔳🔳🔳🔳🔳🔳🔳🔳🔳

TRIPLE-CHOCOLATE BROWNIE COOKIES

Linda Robinson, New Braunfels, Texas

Our family of chocolate lovers gets triply excited when these cookies come out of the oven. They have the texture and taste of fudge brownies.

✓ Uses less fat, sugar or salt. Includes Nutrition Facts.

- 3/4 cup butter, cubed
- 4 squares (1 ounce *each*) unsweetened chocolate
- 2 cups sugar
- 4 eggs
- 1-1/2 cups all-purpose flour
- 1/2 cup baking cocoa

2 teaspoons baking powder
1/2 teaspoon salt
2 cups (12 ounces) semisweet chocolate chips, *divided*
2 teaspoons shortening

In a small saucepan over low heat, melt butter and unsweetened chocolate; cool. Transfer to a large mixing bowl; add sugar and eggs. Beat until smooth. Combine the flour, cocoa, baking powder and salt; gradually add to chocolate mixture. Stir in 1-1/2 cups chocolate chips. Cover and refrigerate for 2 hours or until easy to handle.

Drop by tablespoonfuls 2 in. apart onto greased baking sheets. Bake at 350° for 7-9 minutes or until edges are set and tops are slightly cracked. Cool for 2 minutes before removing from pans to wire racks to cool completely.

In a microwave-safe bowl, heat shortening and remaining chocolate chips on high for 1 minute or until chips are melted; stir until smooth. Drizzle over cookies. Let stand for 30 minutes or until chocolate is set. Store in an airtight container. **Yield:** 6 dozen.

Nutrition Facts: 1 cookie equals 79 calories, 4 g fat (2 g saturated fat), 17 mg cholesterol, 51 mg sodium, 11 g carbohydrate, 1 g fiber, 1 g protein.

BROWNIE BOURBON BITES

Paula Kirchenbauer, Newton, New Jersey

Chocolate and chopped pecans flavor these simple, spirited treats. I recommend making a double batch so you can give some as gifts and savor the rest!

✓ Uses less fat, sugar or salt. Includes Nutrition Facts.

1/2 cup butter, softened
1/2 cup packed brown sugar
1/4 cup bourbon
1 cup all-purpose flour
3 tablespoons baking cocoa
1/2 cup miniature semisweet chocolate chips
1 cup coarsely chopped pecans

In a small mixing bowl, cream butter and brown sugar until light and fluffy, about 5 minutes. Beat in bourbon. Combine flour and cocoa; gradually add to creamed mixture, beating until smooth. Stir in chocolate chips. Cover and refrigerate for 1-2 hours.

Shape into 1-in. balls; roll in pecans. Place 2 in. apart on ungreased baking sheets. Bake at 350° for 8-10 minutes or until cookies are set. Cool for 5 minutes before carefully removing from pans to wire racks to cool completely. Store in an air-

tight container. **Yield:** about 2 dozen.

Nutrition Facts: 1 each equals 110 calories, 7 g fat (3 g saturated fat), 9 mg cholesterol, 35 mg sodium, 10 g carbohydrate, 1 g fiber, 1 g protein.

SNOWFLAKE COOKIES
(Pictured below)

Morven Baker, Ashland, Ohio

Warm from the oven, these sugary snowflakes are guaranteed to melt in your mouth. One cookie is never enough. So bake up a blizzard!

✓ Uses less fat, sugar or salt. Includes Nutrition Facts.

2 cups butter, softened
1-1/4 cups sugar, *divided*
1 teaspoon vanilla extract
4 cups cake flour
2 tablespoons edible glitter

In a large mixing bowl, cream butter and 1 cup sugar. Beat in vanilla. Gradually add flour and mix well. Divide in half. Cover and refrigerate for 2 hours or until easy to handle.

On a lightly floured surface, roll out one portion of dough to 1/4-in. thickness. Cut with a floured 4-in. snowflake-shaped cookie cutter. Place 1 in. apart on ungreased baking sheets. Bake at 325° for 7-10 minutes or until firm. Repeat with remaining dough. Chill and reroll scraps if desired.

In a small resealable plastic bag, combine edible glitter and remaining sugar. Seal bag; crush mixture to break glitter into smaller pieces. Sprinkle over warm cookies. Cool for 5 minutes before removing to wire racks to cool completely. **Yield:** 4 dozen.

Nutrition Facts: 1 cookie equals 131 calories, 8 g fat (5 g saturated fat), 20 mg cholesterol, 78 mg sodium, 15 g carbohydrate, trace fiber, 1 g protein.

Cinnamon Oatmeal Cookies
(Pictured below)

Anna Brydl, Tobias, Nebraska

My family just loves these big, traditional cookies. They're crisp, yet still chewy in the center, and the cinnamon makes them a little different from typical oatmeal cookies.

☑ Uses less fat, sugar or salt. Includes Nutrition Facts.

   1 cup butter, softened
   1 cup sugar
   1 cup packed brown sugar
   2 eggs
   1 teaspoon vanilla extract
1-1/2 cups all-purpose flour
   1 teaspoon baking soda
   1 teaspoon ground cinnamon
 1/2 teaspoon baking powder
 1/2 teaspoon salt
   3 cups quick-cooking oats

In a large mixing bowl, cream butter and sugars. Beat in eggs and vanilla. Combine the flour, baking soda, cinnamon, baking powder and salt; gradually add to creamed mixture and mix well. Stir in oats.

Shape into 1-1/2-in. balls. Place 2 in. apart on ungreased baking sheets. Bake at 350° for 10-12 minutes or until golden brown. Cool for 1 minute before removing to wire racks. **Yield:** 4 dozen.

Nutrition Facts: 2 cookies equals 208 calories, 9 g fat (5 g saturated fat), 38 mg cholesterol, 196 mg sodium, 30 g carbohydrate, 1 g fiber, 3 g protein.

Fruited Jewel Cookies
(Pictured above)

Patricia Marsh, Phoenix, Arizona

When guests drop in, be ready with these cheerful, citrus-flavored tidbits. Finely chopped walnuts can be substituted for pecans in the cookie coating.

☑ Uses less fat, sugar or salt. Includes Nutrition Facts.

 1/2 cup butter, softened
 1/2 cup confectioners' sugar
   1 egg, *separated*
 1/4 cup pineapple preserves
   5 teaspoons grated orange peel
   1 teaspoon vanilla extract
   1 cup all-purpose flour
 1/4 teaspoon salt
1-1/4 cups finely chopped pecans
Red *and/or* green candied cherries, halved

In a large mixing bowl, cream butter and confectioners' sugar. Beat in the egg yolk, preserves, orange peel and vanilla. Combine flour and salt; gradually add to creamed mixture and mix well. Cover and refrigerate for 2 hours or until easy to handle.

Roll dough into 1-in. balls. In a shallow bowl, beat egg white until foamy. Place pecans in another shallow bowl. Dip each ball into egg white, then into pecans.

Place 2 in. apart on ungreased baking sheets. Bake at 350° for 10-12 minutes or until lightly browned. While still warm, press a cherry half into the center of each cookie. Remove to wire racks to cool. **Yield:** 3 dozen.

Nutrition Facts: 1 cookie equals 78 calories, 6 g fat (2 g saturated fat), 13 mg cholesterol, 44 mg sodium, 6 g carbohydrate, 1 g fiber, 1 g protein.

SORGHUM COOKIES

Jennifer Kramer, Lynnville, Iowa

Our family makes lots of syrup from our homegrown sorghum cane. I use it in baking recipes such as these soft, old-fashioned cookies.

✓ Uses less fat, sugar or salt. Includes Nutrition Facts.

1 cup butter, softened
1-1/3 cups sugar
2 eggs
1/4 cup sorghum syrup
1 teaspoon grated orange peel
3 cups all-purpose flour
1 teaspoon baking soda
1 teaspoon baking powder
1 teaspoon ground cinnamon
1/4 teaspoon salt
1/4 teaspoon *each* ground cloves, cardamom and nutmeg

In a large mixing bowl, cream butter and sugar. Beat in the eggs, syrup and orange peel. Combine the flour, baking soda, baking powder, cinnamon, salt, cloves, cardamom and nutmeg; gradually add to creamed mixture.

Drop by tablespoonfuls 2 in. apart onto ungreased baking sheets. Bake at 375° for 10-12 minutes or until set. Remove to wire racks. **Yield:** about 2-1/2 dozen.

Nutrition Facts: 1 cookie equals 137 calories, 6 g fat (4 g saturated fat), 29 mg cholesterol, 133 mg sodium, 19 g carbohydrate, trace fiber, 2 g protein.

ICED CINNAMON CHIP COOKIES

(Pictured above right)

Katie Jean Boyd, Roachdale, Indiana

I take these cookies to family gatherings and socials and give them as gifts to friends. They are wonderful with or without the soft icing.

✓ Uses less fat, sugar or salt. Includes Nutrition Facts.

1 cup butter, softened
3/4 cup sugar
3/4 cup packed brown sugar
2 eggs
1 teaspoon vanilla extract
3 cups all-purpose flour
1 teaspoon baking soda
1 teaspoon salt
1 package (10 ounces) cinnamon baking chips

ICING:
1/4 cup butter, melted
1/4 cup shortening
1-1/4 cups confectioners' sugar
1 tablespoon milk
3/4 teaspoon vanilla extract

In a large mixing bowl, cream butter and sugars. Beat in eggs and vanilla. Combine the flour, baking soda and salt; gradually add to creamed mixture and mix well. Fold in cinnamon chips.

Drop by rounded tablespoonfuls 2 in. apart onto ungreased baking sheets. Bake at 350° for 10-12 minutes or until golden brown. Remove to wire racks to cool.

In a small mixing bowl, combine icing ingredients; beat on high speed for 1-2 minutes or until fluffy. Spread over cookies. **Yield:** about 3-1/2 dozen.

Nutrition Facts: 1 cookie equals 158 calories, 8 g fat (4 g saturated fat), 23 mg cholesterol, 148 mg sodium, 20 g carbohydrate, trace fiber, 2 g protein.

FRESHLY BAKED WITHOUT FUSS

When making cookies, lots of family cooks, bake a sheet or two, then set cookie-size portions of the rest of the dough onto paper-lined cookie sheets to freeze. Once the dough is frozen, they store the portions in resealable freezer bags. This way, a batch of fresh cookies is always at hand for drop-in guests, after-school snacks or last-minute desserts.

MINI MERINGUE PUMPKINS
(Pictured above)

Cast a sweet spell over Halloween party guests by making a pumpkin patch worth of treats from our Test Kitchen. Using a basic meringue recipe spiced with pumpkin flavor, you, too, can scare up the festive, fun-to-eat cookies.

 Uses less fat, sugar or salt. Includes Nutrition Facts.

  2 egg whites
1/4 teaspoon cream of tartar
1/8 teaspoon salt
1/2 cup sugar
1/2 teaspoon pumpkin pie spice
1/2 teaspoon vanilla extract
  2 teaspoons orange colored sugar
  2 teaspoons orange edible glitter
  3 pieces green Fruit by the Foot fruit roll
  2 teaspoons vanilla frosting

Place the egg whites in a small mixing bowl; let stand at room temperature for 30 minutes. Add cream of tartar and salt; beat until soft peaks form. Gradually beat in sugar, 1 tablespoon at a time, on high until stiff peaks form. Add pumpkin pie spice and vanilla.

Place egg white mixture in a pastry bag fitted with a large star tip. Pipe 1-1/2-in.-diameter pumpkins onto parchment paper-lined baking sheets. In a small resealable plastic bag, combine the orange sugar and glitter. Seal bag; crush mixture to break glitter into small pieces. Sprinkle over pumpkins.

Bake at 250° for 40-45 minutes or until set and dry. Turn oven off; leave meringues in oven for 1-1/2 hours.

Carefully remove meringues from parchment paper. Cut leaf and vine shapes from fruit roll; attach to pumpkins with a dab of frosting. Store in an airtight container. **Yield:** 2 dozen.

Nutrition Facts: 1 pumpkin equals 32 calories, trace fat (trace saturated fat), 0 cholesterol, 23 mg sodium, 7 g carbohydrate, trace fiber, trace protein.

Editor's Note: Orange edible glitter is available from Wilton Industries, Inc.

CHOCOLATE-COVERED CHERRY COOKIES

Marie Kinyon, Mason, Michigan

I always bake these cookies for family gatherings, and they never last very long. They require a little extra effort, but they're worth it.

☑ Uses less fat, sugar or salt. Includes Nutrition Facts.

1/2 cup butter
  1 cup sugar
  1 egg
1-1/2 teaspoons vanilla extract
1-1/2 cups all-purpose flour
1/2 cup baking cocoa
1/4 teaspoon salt
1/4 teaspoon baking powder
1/4 teaspoon baking soda
 48 maraschino cherries, blotted dry
FROSTING:
  1 cup (6 ounces) semisweet chocolate chips
1/2 cup sweetened condensed milk
  1 to 3 teaspoons maraschino cherry juice

In a mixing bowl, cream together butter and sugar until fluffy; beat in egg and vanilla. Combine the dry ingredients; gradually add to creamed mixture (batter will be very firm). Shape into 48 balls, about 1 in. round, and place on ungreased baking sheets. Push one cherry halfway into each ball.

For frosting, melt chocolate chips in milk in a small saucepan over low heat, stirring constantly. Remove from the heat; add cherry juice and stir until smooth. Spoon 1 teaspoon of frosting over each cherry (the frosting will spread over cookie during baking).

Bake at 350° for 10-12 minutes. Cool on wire racks. **Yield:** 4 dozen.

Nutrition Facts: 2 cookies equals 177 calories, 7 g fat (4 g saturated fat), 21 mg cholesterol, 92 mg sodium, 29 g carbohydrate, 1 g fiber, 2 g protein.

LEMON OATMEAL COOKIES

Michelle Naber, Tonawanda, New York

My grandmother always made these cookies for us for Christmas, and now I have inherited that task. With rich cream cheese in the dough and the sugary almond topping, a batch doesn't last long at our house!

☑ Uses less fat, sugar or salt. Includes Nutrition Facts.

  1 cup butter-flavored shortening
  1 package (3 ounces) cream cheese, softened

1-1/4 cups sugar
   1 egg yolk
   2 teaspoons grated lemon peel
   1 teaspoon lemon extract
1-1/3 cups all-purpose flour
1-1/3 cups quick-cooking oats
   1/2 teaspoon salt
TOPPING:
   1 egg
   1 egg white
Sugar
   1/2 cup sliced almonds

In a large mixing bowl, cream the shortening, cream cheese and sugar. Add the egg yolk, lemon peel and extract; mix well. Combine the flour, oats and salt; gradually add to creamed mixture.

Drop by heaping teaspoonfuls 2 in. apart onto greased baking sheets. Beat egg and egg white; brush over dough. Sprinkle with sugar; top with almonds. Bake at 350° for 10-12 minutes or until edges are lightly browned. Remove to wire racks. **Yield:** 4-1/2 dozen.

Nutrition Facts: 1 cookie equals 83 calories, 5 g fat (1 g saturated fat), 10 mg cholesterol, 29 mg sodium, 9 g carbohydrate, trace fiber, 1 g protein.

CHOCOLATE ALMOND LOGS

Debbi Groeler, Watertown, Wisconsin

These awesome, almond and chocolate treats are always popular at our annual church cookie sale. The tray empties in no time!

   1/2 cup butter, softened
   1/2 cup plus 1 tablespoon butter-flavored
      shortening, *divided*
   1 cup sugar
   1 egg
   1 teaspoon almond extract
2-1/4 cups all-purpose flour
   1/2 cup baking cocoa
   1/2 teaspoon salt
   1 cup white chips *or* 6 ounces white candy
      coating, chopped
   1/2 cup chopped almonds

In a small mixing bowl, cream butter, 1/2 cup shortening and sugar. Beat in egg and extract. Combine the flour, cocoa and salt; gradually add to creamed mixture.

Shape rounded tablespoonfuls of dough into 2-1/2-in. logs. Place 2 in. apart on ungreased baking sheets. Bake at 375° for 8-10 minutes or until set. Cool on wire racks.

In a small saucepan over low heat, melt white chips and remaining shortening. Dip one end of each cookie in melted chips; allow excess to drip off. Roll in almonds. Place on waxed paper to firm. **Yield:** about 3 dozen.

FROSTED CASHEW COOKIES
(Pictured below)

Sheila Wyum, Rutland, North Dakota

My sister's sister-in-law discovered this recipe. We enjoy the cookies at Christmas, but they're rich and elegant for a coffee event, too.

   1/2 cup butter, softened
   1 cup packed brown sugar
   1 egg
   1/3 cup sour cream
   1/2 teaspoon vanilla extract
   2 cups all-purpose flour
   3/4 teaspoon *each* baking powder, baking
      soda and salt
1-3/4 cups salted cashew halves
BROWNED BUTTER FROSTING:
   1/2 cup butter
   3 tablespoons half-and-half cream
   1/4 teaspoon vanilla extract
   2 cups confectioners' sugar
Additional cashew halves, optional

In a mixing bowl, cream the butter and brown sugar. Beat in egg, sour cream and vanilla; mix well. Combine dry ingredients; add to creamed mixture and mix well. Fold in the cashews.

Drop by rounded teaspoonfuls onto greased baking sheets. Bake at 375° for 8-10 minutes or until lightly browned. Cool on a wire rack.

For the frosting, lightly brown butter in a small saucepan. Remove from the heat; add cream and vanilla. Beat in confectioners' sugar until smooth and thick. Frost cookies. Top each with a cashew half if desired. **Yield:** about 3 dozen.

CHOCOLATE CHIP RASPBERRY BARS

(Pictured below)

Bev Cudrak, Coaldale, Alberta

My husband found this recipe in a farm paper, so I made it for him. The results were out of this world.

☑ Uses less fat, sugar or salt. Includes Nutrition Facts.

1-3/4 cups all-purpose flour
   1 cup sugar
   1 cup cold butter
   1 egg
  1/2 teaspoon almond extract
   1 cup seedless raspberry jam
  1/2 cup miniature semisweet chocolate chips

In a large bowl, combine flour and sugar. Cut in butter until mixture resembles coarse crumbs. Stir in egg and extract just until moistened. Set aside 1 cup crumb mixture for topping.

Press the remaining mixture into a greased 11-in. x 7-in. x 2-in. baking pan. Bake at 350° for 5 minutes. Spread with jam and sprinkle with reserved crumb mixture. Bake 35-40 minutes longer or until golden brown.

Sprinkle with chocolate chips. Return to the oven for 30 seconds or until chips are glossy. Cool completely on a wire rack. Cut into bars. **Yield:** about 3 dozen.

Nutrition Facts: 1 bar equals 112 calories, 5 g fat (3 g saturated fat), 18 mg cholesterol, 48 mg sodium, 16 g carbohydrate, trace fiber, 1 g protein.

 # WALNUT BARS

(Pictured above)

Chante Jones, Antioch, California

I grew up on a "walnut acre," and when I use walnuts, I always think back to my family and harvesttime. I hope you enjoy these bars as much as we do.

☑ Uses less fat, sugar or salt. Includes Nutrition Facts.

  1/2 cup butter, softened
  1/4 cup sugar
   1 egg
  1/2 teaspoon vanilla extract
1-1/4 cups all-purpose flour
  1/2 teaspoon salt
FILLING:
   2 eggs
1-1/2 cups packed brown sugar
   2 tablespoons all-purpose flour
   1 teaspoon vanilla extract
  1/2 teaspoon salt
  1/2 teaspoon baking powder
1-1/2 cups chopped walnuts
LEMON GLAZE:
1-1/2 cups confectioners' sugar
   2 to 3 tablespoons lemon juice

In a small mixing bowl, cream butter and sugar. Beat in egg and vanilla. Combine flour and salt; add to creamed mixture and mix well. Press onto the bottom of a greased 13-in. x 9-in. x 2-in. baking pan. Bake at 350° for 20 minutes or until edges are lightly browned.

For filling, in a bowl, combine the eggs, brown sugar, flour, vanilla, salt and baking powder. Stir in walnuts. Spread over crust. Bake for 25 minutes or until filling is golden brown. Cool on a wire rack.

Combine glaze ingredients; spread over filling. Let stand until set before cutting. **Yield:** 2-1/2 dozen.

Nutrition Facts: 1 bar equals 165 calories, 7 g fat (2 g saturated fat), 29 mg cholesterol, 127 mg sodium, 24 g carbohydrate, trace fiber, 3 g protein.

SIMPLE SNOWFLAKES

Denis Ann Bontrager, Goshen, Indiana

To make these treats, I simply cut tortillas into flake shapes, bake and dust them with sugar. You can serve them on a plate or tie on strings and hang them as ornaments.

✓ Uses less fat, sugar or salt. Includes Nutrition Facts.

    6 flour tortillas (6 inches), warmed
    2 teaspoons vegetable oil
Confectioners' sugar

Fold a tortilla in half, then in half again and once again. Using a clean scissors or sharp knife, cut small triangles on folded and outside edges. Unfold tortilla; brush both sides with oil. Place on a greased baking sheet. Repeat with remaining tortillas and oil.

Bake at 400° for 7-8 minutes or until lightly browned. Dust both sides of tortillas with confectioners' sugar while still warm. **Yield:** 6 servings.

Nutrition Facts: 1 snowflake equals 103 calories, 5 g fat (trace saturated fat), 0 cholesterol, 224 mg sodium, 13 g carbohydrate, 0 fiber, 3 g protein.

PEANUT BUTTER CHOCOLATE COOKIES

June Formanek, Belle Plaine, Iowa

This recipe was featured in our Sunday paper and I just had to try it. Kids of all ages really love the peanut butter surprise inside the cookie.

    1/2 cup butter, softened
    1/2 cup sugar
    1/2 cup packed brown sugar
      1 cup creamy peanut butter, *divided*
      1 egg, lightly beaten
      1 teaspoon vanilla extract
1-1/2 cups all-purpose flour
    1/2 cup baking cocoa
    1/2 teaspoon baking soda
    3/4 cup confectioners' sugar

In a large mixing bowl, cream butter, sugars and 1/4 cup peanut butter. Added egg and vanilla; mix well. Combine flour, cocoa and baking soda; add to creamed mixture and mix well.

Blend confectioners' sugar with remaining peanut butter until smooth. Roll into 24 balls, 1 in. each. Divide dough into 24 pieces; flatten each into a 3-in. circle.

Place one peanut butter ball on each circle; bring edges over to completely cover it. (Dough may crack; reshape cookies as needed.) Place cookies with seam side down on ungreased baking sheets. Flatten each cookie slightly with the bottom of a glass dipped in sugar. Bake at 375° for 7-9 minutes or until set. **Yield:** 2 dozen.

ANISE BUTTER COOKIES
(Pictured below)

Mari Lynn Van Ginkle, Sandia Park, New Mexico

Here in New Mexico, these cookies are known as "bizcochitos," which means "small biscuits." There are many variations of the recipe, which has been passed down through the generations.

      2 cups butter, softened
1-3/4 cups sugar, *divided*
      4 teaspoons aniseed, crushed
      2 eggs
    1/4 cup orange juice concentrate
      6 cups all-purpose flour
      3 teaspoons baking powder
    1/2 teaspoon salt
      1 teaspoon ground cinnamon

In a large mixing bowl, cream the butter, 1-1/2 cups sugar and aniseed. Add eggs, one at a time, beating well after each addition. Beat in orange juice concentrate. Combine the flour, baking powder and salt; gradually add to creamed mixture.

On a lightly floured surface, roll out dough to 1/4-in. thickness. Cut with a floured 2-1/2-in. round cookie cutter. Place 1 in. apart on ungreased baking sheets.

Combine the cinnamon and remaining sugar; sprinkle over cookies. Bake at 350° for 12-15 minutes or until golden brown. Remove to wire racks. **Yield:** 5 dozen.

Dazzling Desserts

PEACH MELBA MOUNTAIN
(Pictured at left and on front cover)

Sally Sibthorpe, Shelby Township, Michigan

Over the years, I've competed in several state fair cooking contests, and this cake is one of my most impressive entries. It tastes as fantastic as it looks.

- 1 package (16 ounces) angel food cake mix
- 1 package (3 ounces) peach gelatin
- 1 cup boiling water
- 1 package (8 ounces) cream cheese, softened
- 1 teaspoon almond extract
- 1 carton (12 ounces) frozen whipped topping, thawed
- 1 cup sliced almonds, toasted, *divided*
- 3 cups sliced peeled fresh peaches
- 3 cups fresh raspberries

Prepare and bake cake according to package directions, using an ungreased 10-in. tube pan. Immediately invert pan; cool completely.

In a small bowl, dissolve gelatin in boiling water; cool. In a large mixing bowl, beat cream cheese and extract until fluffy. Gradually beat in gelatin. Fold in whipped topping and 3/4 cup almonds. Cover and refrigerate for 30 minutes.

Cut cake into three horizontal layers. Place bottom layer on a serving plate; spread with a third of the cream mixture. Top with 1 cup of peaches and 1 cup of raspberries. Repeat layers. Sprinkle with remaining almonds. Chill for at least 30 minutes before serving. Refrigerate leftovers. **Yield:** 12-14 servings.

CHERRY CREAM PIE

Carol Wencka
Greenfield, Wisconsin

A favorite vacation spot in Wisconsin, Door County, is known for its abundance of cherry orchards, and that's where this recipe originated. We think it is a delectable dessert, with a nutty crumb crust, real whipped cream and, of course, cherries.

CRUST:
- 1 cup all-purpose flour
- 1 cup finely chopped walnuts
- 1/2 cup butter, softened
- 1/4 cup packed brown sugar

FILLING:
- 1 package (8 ounces) cream cheese, softened
- 1 cup confectioners' sugar
- 1/4 teaspoon almond extract
- 1/2 cup heavy whipping cream, whipped
- 1 can (21 ounces) cherry pie filling

In a small bowl, combine the flour, walnuts, butter and brown sugar. Transfer to a 13-in. x 9-in. x 2-in. baking pan. Bake at 375° for 15 minutes, stirring once. Set aside 1 cup of crumbs. While warm, press the remaining crumbs into a greased 9-in. pie plate, firmly pressing onto the bottom and up the sides. Chill for 30 minutes.

In a small mixing bowl, beat the cream cheese, confectioners' sugar and almond extract until smooth. Spread over bottom of crust. Gently fold whipped cream into the pie filling; spread over cream cheese layer. Sprinkle with reserved crumbs. Chill for at least 4 hours before serving. **Yield:** 6-8 servings.

CHAI RICE PUDDING

Chai refers to tea cooked in warm milk and flavored with spices such as cardamom, ginger and cinnamon. These same flavors are a wonderful addition to this version of old-fashioned rice pudding from our Test Kitchen.

- 8 cups 1% milk
- 1 cup uncooked basmati rice
- 1/2 cup sugar
- 1/4 teaspoon salt
- 1/2 teaspoon ground cinnamon
- 1/4 teaspoon ground cardamom
- 1/4 teaspoon ground ginger
- 1/8 teaspoon ground allspice

In a heavy saucepan, combine the milk, rice, sugar and salt. Bring to a boil. Reduce heat; simmer, uncovered, for 35-40 minutes or until slightly thickened, stirring frequently.

Remove from heat; stir in the spices. Serve warm or chilled. Refrigerate leftovers. **Yield:** 10 servings.

MOCHA CHIP PIE
(Pictured below)

Sheila Watson, Stettler, Alberta

This mocha pie is chocolaty from top to bottom. The only thing hard about making it is waiting for it to set!

1-1/2 cups chocolate wafer crumbs
  1/4 cup butter, *softened*
    1 envelope unflavored gelatin
  1/2 cup milk
  1/2 cup plus 1 tablespoon sugar, *divided*
  1/2 cup strong brewed coffee
  1/4 cup water
  1/4 teaspoon salt
    2 squares (1 ounce *each*) unsweetened chocolate, melted and cooled
    1 teaspoon vanilla extract
    2 cups heavy whipping cream, *divided*
Toasted sliced almonds, optional

In a small bowl, combine wafer crumbs and butter. Press onto the bottom and up the sides of a greased 9-in. pie plate. Bake at 375° for 5-7 minutes or until lightly browned. Cool on a wire rack.

In a small saucepan, sprinkle gelatin over milk; let stand for 1 minute. Cook and stir over low heat until gelatin is completely dissolved. Add 1/2 cup sugar, coffee, water and salt; cook and stir for 5 minutes or until sugar is dissolved. Remove from the heat; stir in melted chocolate and vanilla. Transfer to a large bowl; cover and refrigerate until slightly thickened, stirring occasionally.

In a small mixing bowl, beat 1 cup cream until stiff peaks form; fold into chocolate mixture. Spread evenly into crust. Refrigerate for 4 hours or until set.

Just before serving, in a small mixing bowl, beat remaining cream until it begins to thicken. Add remaining sugar; beat until stiff peaks form. Pipe over pie. Garnish with almonds if desired. Refrigerate leftovers. **Yield:** 8 servings.

DESSERT CUSTARD SAUCE

Bunny Richardson, Russellville, Alabama

There's no need to stand over the stove to make a custard sauce. This no-cook version goes great over fresh fruit or cake.

✓ Uses less fat, sugar or salt. Includes Nutrition Facts.

    2 cups cold milk, *divided*
  1/4 cup plus 2 teaspoons instant vanilla pudding mix
  1/2 cup heavy whipping cream
  1/4 cup sugar
  1/2 teaspoon vanilla extract

In a small mixing bowl, beat 1 cup milk and pudding mix on medium speed for 2 minutes. Add the cream, sugar, vanilla and remaining milk; beat on low speed for 2 minutes.

Transfer to a pitcher; refrigerate 1-2 hours before serving. **Yield:** 3 cups.

Nutrition Facts: 1/3 cup equals 121 calories, 7 g fat (4 g saturated fat), 25 mg cholesterol, 107 mg sodium, 13 g carbohydrate, trace fiber, 2 g protein.

DUTCH APPLE SOUR CREAM PIE

Laura Thompson, Morristown, Tennessee

This delicious pie is a favorite of family and friends who come to call. It also goes well with my apple-themed kitchen.

    1 egg, lightly beaten
1-1/2 cups (12 ounces) sour cream
    1 cup sugar
    3 tablespoons all-purpose flour
  1/2 teaspoon vanilla extract
    3 cups thinly sliced peeled tart apples
    1 unbaked pastry shell (9 inches)
CRUMB TOPPING:
  1/2 cup packed brown sugar
  1/2 cup all-purpose flour
  1/4 cup cold butter

In a large bowl, combine the egg, sour cream, sugar, flour and vanilla. Stir in apples. Pour into pastry shell. Bake at 375° for 30 minutes.

Meanwhile, combine brown sugar and flour. Cut in butter until mixture resembles coarse crumbs. Sprinkle over pie. Return to the oven for 10-15 minutes or until filling is set and topping is golden brown. Cool completely on a wire rack. Refrigerate leftovers. **Yield:** 6-8 servings.

of the pecan mixture; top with remaining batter and pecan mixture.

Bake at 350° for 45-50 minutes or until a toothpick inserted near the center comes out clean. Cool for 10 minutes before removing from pan to a wire rack to cool completely. In a bowl, whisk the glaze ingredients until smooth; drizzle over cake. **Yield:** 12-14 servings.

CINNAMON PEACH ENCHILADAS
(Pictured below)

Irene Glembotskaya, Brooklyn, New York

These sweet enchiladas are a pleasant change from traditional peach pie—and a whole lot easier to prepare. Simply fill warmed tortillas with the cinnamon-peach mixture, then wait for the compliments.

✓ Uses less fat, sugar or salt. Includes Nutrition Facts and Diabetic Exchanges.

    4 cups sliced peeled fresh peaches
1/3 cup sugar
    1 teaspoon ground cinnamon
    4 flour tortillas (8 inches)
Butter-flavored cooking spray

In a bowl, combine the peaches, sugar and cinnamon; let stand for 5 minutes. Spritz tortillas with butter-flavored spray.

In a nonstick skillet, cook tortillas over medium heat until warmed and lightly browned on both sides. Fill each with about 3/4 cup peaches and roll up. Cut in half to serve. **Yield:** 8 servings.

Nutrition Facts: 1 enchilada equals 143 calories, 2 g fat (trace saturated fat), 0 cholesterol, 125 mg sodium, 31 g carbohydrate, 2 g fiber, 3 g protein. **Diabetic Exchanges:** 1 starch, 1 fruit.

CRANBERRY PEAR CAKE
(Pictured above)

Jeanne Holt, Mendota Heights, Minnesota

If you want a change-of-pace cake that's full of fall flavors, try this pairing of cranberries and pears. The nutty filling and sweet glaze elevate it from a coffee cake to a special dessert.

    1 cup packed brown sugar
3/4 cup chopped pecans
1/3 cup chopped dried cranberries
    1 teaspoon apple pie spice
BATTER:
1/2 cup butter, softened
    1 cup sugar
    3 eggs
    1 teaspoon vanilla extract
    2 cups all-purpose flour
    2 teaspoons baking powder
    1 teaspoon baking soda
1/2 teaspoon salt
    1 cup (8 ounces) sour cream
    2 cups chopped peeled ripe pears
GLAZE:
    1 cup confectioners' sugar
    5 teaspoons milk
4-1/2 teaspoons butter, melted
1/4 teaspoon apple pie spice
1/4 teaspoon vanilla extract

In a small bowl, combine the brown sugar, pecans, cranberries and apple pie spice; set aside. In a large mixing bowl, cream butter and sugar until fluffy. Add eggs, one at a time, beating after each addition. Beat in vanilla. Combine the flour, baking powder, baking soda and salt; add to creamed mixture alternately with sour cream. Beat just until combined. Fold in pears.

Pour half of the batter into a greased and floured 10-in. fluted tube pan. Sprinkle with half

Cherry-Topped Chocolate Cake

(Pictured above)

Bonnie Cochran, Bryson City, North Carolina

My husband and I love this rich, moist, "special occasion" dessert. The cherry pie filling and whipped topping really dress it up...and it's sure to satisfy any sweet tooth!

- **5 teaspoons baking cocoa, *divided***
- **1 cup butter, cubed**
- **9 squares (1 ounce *each*) semisweet chocolate, chopped**
- **5 eggs**
- **1/2 cup plus 1 tablespoon sugar, *divided***
- **2 teaspoons vanilla extract**
- **1 can (21 ounces) cherry pie filling**
- **1/2 cup heavy whipping cream, whipped**

Coat a 9-in. springform pan with cooking spray; line with waxed paper and spray the paper. Dust with 2 teaspoons cocoa. Place pan on a double thickness of heavy-duty foil (about 18 in. square); securely wrap foil around pan.

In a heavy saucepan over low heat, melt butter and chocolate. Cool to lukewarm. In a large mixing bowl, beat eggs and 1/2 cup sugar until thick and lemon-colored. Combine the remaining cocoa and sugar; beat into eggs. Add vanilla. Gradually beat in cooled chocolate mixture. Pour into prepared pan.

Place pan in a large baking pan; add 3/4 in. of hot water to larger pan. Bake at 325° for 35-40 minutes or until a toothpick inserted near the center comes out clean. Cool on a wire rack for 20 minutes.

Carefully run a knife around edge of pan; cool completely. Serve with cherry pie filling and whipped cream. Refrigerate leftovers. **Yield:** 12-14 servings.

Editor's Note: This recipe does not use flour.

Chocolate-Hazelnut Cream Puffs

(Pictured above)

Mary Lou Wayman, Salt Lake City, Utah

Chocoholics will think you fussed when they taste these mini cream puffs filled with a creamy sensation.

- **2 packages (3 ounces *each*) cream cheese, softened**
- **4 tablespoons sugar, *divided***
- **2/3 cup chocolate hazelnut spread**
- **1/4 cup heavy whipping cream**
- **1/2 cup chopped hazelnuts *or* pecans, toasted**

1 cup all-purpose flour
3 tablespoons baking cocoa
1 cup water
1/2 cup butter
1/4 teaspoon salt
4 eggs
Confectioners' sugar

For filling, in a small mixing bowl, beat cream cheese and 2 tablespoons sugar until smooth. Gradually beat in hazelnut spread and cream until blended. Stir in nuts. Cover and refrigerate.

In a bowl, combine the flour, cocoa and remaining sugar. In a large saucepan, bring water, butter and salt to a boil. Add flour mixture all at once and stir until a smooth ball forms. Remove from the heat; let stand for 5 minutes. Add eggs, one at a time, beating well after each addition. Continue beating until mixture is smooth and shiny.

Drop by rounded tablespoonfuls 2 in. apart onto greased baking sheets. Bake at 400° for 20-25 minutes or until set and browned. Remove to wire racks. Immediately split puffs open; remove and discard soft dough from inside. Cool completely.

Spoon filling into cream puffs; replace tops. Dust with confectioners' sugar. Refrigerate leftovers. **Yield:** 2 dozen.

SOUR CREAM BAVARIAN
(Pictured above left)

Judi Janczewski, Berwyn, Illinois

Are you sweet on someone who's counting calories? Show them you care with this light and refreshing dessert. It's sinfully creamy and so pretty with the tart raspberry sauce. No one would ever guess that it's nearly fat-free!

✓ Uses less fat, sugar or salt. Includes Nutrition Facts.

1 envelope unflavored gelatin
3/4 cup cold water
2/3 cup sugar
1 cup (8 ounces) fat-free sour cream
1 teaspoon vanilla extract
2 cups fat-free whipped topping
RASPBERRY SAUCE:
1 package (10 ounces) frozen raspberries in syrup, thawed
1 tablespoon cornstarch
1 tablespoon sugar

In a small saucepan, sprinkle gelatin over cold water; let stand for 1 minute. Add sugar; cook and stir over low heat until gelatin and sugar are completely dissolved. Remove from the heat. Whisk in sour cream and vanilla. Refrigerate until slightly thickened.

Fold in whipped topping. Pour into a 4 cup heart-shaped or other shape mold coated with cooking spray. Refrigerate until firm.

For sauce, drain raspberries, reserving syrup; set berries aside. Add enough water to the syrup to measure 3/4 cup. In a small saucepan, combine cornstarch and sugar. Stir in syrup mixture until smooth. Bring to a boil; cook and stir for 2 minutes or until thickened. Remove from the heat; stir in berries. Refrigerate until serving.

To serve, unmold dessert onto a serving plate; top with the raspberry sauce. **Yield:** 8 servings (1-1/4 cups sauce).

Nutrition Facts: 1 piece equals 180 calories, trace fat (trace saturated fat), 5 mg cholesterol, 37 mg sodium, 40 g carbohydrate, 2 g fiber, 3 g protein.

PINEAPPLE SOUR CREAM PIE
(Pictured below)

Jaye Bloomer, Canoga Park, California

It's hard to believe that this delightful treat comes from just handful of items. The refrigerated pie is a refreshing summer dessert, but you'll want to make it a year-round staple.

1 package (3.4 ounces) instant vanilla pudding mix
2 cups (16 ounces) sour cream
1 can (8 ounces) crushed pineapple, undrained
1 graham cracker crust (9 inches)
Whipped cream, optional

In a small bowl, combine the pudding mix and sour cream. Stir in the pineapple. Spread into crust. Cover and refrigerate for 3 hours or until set. Serve with whipped cream if desired. **Yield:** 6-8 servings.

Cool Down with a Frosty Treat

NOTHING beats the summer heat like an icy cold sensation…particularly one that satisfies the sweet tooth! Consider these after-dinner delights the next time you're in the mood for a taste of fun.

★★★★★★★★★★

WATERMELON SORBET
(Pictured at far right)

Kory Figura, Waverly, Iowa

No ice cream maker is needed for this easy, four-ingredient delight. We can't store enough watermelon in the house to keep up with the demand!

☑ Uses less fat, sugar or salt. Includes Nutrition Facts.

  1 cup sugar
  1 cup water
  8 cups cubed seedless watermelon
  2 tablespoons lemon juice

In a small saucepan, bring sugar and water to a boil. Cook and stir until sugar is dissolved; set aside.

In a blender or food processor, process the watermelon in batches until pureed. Transfer to a large bowl; stir in the sugar syrup and lemon juice.

Pour into a 13-in. x 9-in. x 2-in. dish; cover and freeze for 8 hours or until firm. Just before serving, puree watermelon mixture in batches until smooth. **Yield:** 1-1/2 quarts.

Nutrition Facts: 1 cup equals 184 calories, 0 fat (0 saturated fat), 0 cholesterol, 7 mg sodium, 52 g carbohydrate, 1 g fiber, 1 g protein.

★★★★★★★★★★

STRAWBERRY CRUMBLE PARFAITS
(Pictured above, far right)

Carol Anderson, Salt Lake City, Utah

Time to take out those parfaits glasses! This is one of those elegant, but effortless recipes perfect for simple summer entertaining. It's always so delicious and refreshing on a warm summer's evening.

  1 cup all-purpose flour
1/4 cup packed brown sugar
1/2 cup chopped pecans
1/2 cup cold butter
  1 can (14 ounces) sweetened condensed milk
  3 tablespoons lemon juice
  3 tablespoons orange juice
  2 cups chopped fresh strawberries
  1 cup heavy whipping cream, whipped

In a bowl, combine the flour, brown sugar and pecans; cut in butter until mixture resembles coarse crumbs. Spread into an ungreased 15-in. x 10-in. x 1-in. baking pan. Bake at 350° for 15-18 minutes or until golden brown.

In a large bowl, combine the milk, lemon juice and orange juice. Add strawberries; mix well. Fold in whipped cream.

Spoon 1 tablespoon of crumb mixture into each parfait glass; top with a scant 3 tablespoonfuls of berry mixture. Repeat layers. Sprinkle with remaining crumb mixture. Freeze until firm. Remove from the freezer 20-30 minutes before serving. **Yield:** 10 servings.

★★★★★★★★★★

RAINBOW SHERBET CAKE ROLL
(Pictured above right)

Nancy Geissler, Pittsburgh, Pennsylvania

Years ago I saw a cake mix recipe and decided to put my own spin on it. Now I keep the sherbet in the freezer so I can whip up the pretty dessert regularly.

  4 eggs, *separated*
3/4 cup sugar, *divided*
3/4 teaspoon vanilla *or* lemon extract
3/4 cup cake flour
  1 teaspoon baking powder
1/2 teaspoon salt
Confectioners' sugar
  2 cups raspberry sherbet, softened
  2 cups orange sherbet, softened
  2 cups lime sherbet, softened

Line a greased 15-in. x 10-in. x 1-in. baking pan with waxed paper; grease the paper and set aside.

In a large mixing bowl, beat egg yolks, 1/2 cup sugar and extract until thickened. In a small mixing bowl, beat egg whites until foamy. Gradually add remaining sugar, beating until stiff peaks form. Fold into yolk mixture. Combine the flour, baking powder and salt; fold into yolk mixture. Pour into prepared pan.

Bake at 375° for 13-15 minutes or until cake springs back when lightly touched. Cool for 5 minutes. Turn cake onto a kitchen towel dusted with confectioners' sugar. Gently peel off waxed paper. Roll up cake in the towel jelly-roll style, starting with a short side. Cool completely on a wire rack.

Unroll cake. Spread raspberry sherbet widthwise over a third of the cake to within 1/2 in. of edges. Repeat with orange and lime sherbet.

Roll up carefully; place seam side down on a sheet of foil and wrap securely in foil. Freeze until firm, about 6 hours.

Remove from the freezer 15 minutes before serving. Sprinkle with confectioners' sugar. **Yield:** 10-15 servings.

NEVER FAIL CAKE ROLLS

To prevent the cake from cracking when making a cake roll, spread the batter evenly in the pan. This keeps the cake moist so it's less likely to crack. Also, be careful to not overbake the cake. Batter in a 15-in. x 10-in. x 1-in. pan takes about 10 to 15 minutes to bake. Check your cake after 8 or 9 minutes and watch closely until it tests done.

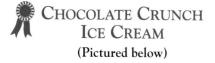

CHOCOLATE CRUNCH ICE CREAM

(Pictured below)

Rosalie Peters, Caldwell, Texas

Featuring chocolate chips, toasted almonds and toffee bits, this homemade treat hits the spot on casual nights at home.

   1-1/2 cups milk
     3/4 cup sugar, *divided*
       4 egg yolks
   2-1/2 teaspoons instant coffee granules
       2 cups 60% cocoa bittersweet chocolate baking chips, melted and cooled
   1-1/2 cups heavy whipping cream
       1 teaspoon vanilla extract
     3/4 cup semisweet chocolate chips, melted
     3/4 cup slivered almonds, toasted
     1/3 cup milk chocolate toffee bits

In a large saucepan, heat milk to 175°; stir in 1/2 cup sugar until dissolved. In a bowl, whisk egg yolks and remaining sugar. Stir in coffee granules and bittersweet chocolate. Whisk in a small amount of hot milk mixture. Return all to the pan, whisking constantly. Cook and stir over low heat

until mixture reaches at least 160° and coats the back of a metal spoon. Remove from the heat.

Cool quickly by placing pan in a bowl of ice water; let stand for 30 minutes, stirring frequently. Transfer to a bowl; stir in cream and vanilla. Press plastic wrap onto surface of custard. Refrigerate for several hours or overnight.

Line a baking sheet with waxed paper; spread melted semisweet chocolate to 1/8-in. thickness. Refrigerate for 20 minutes; chop coarsely.

Fill cylinder of ice cream freezer two-thirds full with custard; freeze according to manufacturer's directions. Stir in some of the chopped chocolate, almonds and toffee bits. Refrigerate remaining custard until ready to freeze. Stir in remaining chocolate, almonds and toffee bits. Allow to ripen in ice cream freezer or firm up in the refrigerator freezer for 2-4 hours before serving. **Yield:** 1-1/2 quarts.

CHEESECAKE WITH RASPBERRY SAUCE

Jeanette Volker, Walton, Nebraska

It is a family tradition to make this for our Christmas dinner. And when my daughter was away from home, I actually made it for her birthday and shipped it on dry ice.

   1-3/4 cups graham cracker crumbs
     1/4 cup sugar
     1/3 cup butter, melted
FILLING:
       5 packages (8 ounces *each*) cream cheese, softened
       1 cup sugar
       1 cup (8 ounces) sour cream
     1/2 cup heavy whipping cream
       2 teaspoons vanilla extract
       7 eggs, lightly beaten
SAUCE/TOPPING:
       1 package (12 ounces) frozen unsweetened raspberries, thawed
     1/2 cup sugar
       2 cups heavy whipping cream
     1/2 cup confectioners' sugar
       1 teaspoon vanilla extract

In a small bowl, combine cracker crumbs and sugar; stir in butter. Press onto the bottom and 1 in. up the sides of a greased 10-in. springform pan. Place on a baking sheet. Bake at 350° for 5-8 minutes. Cool on a wire rack.

In a large mixing bowl, beat cream cheese and sugar until smooth. Beat in the sour cream, heavy cream and vanilla. Add eggs; beat on low speed just until combined. Pour into crust. Place pan on

a double thickness of heavy-duty foil (about 17 in. square); securely wrap foil around pan.

Place in a large baking pan; add 1 in. of hot water to larger pan. Bake at 350° for 50-60 minutes or until center is almost set. Remove pan from water bath. Cool on a wire rack for 10 minutes. Carefully run a knife around edge of pan to loosen. Cool 1 hour longer. Refrigerate overnight.

For sauce, place raspberries and sugar in a food processor; cover and process until smooth. For topping, in a small mixing bowl, beat heavy cream until it begins to thicken. Add confectioners' sugar and vanilla; beat until soft peaks form. Serve cheesecake with raspberry sauce and topping. **Yield:** 16 servings.

MACADAMIA-CRUSTED CUSTARDS
(Pictured above)

Anna Erickson, Terrebonne, Oregon

Sized just right for a twosome, these elegant custards make a simple but scrumptious finale for any meal. Best of all, they whip up in a heartbeat for busy weeknights.

2 egg yolks
1 egg
3/4 cup half-and-half cream
4-1/2 teaspoons sugar
1/2 teaspoon rum extract
1/8 teaspoon salt
1/4 cup finely chopped macadamia nuts,
   walnuts *or* pecans

In a small mixing bowl, beat egg yolks, egg, cream, sugar, extract and salt until blended. Pour into two ungreased 6-oz. custard cups. Sprinkle with nuts.

Place cups in a baking pan; add 1 in. of boiling water to pan. Bake, uncovered, at 350° for 25-30 minutes or until a knife inserted near the cen-

ter comes out clean. Remove from pan to a wire rack; cool for 15 minutes. Refrigerate until chilled. **Yield:** 2 servings.

MAPLE MOUSSE
(Pictured below)

Jane Fuller, Ivoryton, Connecticut

I love to make this dessert with maple syrup produced in our area. A change from heavy cakes and pies, it's a refreshing ending to meals.

3/4 cup plus 6 teaspoons maple syrup,
   divided
3 egg yolks, beaten
2 cups heavy whipping cream
2 tablespoons chopped hazelnuts, toasted

In a small saucepan over medium heat, heat 3/4 cup syrup just until it simmers. Reduce heat to low. Stir a small amount of hot syrup into egg yolks; return all to the pan, stirring constantly. Cook and stir until mixture is thickened and reaches 160°. Transfer to a large bowl; set bowl in ice water and stir for 2 minutes. Cool to room temperature.

In a large mixing bowl, beat cream until stiff peaks form. Gently fold into the syrup mixture. Spoon into dessert dishes. Chill for at least 2 hours. Just before serving, drizzle with remaining syrup and sprinkle with hazelnuts. **Yield:** 6 servings.

in a corner of bag. Drizzle over apples.

Repeat with vanilla chips. Chill until set. Remove from the refrigerator 5 minutes before serving. **Yield:** 6 servings.

Editor's Note: We recommend that you test your candy thermometer before each use by bringing water to a boil; the thermometer should read 212°. Adjust your recipe temperature up or down based on your test.

▰▰▰▰▰▰▰▰▰▰▰▰

CHOCOLATE MERINGUE BREAD PUDDING

Doris Heath, Franklin, North Carolina

The sweet chocolate layer and pretty golden meringue set this bread pudding apart from the rest. We love its custard-like consistency. It's a great dessert for any occasion.

>   8 slices day-old white bread, cubed (about
>   4 cups)
>   2 cups milk
> 1/2 cup plus 2 tablespoons sugar, *divided*
>   3 eggs, *separated*
>   2 tablespoons butter, melted
>   1 teaspoon vanilla extract
>   1 cup (6 ounces) semisweet chocolate
>   chips

Place the bread cubes in a greased 9-in. square baking dish. Combine the milk, 1/2 cup sugar, egg yolks, butter and vanilla; pour over bread. Sprinkle with chocolate chips.

Cover and bake at 350° for 25-30 minutes or until a knife inserted near the center comes out clean.

In a small mixing bowl, beat egg whites on medium speed until soft peaks form. Gradually beat in remaining sugar, 1 tablespoon at a time, on high until stiff peaks form.

Spread evenly over hot filling, sealing meringue to sides of dish. Bake, uncovered, for 10-12 minutes or until meringue is golden. Serve warm. Refrigerate leftovers. **Yield:** 9 servings.

▰▰▰▰▰▰▰▰▰▰▰▰

VANILLA CUSTARD PIE
(Pictured at right)

Mrs. Bernard Parys, Ixonia, Wisconsin

With a graham cracker crust, custard filling and meringue topping, this pie was one of my favorites when I was growing up, and it still is today. My grandmother passed down this recipe to my mother, who in turn passed it to me. Now my daughter is making it for her family.

▰▰▰▰▰▰▰▰▰▰▰▰

SWEET SHOPPE CARAMEL APPLES
(Pictured above)

Mary Bilyeu, Ann Arbor, Michigan

My hand-dipped apples are as beautiful as the ones you'll find at fancy candy counters, only they're fresher, better-tasting and more economical. Try them for Halloween or fall get-togethers.

>   6 large McIntosh apples
>   6 Popsicle sticks
>   2 cups sugar
>   2 cups half-and-half cream
>   1 cup light corn syrup
> 1/2 cup butter, cubed
> 1-1/4 cups English toffee bits *or* almond
>   brickle chips
>   1 cup semisweet chocolate chips
>   1 cup vanilla *or* white chips

Line a baking sheet with waxed paper and grease the paper; set aside. Wash and thoroughly dry apples. Insert a Popsicle stick into each; place on prepared pan. Chill.

In a heavy 3-qt. saucepan, combine the sugar, cream, corn syrup and butter; bring to a boil over medium-high heat. Cook and stir until a candy thermometer reads 245°, about 1 hour.

Remove from the heat. Working quickly, dip each apple into hot caramel mixture to completely coat, then dip the bottom into toffee bits. Return to baking sheet; chill.

In a small microwave-safe bowl, microwave chocolate chips at 50% power for 1-2 minutes or until melted; stir until smooth. Transfer to a small heavy-duty resealable plastic bag; cut a small hole

1-1/4 cups graham cracker crumbs
 3 tablespoons brown sugar
 1/3 cup butter, melted
FILLING:
 1/2 cup sugar
 1/4 cup all-purpose flour
 1/2 teaspoon salt
 2 cups milk
 2 egg yolks, beaten
 2 teaspoons vanilla extract
MERINGUE:
 2 egg whites
 1/4 teaspoon vanilla extract
 1/8 teaspoon cream of tartar
 1/4 cup sugar
 1/4 cup graham cracker crumbs

Combine the graham cracker crumbs, brown sugar and butter; press onto the bottom and up the sides of an ungreased 9-in. pie plate. Bake at 350° for 8-10 minutes or until lightly browned. Cool on a wire rack.

In a small saucepan, combine the sugar, flour and salt. Stir in milk until smooth. Cook and stir over medium-high heat until thickened and bubbly. Reduce heat; cook and stir 2 minutes longer. Remove from the heat. Stir a small amount of hot filling into egg yolks; return all to the pan. Bring to a gentle boil, stirring constantly; cook and stir 2 minutes longer. Remove from the heat. Gently stir in vanilla. Pour into crust.

In a small mixing bowl, beat the egg whites, vanilla and cream of tartar on medium speed until soft peaks form. Gradually beat in sugar, 1 tablespoon at a time, on high until stiff peaks form. Spread over hot filling, sealing edges to crust. Sprinkle with graham cracker crumbs.

Bake at 350° for 15 minutes or until golden brown. Cool on a wire rack for 1 hour. Refrigerate for at least 3 hours before serving. **Yield:** 8 servings.

BLACK 'N' BLUE BERRY GRUNT
(Pictured above)

Kelly Akin, Johnsonville, New York

If you're looking for something different from cakes and fruit pies, try this old-fashioned dessert. It features a delicious combination of blackberries and blueberries with homemade dumplings on the top.

2-1/2 cups fresh *or* frozen blackberries,
  thawed
2-1/2 cups fresh *or* frozen blueberries, thawed
 3/4 cup sugar
 1/4 cup water
 1 tablespoon lemon juice
 1/8 teaspoon ground cinnamon
 1/8 teaspoon pepper
DUMPLINGS:
 1 cup all-purpose flour
 2 tablespoons sugar
 1 teaspoon baking powder
 1/2 teaspoon baking soda
 1/8 teaspoon salt
 2 tablespoons butter, melted
 1/2 cup buttermilk
 1 tablespoon cinnamon-sugar
Heavy whipping cream, optional

In a large skillet, combine the berries, sugar, water, lemon juice, cinnamon and pepper. Bring to boil. Reduce heat; simmer, uncovered, for 5 minutes.

Meanwhile, in a large mixing bowl, combine the flour, sugar, baking powder, baking soda and salt. Add butter and buttermilk; stir just until moistened. Drop by tablespoonfuls onto berry mixture. Sprinkle with cinnamon-sugar.

Cover tightly; simmer for 10-15 minutes or until a toothpick inserted in a dumpling comes out clean. Serve warm with cream if desired. **Yield:** 6-8 servings.

pan. Cut through batter with a knife to remove air pockets. Bake on the lowest oven rack at 325° for 50-55 minutes or until top springs back when lightly touched and cracks feel dry. Immediately invert baking pan; cool completely.

For topping, in a large mixing bowl, beat cream until it begins to thicken. Add confectioners' sugar; beat until stiff peaks form. Serve with cake; sprinkle with coconut. Refrigerate any leftover topping. **Yield:** 12-16 servings.

▰▰▰▰▰▰▰▰▰▰▰▰▰

SOUTHERN BANANA PUDDING

Jan Campbell, Purvis, Mississippi

This old Southern recipe features a comforting custard layered with bananas and vanilla wafers, then topped with a meringue. I serve it all year-round…it's a nice ending to most any meal.

      3/4 cup sugar
      1/3 cup all-purpose flour
        2 cups milk
        2 egg yolks, beaten
        1 tablespoon butter
        1 teaspoon vanilla extract
       36 vanilla wafers
        3 medium ripe bananas, cut into 1/4-inch
           slices
   MERINGUE:
        2 egg whites
        1 teaspoon vanilla extract
      1/8 teaspoon cream of tartar
        3 tablespoons sugar

In a large saucepan, combine sugar and flour. Stir in milk until smooth. Cook and stir over medium-high heat until thickened and bubbly. Reduce heat; cook and stir 2 minutes longer.

Remove from the heat. Stir a small amount of hot filling into egg yolks; return all to the pan, stirring constantly. Bring to a gentle boil; cook and stir 2 minutes longer. Remove from the heat. Gently stir in butter and vanilla.

In an ungreased 8-in. square baking dish, layer a third of the vanilla wafers, banana slices and filling. Repeat layers twice.

For meringue, in a large mixing bowl, beat the egg whites, vanilla and cream of tartar on medium speed until soft peaks form. Gradually beat in sugar, 1 tablespoon at a time, on high until stiff peaks form. Spread evenly over hot filling, sealing edges to sides of baking dish.

Bake at 350° for 12-15 minutes or until meringue is golden. Cool on a wire rack for 1 hour. Refrigerate for at least 3 hours before serving. Refrigerate leftovers. **Yield:** 8 servings.

▰▰▰▰▰▰▰▰▰▰▰▰▰

CHIPPY MACAROON ANGEL CAKE

(Pictured above)

Joyce Platfoot, Wapakoneta, Ohio

This homemade angel cake, filled with coconut and chocolate chips, is as light as a cloud. It's so pretty with the whipped cream "frosting" piped alongside it.

   1-1/2 cups egg whites (about 10)
   1-1/2 cups confectioners' sugar
        1 cup cake flour
   1-1/2 teaspoons cream of tartar
        1 teaspoon almond extract
        1 teaspoon vanilla extract
      1/4 teaspoon salt
        1 cup sugar
        1 cup (6 ounces) miniature semisweet
           chocolate chips
      1/2 cup flaked coconut
   TOPPING:
        1 cup heavy whipping cream
        2 tablespoons confectioners' sugar
      1/2 cup flaked coconut, toasted

Place egg whites in a large mixing bowl; let stand at room temperature for 30 minutes. Sift confectioners' sugar and flour together twice; set aside.

Add cream of tartar, extracts and salt to egg whites; beat on medium speed until soft peaks form. Gradually add sugar, about 2 tablespoons at a time, beating on high until glossy peaks form and sugar is dissolved. Gradually fold in flour mixture, about 1/2 cup at a time. Fold in chocolate chips and coconut.

Gently spoon into an ungreased 10-in. tube

BLUEBERRY CREAM DESSERT
(Pictured below)

Susan Kruspe, Shortsville, New York

Here is a tasty, cool treat I especially enjoy serving after spring or summer luncheons. Feel free to adjust the flavor to strawberry, orange, raspberry or whatever fruit is in season.

      1 cup (8 ounces) sour cream
      1 carton (6 ounces) blueberry yogurt
      1 envelope unflavored gelatin
    3/4 cup cold water
    3/4 cup sugar, *divided*
    1/2 teaspoon vanilla extract
  1-1/4 cups graham cracker crumbs
      6 tablespoons butter, melted
      1 cup fresh blueberries
    1/2 cup heavy whipping cream, whipped

In a small bowl, combine sour cream and yogurt; set aside. In a small saucepan, sprinkle gelatin over cold water; let stand for 1 minute. Add 1/2 cup sugar. Cook and stir over low heat until gelatin is completely dissolved.

Remove from the heat; stir in vanilla and sour cream mixture until blended. Transfer to a large bowl. Chill until partially set.

Meanwhile, in a small bowl, combine the graham cracker crumbs, butter and remaining sugar; set aside 1/4 cup for topping. Press the remaining crumb mixture into an ungreased 8-in. square dish; set aside.

Stir blueberries into gelatin mixture; fold in whipped cream. Spoon into crust. Sprinkle with reserved crumb mixture. Chill until set. Refrigerate leftovers. **Yield:** 9 servings.

CARAMEL PECAN PIE
(Pictured above)

Diana Bartelings, Rock Creek, British Columbia

Of all my pecan pie recipes, this is the most decadent. It oozes goodness. Even my two young sons eat it slowly to enjoy every bite.

  1-2/3 cups all-purpose flour
    1/4 teaspoon salt
    1/2 cup cold butter
    1/3 cup sweetened condensed milk
      2 egg yolks
FILLING:
  1-1/2 cups sugar
    1/2 cup plus 2 tablespoons butter
    1/3 cup maple syrup
      3 eggs
      3 egg whites
    1/2 teaspoon vanilla extract
      2 cups ground pecans

In a bowl, combine flour and salt; cut in butter until mixture resembles coarse crumbs. Combine milk and egg yolks; stir into crumb mixture until dough forms a ball. Press onto the bottom and up the sides of an ungreased 9-in. deep-dish pie plate; flute edges. Cover and refrigerate.

In a large saucepan, combine the sugar, butter and syrup; bring to a boil over medium heat, stirring constantly. Remove from the heat.

In a large mixing bowl, beat the eggs, egg whites and vanilla. Gradually add hot syrup mixture. Stir in pecans. Pour into pastry shell.

Cover edges loosely with foil. Bake at 350° for 35-40 minutes or until set. Cool on a wire rack. Refrigerate leftovers. **Yield:** 6-8 servings.

HOT FUDGE CAKE
(Pictured below)

Marleen Adkins, Placentia, California

A cake baked in a slow cooker may seem unusual, but chocolaty smiles around the table prove how tasty it is. Sometimes, for a change of pace, I substitute butterscotch chips for the chocolate.

1-3/4 cups packed brown sugar, *divided*
   1 cup all-purpose flour
   6 tablespoons baking cocoa, *divided*
   2 teaspoons baking powder
1/2 teaspoon salt
1/2 cup milk
   2 tablespoons butter, melted
1/2 teaspoon vanilla extract
1-1/2 cups semisweet chocolate chips
1-3/4 cups boiling water
Vanilla ice cream

In a bowl, combine 1 cup brown sugar, flour, 3 tablespoons cocoa, baking powder and salt. In another bowl, combine the milk, butter and vanilla; stir into dry ingredients just until combined. Spread evenly into a 3-qt. slow cooker coated with cooking spray. Sprinkle with chocolate chips.

In a bowl, combine the remaining brown sugar and cocoa; stir in boiling water. Pour over batter (do not stir). Cover and cook on high for 4 to 4-1/2 hours or until a toothpick inserted near the center of cake comes out clean. Serve warm with ice cream. **Yield:** 6-8 servings.

Editor's Note: This recipe does not use eggs.

PEANUT BUTTER CREAM PIE

Dolores Corke, Goodland, Kansas

This peanut buttery treat is a specialty pie I make as manager and baker of our municipal airport's cafe. Pilot friends plot their flight plan to include a stop here in rural Kansas to refuel their planes and enjoy a slice of pie!

1/2 cup semisweet chocolate chips
   1 tablespoon plus 1 cup butter, *divided*
   1 tablespoon water
1/4 cup confectioners' sugar
   1 pastry shell (9 inches), baked
   1 cup packed brown sugar
   1 cup creamy peanut butter
   1 carton (12 ounces) frozen whipped topping, thawed
TOPPING:
1/2 cup semisweet chocolate chips
   1 tablespoon butter
2-1/2 teaspoons milk
1-1/2 teaspoons light corn syrup
Whipped topping and salted peanuts

In a small saucepan, combine chocolate chips, 1 tablespoon butter and water. Cook and stir over low heat until smooth. Whisk in the confectioners' sugar until smooth. Spread over sides and bottom of pastry shell. Refrigerate until set.

For filling, in a saucepan, combine brown sugar and remaining butter. Cook and stir over medium heat until smooth. Transfer to a large mixing bowl. Refrigerate for 10 minutes or until cool. Add peanut butter; beat on medium-high speed for 1 minute. Fold in whipped topping; spoon into crust. Refrigerate.

For topping, in a small saucepan, combine the chocolate chips, butter, milk and corn syrup. Cook and stir over low heat until smooth. Carefully spread over filling. Refrigerate for at least 2 hours. Garnish with whipped topping and peanuts. **Yield:** 10-12 servings.

WHITE CHOCOLATE RASPBERRY CHEESECAKE
(Pictured above right)

Wendy Barkman, Breezewood, Pennsylvania

As a dairy farmer's wife, I have lots of experience making cheesecake and this pretty dessert is a favorite of ours.

1-1/2 cups graham cracker crumbs
   1/4 cup sugar
   1/3 cup butter, melted

FILLING:

- 3 packages (8 ounces *each*) cream cheese, softened
- 3/4 cup sugar
- 1/3 cup sour cream
- 3 tablespoons all-purpose flour
- 1 teaspoon vanilla extract
- 3 eggs, lightly beaten
- 1 package (10 to 12 ounces) vanilla *or* white chips
- 1/4 cup seedless raspberry jam

In a small bowl, combine the graham cracker crumbs, sugar and butter. Press onto the bottom of a greased 9-in. springform pan; set aside.

In a large mixing bowl, beat cream cheese and sugar until smooth. Beat in the sour cream, flour and vanilla. Add eggs; beat on low speed just until combined. Fold in the chips. Pour over crust.

In a microwave-safe bowl, melt raspberry jam; stir until smooth. Drop by teaspoonfuls over batter; cut through batter with a knife to swirl.

Place pan on a double thickness of heavy-duty foil (about 16 in. square). Securely wrap foil around pan. Place in a large baking pan; add 1 in. of hot water to larger pan.

Bake at 325° for 80-85 minutes or until center is just set. Cool on a wire rack for 10 minutes. Carefully run a knife around edge of pan to loosen; cool 1 hour longer. Refrigerate overnight. Remove sides of pan. **Yield:** 12 servings.

<hr>

TUXEDO CREAM DESSERT
(Pictured at right)

Camilla Saulsbury, Nacogdoches, Texas

My adaptation of my grandmother's signature dessert always garners oohs and aahs. It's pretty and deliciously rich and creamy. Gran and I both consider it a staple for entertaining because it can be prepared a day ahead of time.

- 1-3/4 teaspoons unflavored gelatin
- 2 tablespoons cold water
- 1-1/2 cups heavy whipping cream, *divided*
- 3/4 cup semisweet chocolate chips

VANILLA LAYER:

- 1-3/4 teaspoons unflavored gelatin
- 2 tablespoons cold water
- 1-2/3 cups heavy whipping cream, *divided*
- 1/4 cup sugar
- 2 teaspoons vanilla extract

STRAWBERRY SAUCE:

- 2 cups sliced fresh strawberries
- 2 to 3 tablespoons sugar

In a small bowl, sprinkle gelatin over cold water; let stand for 1 minute. In a small saucepan, bring 1 cup cream to a simmer. Stir 1/2 cup into gelatin mixture until gelatin is completely dissolved. Stir chocolate chips into remaining warm cream until melted. Stir in gelatin mixture and remaining cream.

Transfer to an 8-in. x 4-in. x 2-in. loaf pan coated with cooking spray. Cover and refrigerate for 30 minutes or until firm.

For vanilla layer, in a small bowl, sprinkle gelatin over cold water; let stand for 1 minute. In a small saucepan, bring 1 cup cream and sugar to a simmer. Stir in gelatin mixture until gelatin is completely dissolved. Stir in vanilla and remaining cream. Carefully spoon over chocolate layer. Cover and refrigerate for at least 2 hours or until firm.

For sauce, in a blender or food processor, puree strawberries and sugar. Transfer to a bowl; cover and refrigerate until serving.

Just before serving, unmold dessert and cut into slices. Serve with strawberry sauce. **Yield:** 6-8 servings.

Pears Add Sweet Flair to Desserts

ENJOYING summer's sweet sensations is easy when you pick juicy pears as the focal point of family-favorite desserts. Here, you'll find a must-try collection of delights that are sure to please.

OLD-FASHIONED PEAR DESSERT

(Pictured below)

Eileen Ueberroth, Toledo, Ohio

This never-fail pear recipe turns out moist, firm and fruity every time. Some members of our family request these rich squares instead of cake for their birthdays.

2-1/4 cups all-purpose flour
    5 tablespoons sugar, *divided*
  3/4 teaspoon salt
  3/4 cup cold butter
    3 egg yolks
4-1/2 teaspoons lemon juice
FILLING:
  1/2 cup sugar
    4 tablespoons cornstarch, *divided*
  1/2 teaspoon salt
  1/2 teaspoon ground cinnamon
  3/4 cup water
    2 tablespoons plus 1-1/2 teaspoons lemon juice
    2 tablespoons butter
    1 teaspoon vanilla extract
    5 cups chopped peeled ripe pears

In a bowl, combine the flour, 3 tablespoons sugar and salt; cut in butter until crumbly. In a small bowl, whisk egg yolks and lemon juice; stir into dry ingredients with a fork. Remove 1 cup to another bowl; stir in the remaining sugar and set aside for the topping.

Press remaining crumb mixture onto the bottom and up the sides of a greased 8-in. square baking dish. Bake at 375° for 10-12 minutes or until edges are lightly browned.

Meanwhile, for filling, combine the sugar, 2 tablespoons cornstarch, salt and cinnamon in a small saucepan; slowly stir in water and lemon juice until smooth. Bring to a boil over medium heat; cook and stir for 1 minute or until thickened. Remove from the heat; stir in butter and vanilla.

Toss pears with remaining cornstarch; spoon over crust. Top with filling. Sprinkle with reserved topping. Bake for 35-40 minutes or until filling is bubbly and topping is lightly browned. Cool on a wire rack. **Yield:** 9 servings.

ROASTED PEARS IN PECAN SAUCE

(Pictured above right)

Darlene King, Estevan, Saskatchewan

Whenever I bring home pears from the store, my family begs me to make this recipe. They love the tender roasted fruit smothered in creamy pecan sauce. The sauce is also luscious over ice cream or cake.

    4 medium pears, peeled and cut into wedges
    3 tablespoons brown sugar
    3 tablespoons unsweetened apple juice
    3 tablespoons butter, melted
  1/4 cup chopped pecans
    3 tablespoons heavy whipping cream
Vanilla ice cream, optional

Place pears in an ungreased 13-in. x 9-in. x 2-in. baking dish. In a small bowl, combine the brown sugar, apple juice and butter; pour over pears. Bake, uncovered, at 400° for 20 minutes, basting occasionally.

Sprinkle with pecans. Bake 10-15 minutes longer or until pears are tender. Transfer pears to serving dishes. Pour cooking juices into a small bowl; whisk in cream until blended. Drizzle over pears. Serve with ice cream if desired. **Yield:** 4 servings.

CHOCOLATE PEARS IN CARAMEL SAUCE

Margaret Pache, Mesa, Arizona

Baked pears get an elegant touch with a chocolate topping and my tasty, caramel plate garnish.

     2 medium ripe pears
 1-1/2 teaspoons lemon juice
     3 tablespoons butter, melted, *divided*
     1 tablespoon sugar
     2 squares (1 ounce *each*) semisweet
        chocolate
 1-1/2 teaspoons heavy whipping cream
     6 tablespoons caramel ice cream topping
   1/4 cup chopped macadamia nuts, toasted

Core pears from bottom, leaving stem intact. Peel pears. If necessary, cut 1/4 in. from bottom to level. Place in a small baking dish. Brush pears with lemon juice and 1 tablespoon butter. Sprinkle with sugar. Bake, uncovered, at 375° for 25 minutes or until tender, basting occasionally.

In a small saucepan, combine the chocolate, cream and remaining butter. Heat over low heat until smooth, stirring occasionally. Combine caramel topping and macadamia nuts; spoon onto dessert plates. Place pears upright on plates; spoon chocolate sauce over pears. **Yield:** 2 servings.

POMEGRANATE POACHED PEARS
(Pictured below)

Bev Jones, Brunswick, Missouri

These pears can benefit from an overnight marinade of poaching liquid in the fridge. They'll pick up more flavor and the pomegranate's ruby color. Guests will enjoy identifying the subtle tastes in the reduction sauce from wine, rosemary and fruit juice.

     3 cups dry red wine *or* red grape juice
     1 bottle (16 ounces) pomegranate juice
     1 cup water
   1/2 cup sugar
   1/4 cup orange juice
     2 tablespoons grated orange peel
     3 fresh rosemary sprigs (4 inches)
     1 cinnamon stick (3 inches)
     6 medium pears
     6 orange slices
     6 tablespoons Mascarpone cheese

In a Dutch oven, combine the first eight ingredients. Core pears from the bottom, leaving stems intact. Peel pears; place on their sides in the pan. Bring to a boil. Reduce heat; cover and simmer for 25-30 minutes or until pears are almost tender. Remove with a slotted spoon; cool.

Strain poaching liquid and return to Dutch oven. Bring to a boil; cook until reduced to 1 cup, about 45 minutes. Discard rosemary and cinnamon. Place an orange slice on each serving plate; top with 1 tablespoon cheese and a pear. Drizzle with poaching liquid. **Yield:** 6 servings.

Remove from the heat. Cool quickly by placing pan in a bowl of ice water; stir for 2 minutes. Stir in cream and vanilla. Transfer to a bowl. Press plastic wrap onto surface of custard. Refrigerate for several hours or overnight.

Fill cylinder of ice cream freezer two-thirds full; freeze according to manufacturer's directions. Refrigerate remaining mixture until ready to freeze. Transfer to a freezer container; freeze for 2-4 hours before serving.

In a heavy skillet, melt butter over medium heat. Stir in brown sugar, cinnamon and nutmeg; cook and stir until sugar is dissolved. Add pecans; cook and stir for 2-3 minutes or until coated. Spread pecans onto a greased foil-lined baking sheet. Cool completely.

For sauce, combine butter, water and corn syrup in a heavy saucepan. Cook and stir over medium-low heat until butter is melted. Add sugar; cook and stir until sugar is dissolved. Bring to a boil over medium-high heat without stirring. Boil for 4 minutes. Stir for 6-8 minutes or until mixture is caramel-colored. Remove from the heat. Carefully stir in cream until smooth. Serve caramel sauce and candied pecans over ice cream. **Yield:** about 1-1/2 quarts ice cream (1-1/2 cups sauce).

PRALINE CRUNCH ICE CREAM
(Pictured above)

Julia Register, Huntersville, North Carolina

If you're a caramel lover, you'll want to try my home-made ice cream topped with pralines and a rich caramel sauce. It always goes over well at ice cream socials at my church.

  1-3/4 cups milk
    2/3 cup sugar
      2 eggs, beaten
      2 cups heavy whipping cream
      1 teaspoon vanilla extract
CANDIED PECANS:
      1 tablespoon butter
    1/4 cup packed brown sugar
    1/4 teaspoon ground cinnamon
Dash ground nutmeg
    1/2 cup chopped pecans
CARAMEL SAUCE:
      1 cup butter, cubed
    1/2 cup water
      1 tablespoon light corn syrup
      2 cups sugar
      1 cup heavy whipping cream

In a heavy saucepan, heat milk to 175°; stir in sugar until dissolved. Whisk a small amount of hot mixture into eggs; return all to the pan, whisking constantly. Cook and stir over low heat until mixture reaches at least 160° and coats the back of a metal spoon.

ALMOND RICE PUDDING (RIS A L'AMANDE)

Jytte Klarlund, Lawson, Missouri

This rich and creamy rice pudding is traditionally served at Christmas Eve dinner in Scandinavia. I think the cherries give it holiday flair.

      8 cups milk
  1-1/2 cups uncooked medium grain rice
    3/4 cup sugar
      1 teaspoon salt
    1/2 cup chopped almonds, toasted
  1-1/2 teaspoons almond extract
  1-1/2 cups heavy whipping cream, whipped
      1 can (21 ounces) cherry or raspberry pie filling
Toasted slivered almonds

In a large heavy saucepan, combine the milk, rice, sugar and salt. Bring to a boil. Reduce heat; simmer, uncovered, for 35-40 minutes or until slightly thickened, stirring frequently. Remove from the heat; transfer to a large bowl. Cover and refrigerate until chilled.

Just before serving, stir in chopped almonds and extract. Fold in whipped cream. Garnish with pie filling and slivered almonds. **Yield:** 12 servings.

PUMPKIN SPICE TORTE
(Pictured below)

Kathy Michel, Dubuque, Iowa

Instead of pumpkin pie, why not try this pretty dessert for Thanksgiving? The maple frosting nicely complements the autumnal flavor of the cake.

    3/4 cup butter, softened
1-1/2 cups sugar
      3 eggs
1-1/2 cups canned pumpkin
1-1/2 teaspoons vanilla extract
      3 cups all-purpose flour
1-1/2 teaspoons ground cinnamon
      1 teaspoon baking powder
      1 teaspoon baking soda
    3/4 teaspoon ground nutmeg
    1/2 teaspoon salt
    1/4 teaspoon ground ginger
    1/4 teaspoon ground cloves
      1 cup buttermilk
FROSTING:
      2 packages (one 8 ounces, one 3 ounces)
        cream cheese, softened
    1/2 cup butter, softened
3-1/2 cups confectioners' sugar
      2 to 3 teaspoons maple flavoring
     10 to 12 walnut halves, toasted

In a large mixing bowl, cream butter and sugar. Beat in eggs, pumpkin and vanilla. Combine the flour, cinnamon, baking powder, baking soda, nutmeg, salt, ginger and cloves; add to pumpkin mixture alternately with the buttermilk.

Pour into three greased and floured 9-in. round baking pans. Bake at 325° for 20-25 minutes or until a toothpick inserted near the center comes out clean. Cool for 5 minutes before removing from pans to wire racks to cool completely.

In a large mixing bowl, beat cream cheese and butter until smooth. Add confectioners' sugar and enough maple flavoring to achieve spreading consistency. Place one cake layer on a serving plate; spread with 1 cup frosting. Repeat with remaining layers and frosting. Garnish with walnuts. Store in the refrigerator. **Yield:** 10-12 servings.

STOVETOP RICE PUDDING
(Pictured above)

Mandy Barnhart, Pensacola, Florida

This is my mom's recipe, which she called Creamy Steamed Rice. Although many people would eat it for dessert, it was one of my favorite breakfasts when I was growing up. My family considers it a real treat.

✓ Uses less fat, sugar or salt. Includes Nutrition Facts.

1-1/2 cups water
    3/4 cup uncooked long grain rice
    1/2 teaspoon salt
      4 cups milk
    1/2 cup sugar
      2 tablespoons butter
    1/2 teaspoon ground cinnamon
Cinnamon sticks and fresh fruit, optional

In a large heavy saucepan, bring water to a boil over medium-high heat; stir in rice and salt. Reduce heat; cover and simmer for 15 minutes or until water is absorbed.

Stir in milk and sugar. Cook, uncovered, over medium heat for 30-40 minutes or until thickened, stirring frequently. Remove from the heat; stir in butter.

Serve warm or chilled. Sprinkle with cinnamon. Garnish with cinnamon sticks and fruit if desired. **Yield:** 4-6 servings.

Nutrition Facts: 1 serving equals 283 calories, 9 g fat (6 g saturated fat), 32 mg cholesterol, 316 mg sodium, 43 g carbohydrate, trace fiber, 7 g protein.

■■■■■■■■■■■■■■

CINNAMON APPLE DUMPLINGS

(Pictured below)

Marie Hattrup, Moro, Oregon

When Mom made pies to feed the crew during wheat harvest, she always had plenty of dough left over, so she treated us kids to apple dumplings. I've carried on this tradition in my own family. Now my husband and I enjoy this special dessert even when I'm not baking pies.

> 1 cup all-purpose flour
> 1/4 teaspoon salt
> 1/3 cup shortening
> 3 tablespoons ice water
> 2 medium baking apples
> 3 tablespoons sugar
> 1/2 teaspoon ground cinnamon

Half-and-half cream

SAUCE:

> 1/3 cup sugar
> 2 tablespoons red-hot candies *or* 1/4 teaspoon ground cinnamon
> 1/2 teaspoon cornstarch
> 2/3 cup water
> 1 tablespoon butter

Additional half-and-half cream, optional

In a bowl, combine flour and salt. Cut in shortening until mixture resembles coarse crumbs. With a fork, stir in water until dough forms a ball. Roll out on a floured surface to a 14-in. x 7-in. rectangle; cut pastry in half.

Peel and core apples; place one on each square of pastry. Combine sugar and cinnamon; spoon

into apples. Moisten edges of pastry and gather around apples; pinch and seal. Place dumplings in an ungreased 9-in. x 5-in. x 3-in. loaf pan or a shallow 1-1/2-qt. baking dish. Brush with cream.

In a small saucepan, combine the sugar, red-hots, cornstarch, water and butter. Bring to a boil over medium-low heat, stirring frequently; boil for 2 minutes. Pour between dumplings.

Bake at 400° for 35-45 minutes or until pastry is golden brown and apples are tender. Serve warm with cream if desired. **Yield:** 2 servings.

■■■■■■■■■■■■■■

LEMON-BUTTERMILK POUND CAKE

Marianna King, Gastonia, North Carolina

Here's the recipe I reach for when I need something tried and true. The old-fashioned cake has a tangy lemon flavor and is a nice dessert for a potluck or most any occasion.

> 1 cup shortening
> 1/2 cup butter, softened
> 2-1/2 cups sugar
> 4 eggs
> 1 teaspoon lemon extract
> 1 teaspoon vanilla extract
> 3-1/2 cups all-purpose flour
> 1/2 teaspoon baking soda
> 1/2 teaspoon salt
> 1 cup buttermilk

LEMON SAUCE:

> 1 cup sugar
> 1/2 cup water
> 1/2 cup lemon juice
> 3 tablespoons grated lemon peel

In a large mixing bowl, cream the shortening, butter and sugar. Add eggs, one at a time, beating well after each addition. Beat in extracts. Combine the flour, baking soda and salt; add to creamed mixture alternately with buttermilk.

Pour into a greased and floured 10-in. tube pan. Bake on the lowest oven rack at 350° for 75-80 minutes or until a toothpick inserted near the center comes out clean. Cool for 10 minutes. Run a knife around side and center tube of pan. Remove cake to a wire rack placed over a sheet of waxed paper.

In a saucepan, combine the sauce ingredients. Bring to a boil. Reduce heat; simmer, uncovered, until sauce is reduced to 1-1/2 cups, about 10 minutes.

Poke holes in top of cake; spoon about 1/4 cup sauce into holes. Let stand for 10 minutes. Poke holes into sides of cake; brush remaining sauce over cake. Cool completely. **Yield:** 12-16 servings.

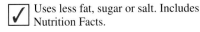

FANTASY STRAWBERRIES
(Pictured below)
Millie Tokarz, Chicago, Illinois

Ever wish strawberries could always be in season? My homemade variety is ripe and ready for "picking" year-round. These sweet confections are real conversation starters. Plus, they demonstrate how special my guests are to me.

☑ Uses less fat, sugar or salt. Includes Nutrition Facts.

- 2 packages (3 ounces *each*) strawberry gelatin
- 1/2 cup sweetened condensed milk
- 1 cup finely chopped pecans
- 1 cup flaked coconut
- 1 teaspoon vanilla extract

Red and green colored sugar
Slivered almonds
Green liquid food coloring

In a small mixing bowl, beat the gelatin powder and milk until smooth. Add pecans, coconut and vanilla; mix just until combined. Shape into strawberries.

Roll sides of strawberries in red sugar and dip tops into green sugar. Tint almonds with green food coloring; insert an almond into the top of each strawberry for stem. Store in an airtight container in the refrigerator. **Yield:** about 2 dozen.

Nutrition Facts: 1 strawberry equals 87 calories, 5 g fat (2 g saturated fat), 2 mg cholesterol, 26 mg sodium, 9 g carbohydrate, 1 g fiber, 1 g protein.

PEACH UPSIDE-DOWN CAKE
(Pictured above)
Susie Fisher, Loganton, Pennsylvania

This is a family favorite and a great summertime dessert that calls for fresh peaches. We love it served warm with whipped cream.

- 1/3 cup butter, melted
- 1/2 cup packed brown sugar
- 2 cups sliced peeled fresh peaches
- 1/3 cup shortening
- 1 cup sugar
- 1 egg
- 1/2 teaspoon lemon juice
- 1/2 teaspoon vanilla extract
- 1-1/3 cups all-purpose flour
- 2 teaspoons baking powder
- 1/2 teaspoon salt
- 2/3 cup milk

Whipped cream, optional

Pour butter into an ungreased 9-in. square baking pan; sprinkle with brown sugar. Arrange peach slices in a single layer over brown sugar.

In a small mixing bowl, cream shortening and sugar. Beat in the egg, lemon juice and vanilla. Combine the flour, baking powder and salt; add to creamed mixture alternately with milk. Spoon over peaches.

Bake at 350° for 45-50 minutes or until a toothpick inserted near the center comes out clean. Cool for 10 minutes before inverting onto a serving plate. Serve warm with whipped cream if desired. **Yield:** 6 servings.

PEACHY PARTICULARS

The peak season for peaches is June through September. However, you can substitute frozen peaches (thawed and drained) or well-drained canned peaches in equal amounts for fresh. One pound of frozen or canned peaches is equal to about three medium peaches.

NO-BAKE LIME CHEESECAKE
(Pictured below)

Robin Spires, Tampa, Florida

Being from the Sunshine State, I love any recipe containing citrus. This one, featuring lime, is quick to mix up and disappears almost as fast. Use orange juice and peel for the lime-flavored ingredients to get another cheesecake variation.

    3 cups graham cracker crumbs
2/3 cup sugar
2/3 cup butter, melted
FILLING:
    2 envelopes unflavored gelatin
    1 cup lime juice
1/4 cup cold water
1-1/2 cups sugar
    5 eggs, lightly beaten
    2 teaspoons grated lime peel
    2 packages (8 ounces *each*) cream cheese, softened
1/2 cup butter, softened
1/2 cup heavy whipping cream

In a large bowl, combine the graham cracker crumbs, sugar and butter. Press onto the bottom and 2 in. up the sides of a greased 9-in. springform pan. Cover and refrigerate for at least 30 minutes.

In a small saucepan, sprinkle gelatin over lime juice and cold water; let stand for 1 minute. Stir in the sugar, eggs and lime peel. Cook and stir over medium heat until mixture reaches 160°. Remove from the heat.

In a large mixing bowl, beat cream cheese and butter until fluffy. Gradually beat in gelatin mixture. Cover and refrigerate for 45 minutes or until partially set, stirring occasionally.

PEAR SORBET
(Pictured above)

Deirdre Dee Zosha, Milwaukee, Wisconsin

A touch of sweet white wine and lemon makes this lovely pear sorbet so refreshing. You can use canned pears when fresh ones aren't available. Lime juice also makes a nice substitute for the lemon.

☑ Uses less fat, sugar or salt. Includes Nutrition Facts.

    5 small pears, peeled and sliced
3/4 cup sweet white wine *or* apple juice
1/3 cup sugar
4-1/2 teaspoons lemon juice

In a large saucepan, combine all of the ingredients. Bring to a boil. Reduce heat; simmer, uncovered, for 8-10 minutes or until the pears are tender. Cool slightly.

Pour into a food processor; cover and process for 1-2 minutes or until smooth. Transfer to a 13-in. x 9-in. x 2-in. dish. Cover and freeze for 4 hours or until firm.

Just before serving, process again in a food processor for 1-2 minutes or until smooth. Spoon into dessert dishes. **Yield:** 4 servings.

Nutrition Facts: 1/2 cup equals 198 calories, 1 g fat (trace saturated fat), 0 cholesterol, 2 mg sodium, 44 g carbohydrate, 4 g fiber, 1 g protein.

In a small mixing bowl, beat cream until stiff peaks form; fold into lime mixture. Spoon into crust. Cover and refrigerate for 3-4 hours or until set. Just before serving, remove sides of pan. Refrigerate leftovers. **Yield:** 12 servings.

FRESH BLUEBERRY PIE
(Pictured above)

Mrs. R. Ricks, Kalamazoo, Michigan

We live in blueberry country, and this pie is a perfect way to showcase the luscious berries. A neighbor made the dessert for us several years ago, and she shared the recipe. Our whole family enjoys it.

☑ Uses less fat, sugar or salt. Includes Nutrition Facts.

    3/4 cup sugar
      3 tablespoons cornstarch
    1/8 teaspoon salt
    1/4 cup water
      4 cups fresh blueberries, *divided*
      1 graham cracker crust (9 inches)
Whipped cream

In a large saucepan, combine the sugar, cornstarch and salt. Gradually add water, stirring until smooth. Stir in 2 cups of blueberries. Bring to a boil; cook and stir for 1-2 minutes or until thickened. Remove mixture from the heat; cool to room temperature.

Spoon remaining blueberries into the crust; top with cooled blueberry mixture. Cover and refrigerate for 1-2 hours or until chilled. Serve with whipped cream. **Yield:** 6-8 servings.

Nutrition Facts: 1 piece equals 230 calories, 6 g fat (1 g saturated fat), 0 cholesterol, 159 mg sodium, 46 g carbohydrate, 2 g fiber, 1 g protein.

SUMMERTIME FRUIT CONES
(Pictured below)

Here's a simple summer dessert that appeals to kids and adults alike. Our home economists also suggest assembling the ingredients in parfait glasses.

☑ Uses less fat, sugar or salt. Includes Nutrition Facts and Diabetic Exchanges.

      2 medium nectarines, chopped
      1 cup whole small fresh strawberries
      1 cup fresh blueberries
      2 tablespoons mashed fresh strawberries
      1 teaspoon crystallized ginger
    1/4 teaspoon ground cinnamon
      1 cup reduced-fat whipped topping
      4 ice cream waffle cones

In a small bowl, combine the nectarines, whole strawberries and blueberries. In another bowl, combine the mashed strawberries, ginger and cinnamon. Fold in whipped topping.

Fill each waffle cone with 1/4 cup fruit mixture; top with 2 tablespoons whipped topping mixture. Repeat layers. Serve immediately. **Yield:** 4 servings.

Nutrition Facts: 1 fruit cone equals 162 calories, 4 g fat (2 g saturated fat), 1 mg cholesterol, 18 mg sodium, 31 g carbohydrate, 3 g fiber, 2 g protein. **Diabetic Exchanges:** 1 starch, 1 fruit, 1/2 fat.

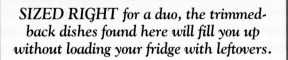

SIZED RIGHT for a duo, the trimmed-back dishes found here will fill you up without loading your fridge with leftovers.

PERFECT FOR A PAIR. Clockwise from center left: Chunky Orange Marmalade Cookies (p. 138), Creamy Fish Chowder (p. 137), Quick Pizza Sandwiches (p. 137) and Green 'n' Red Potato Salad (p. 137).

Cooking for Two

QUICK PIZZA SANDWICHES

Marge Barto, Poquoson, Virginia

I came up with this recipe when I needed a quick supper. The robust subs are great when served with a salad and deli pickles. They are my husband's favorite...as well as my grandchildren's.

- 1/2 pound ground beef
- 1/4 teaspoon salt
- 1/4 teaspoon onion powder
- 1/4 teaspoon garlic powder
- 1/4 teaspoon Italian seasoning
- 1/4 teaspoon rubbed sage
- Dash pepper
- 3/4 cup pizza sauce
- 1 loaf (8 ounces) French bread, halved lengthwise
- 1/4 cup shredded part-skim mozzarella cheese

In a small bowl, mix the beef and seasonings just until combined. Divide into six portions; shape each into a 1-1/2-in. patty.

In a large nonstick skillet, cook patties for 3-1/2 to 4-1/2 minutes on each side or until meat is no longer pink; drain. Pour pizza sauce over patties and heat through. Spoon onto French bread; sprinkle with cheese. Cut into sandwiches. **Yield:** 2 servings.

GREEN 'N' RED POTATO SALAD

De Loris Lawson, Carthage, Missouri

From the first time I made it, this has been my go-to recipe for fresh green beans. I serve it alongside all sorts of meats, poultry and fish. It's even a wonderful way to round out a meal of hamburgers, hot dogs or barbecue sandwiches.

- 1-1/3 cups cubed red potatoes (1-inch pieces)
- 1 cup cut fresh green beans (1-inch pieces)
- 2 tablespoons sliced pimiento-stuffed olives
- 1/8 teaspoon salt
- Dash pepper

MUSTARD DILL DRESSING:
- 1 tablespoon olive oil
- 1 tablespoon Dijon mustard
- 2 teaspoons red wine vinegar
- 1 teaspoon lemon juice
- 1 teaspoon dill weed
- 1/4 teaspoon sugar

Place potatoes in a small saucepan and cover with water. Bring to a boil. Reduce heat; cover and cook for 10-12 minutes or until tender. Meanwhile, place beans in another saucepan and cover with water. Bring to a boil. Cook, uncovered, for 8-10 minutes or until crisp-tender.

Drain potatoes and beans; place in a bowl. Add the olives, salt and pepper. Cover and refrigerate until chilled.

In a small bowl, combine the dressing ingredients. Drizzle over salad and toss to coat. Refrigerate until serving. **Yield:** 2 servings.

CREAMY FISH CHOWDER

Claudette Mogle, Federal Way, Washington

We were tired of the same old vegetable soup, and I had some fish on hand that needed to be cooked. The result was the creation of this easy seafood chowder.

- 1/3 cup chopped onion
- 1 tablespoon butter
- 2 cups chicken broth
- 1-1/2 cups diced potatoes
- 1/2 teaspoon salt
- 1/2 teaspoon pepper
- 2 tablespoons all-purpose flour
- 2 tablespoons mashed potato flakes
- 2 cups milk
- 1/2 pound cod *or* haddock fillets, cut into 1/2-inch pieces
- 2 tablespoons minced fresh parsley

In a large saucepan, saute onion in butter until tender. Add the broth, potatoes, salt and pepper. Bring to a boil. Reduce heat; cover and simmer for 20 minutes or until potatoes are tender.

In a bowl, combine the flour, potato flakes and milk until smooth. Stir into the potato mixture. Bring to a boil. Reduce heat; add fish and parsley. Cover and simmer for 5-10 minutes or until fish is opaque. **Yield:** 3-1/2 cups.

Chunky Orange Marmalade Cookies

(Pictured on page 136)

Mary Small, Monmouth, Maine

My mother had this recipe in her cookie collection, and she and I began baking these when I was a young teen. There is no sugar among the ingredients, just the subtle taste of marmalade to add sweetness. It's a soft cookie with an interesting combination of orange and chocolate.

       1/4 cup shortening
         1 egg yolk
       1/2 cup orange marmalade
       1/2 teaspoon vanilla extract
         1 cup all-purpose flour
       1/2 teaspoon salt
       1/2 teaspoon baking powder
       1/2 teaspoon baking soda
       1/2 teaspoon ground cinnamon
       1/2 teaspoon ground nutmeg
       1/2 cup semisweet chocolate chips
       1/2 cup chopped pecans

In a small mixing bowl, cream the shortening, egg yolk and marmalade until light and fluffy. Beat in vanilla. Combine the flour, salt, baking powder, baking soda, cinnamon and nutmeg; add to creamed mixture and mix well. Stir in chocolate chips and pecans.

Drop by tablespoonfuls 2 in. apart onto greased baking sheets. Bake at 350° for 12-15 minutes or until lightly browned. Remove to wire racks. **Yield:** 2 dozen.

Veggie Rice Saute

Claudia Resac, Holmen, Wisconsin

I came up with this recipe one day when I had nothing but burgers to cook on the grill and not enough of any one vegetable. It was so tasty we ate almost all of it, and the little bit that was leftover I heated in the microwave the following day.

         3 tablespoons vegetable oil, *divided*
         1 egg, lightly beaten
       3/4 cup cut fresh green beans (1/2-inch
             pieces)
       1/4 cup chopped onion
       3/4 cup thinly sliced quartered
             zucchini
       3/4 cup thinly sliced fresh mushrooms
         1 garlic clove, minced
     1-1/2 cups cooked long grain rice
         2 tablespoons soy sauce

In a small skillet, heat 1 tablespoon oil over medium-high heat. Add egg. As egg sets, lift edges, letting uncooked portion flow underneath. Remove egg and chop into small pieces; set aside.

In the same skillet, saute beans and onion in remaining oil for 1-2 minutes. Add the zucchini, mushrooms and garlic; saute 1 minute longer. Add rice; cook and stir for 2-3 minutes or until beans are tender and rice is lightly browned. Stir in soy sauce. Return egg to the pan; heat through. Serve immediately. **Yield:** 2 servings.

Homemade Chocolate Pudding

(Pictured below)

Maribeth Janus, Ivoryton, Connecticut

During the Depression it was hard to find chocolate, but when my mother found some, she made this pudding. I make it now and think of her when I prepare it.

         2 tablespoons sugar
         1 tablespoon cornstarch
         1 cup milk
       1/3 cup semisweet chocolate chips
       1/2 teaspoon vanilla extract

In a small saucepan, combine sugar and cornstarch. Add milk; stir until smooth. Cook and stir over medium heat until mixture comes to a boil. Cook and stir 1-2 minutes longer or until the mixture is thickened.

Stir in chocolate chips; cook and stir until melted. Remove from the heat. Stir in vanilla. Spoon into dessert dishes. Serve warm or chilled. **Yield:** 2 servings.

PASTA WITH SAUSAGE CREAM SAUCE

Ernest Walker, Gallipolis, Ohio

For a hearty linguine dish sized right for two, consider this recipe. Italian sausage keeps the supper satisfying.

1/2 pound bulk Italian sausage
1 cup heavy whipping cream
1 cup frozen peas
1/2 cup sliced fresh mushrooms
2 tablespoons shredded Parmesan cheese
1/8 teaspoon ground nutmeg
2 cups hot cooked linguine

In a skillet, cook sausage over medium heat until no longer pink; drain. Add cream; stir to loosen browned bits from pan. Bring to a boil; cook and stir for 1 minute. Reduce heat. Add the peas, mushrooms, Parmesan cheese and nutmeg; cook and stir until heated through. Serve with linguine. **Yield:** 2 servings.

HOMEMADE CHICKEN AND DUMPLINGS

Claire Bruno, Tucson, Arizona

Here's a meal-in-one that's sized right for a pair. The whole dinner comes together on the stovetop, so you can get out of the kitchen in hurry.

2 boneless skinless chicken breast halves, cut into 1/2-inch cubes
1-1/2 cups chicken broth
1 medium carrot, sliced
1 small potato, peeled and cubed
1/4 cup chopped onion
2 tablespoons chopped celery
1 bay leaf
1/4 teaspoon salt
1/8 teaspoon pepper
DUMPLINGS:
1/4 cup all-purpose flour
1 teaspoon dried parsley flakes
1/2 teaspoon baking powder
Pinch ground cloves
Pinch salt
3 tablespoons milk

In a saucepan, combine the first nine ingredients; bring to a boil. Reduce heat; cover and simmer for 15 minutes or until vegetables are tender. Discard bay leaf.

For dumplings, in a bowl, combine the flour, parsley, baking powder, cloves and salt. Stir in milk just until moistened. Drop by heaping teaspoonfuls onto simmering chicken mixture. Cov-

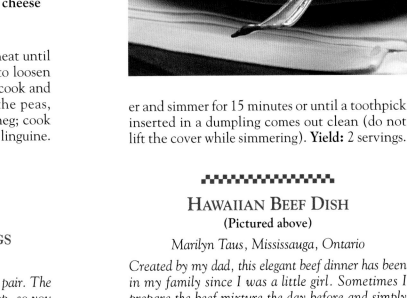

er and simmer for 15 minutes or until a toothpick inserted in a dumpling comes out clean (do not lift the cover while simmering). **Yield:** 2 servings.

HAWAIIAN BEEF DISH
(Pictured above)

Marilyn Taus, Mississauga, Ontario

Created by my dad, this elegant beef dinner has been in my family since I was a little girl. Sometimes I prepare the beef mixture the day before and simply warm it up while I'm cooking the rice.

1/2 pound lean ground beef
1 medium onion, halved and sliced
1/3 cup sliced celery
1/3 cup chopped green pepper
1 garlic clove, minced
2 teaspoons butter
1 can (8 ounces) unsweetened pineapple chunks
1/4 cup packed brown sugar
1 tablespoon all-purpose flour
1 tablespoon white wine vinegar
1/4 teaspoon salt
1 cup hot cooked rice

In a small skillet, cook beef over medium heat until no longer pink; drain and set aside. In the same skillet, saute the onion, celery, green pepper and garlic in butter for 5 minutes or until crisp-tender.

Drain pineapple, reserving juice; set pineapple aside. Add enough water to the juice to measure 1/2 cup. In a bowl, combine the brown sugar, flour, vinegar, salt and pineapple juice mixture until smooth. Add to skillet. Bring to a boil. Cook and stir over medium heat for 2 minutes. Stir in beef and pineapple; heat through. Serve with rice. **Yield:** 2 servings.

RASPBERRY WALNUT BARS
(Pictured above)

Marilyn Forsell, Hydesville, California

Many of my treasured recipes have come from a group of moms I used to meet with for tea and coffee when our children were small. I adapted this recipe from a friend who made it with strawberry jam.

  1 cup butter, softened
  1 cup sugar
  2 egg yolks
  2 cups all-purpose flour
  1 cup finely chopped walnuts
1/2 cup seedless raspberry jam

In a large mixing bowl, cream butter and sugar. Beat in egg yolks. Gradually add flour and walnuts. Pat half of the mixture into a greased 8-in. square baking pan. Spread with jam. Crumble remaining crust mixture over jam.

Bake at 350° for 35-40 minutes or until lightly browned. Cool on a wire rack. **Yield:** 16 bars.

SPAGHETTI SALAD
(Pictured above, far right)

Leona Pecoraro, Ravenden, Arkansas

This dish is surprisingly flavorful, light and offers a refreshing change from mayonnaise-based dressings. In addition, it's a breeze to toss together.

  4 ounces uncooked spaghetti
  1 plum tomato, diced
1/2 cup sliced fresh mushrooms
  2 tablespoons sliced ripe olives
  1 green onion, chopped
  1 garlic clove, minced
1/4 cup Italian salad dressing

Cook pasta according to package directions; drain and rinse in cold water. Place pasta in a bowl; add tomato, mushrooms, olives, onion and garlic. Add dressing and toss to coat. Cover and refrigerate until serving. **Yield:** 2 servings.

CHICKEN PARMIGIANA
(Pictured at right)

Iola Butler, Sun City, California

For years my husband ordered Chicken Parmigiana at restaurants. Then I found this recipe in one of our local newspapers, trimmed it down to serve two and began making it at home.

  1 can (15 ounces) tomato sauce
  2 teaspoons Italian seasoning
1/2 teaspoon garlic powder
  1 egg
1/4 cup seasoned bread crumbs
  3 tablespoons grated Parmesan cheese
  2 boneless skinless chicken breast halves
    (4 ounces *each*)
  2 tablespoons olive oil
  2 slices part-skim mozzarella cheese

In a small saucepan, combine the tomato sauce, Italian seasoning and garlic powder. Bring to a boil. Reduce heat; cover and simmer for 20 minutes.

Meanwhile, in a shallow bowl, lightly beat the egg. In another shallow bowl, combine bread crumbs and Parmesan cheese. Dip chicken in egg, then coat with crumb mixture.

In a skillet, cook chicken in oil over medium heat for 5 minutes on each side or until juices run clear. Top with mozzarella cheese. Cover and cook 3-4 minutes longer or until cheese is melted. Serve with tomato sauce. **Yield:** 2 servings.

ITALIAN BROCCOLI
(Pictured above right)

Kitty Ganser, Hendersonville, North Carolina

I've relied on this well-seasoned side dish for years. I often steam the broccoli ahead of time, cool it quickly in cold water, drain it and then, when ready to serve, warm it in the hot garlic oil.

✓ Uses less fat, sugar or salt. Includes Nutrition Facts.

1/2 pound fresh broccoli spears, cut into
    2-inch pieces
  1 tablespoon olive oil
  2 garlic cloves, thinly sliced
Pinch crushed red pepper flakes, optional
Salt to taste

Place broccoli in a steamer basket; place in a small saucepan over 1 in. of water. Bring to a boil; cover and steam for 5-7 minutes or until crisp-tender.

Meanwhile, in a small skillet, combine the oil, garlic and pepper flakes if desired. Cook over low heat until garlic begins to brown, about 1-2

minutes, stirring occasionally. Using a slotted spoon, remove garlic and discard. Add broccoli and toss to coat. Season with salt. Serve immediately. **Yield:** 2 servings.

Nutrition Facts: 1 cup equals 96 calories, 7 g fat (1 g saturated fat), 0 cholesterol, 30 mg sodium, 7 g carbohydrate, 3 g fiber, 4 g protein.

★★★★★★★★★★★★★★

CLASSIC CHEESECAKE
(Pictured above)

Therese Fortier, Grand Rapids, Michigan

My husband and I love desserts and this is one of our favorites. It is delicious and there are no leftovers! Sometimes, I top each slice with fresh, seasonal berries.

   1/4 cup graham cracker crumbs
      1 teaspoon sugar
4-1/2 teaspoons butter, melted
FILLING:
      1 package (3 ounces) cream cheese,
         softened
   1/4 cup sugar
      1 egg, lightly beaten
      1 teaspoon lemon juice
   1/2 teaspoon grated lemon peel
TOPPING:
   1/4 cup sour cream
      2 teaspoons sugar
   1/4 teaspoon vanilla extract

In a small bowl, combine cracker crumbs and sugar; stir in butter. Press onto the bottom of a greased 4-in. springform pan. Place on a baking sheet. Bake at 350° for 5 minutes. Cool on a wire rack.

In a small mixing bowl, beat cream cheese and sugar until smooth. Add egg; beat on low speed just until combined. Stir in lemon juice and peel.

Pour over crust. Return pan to baking sheet. Bake at 350° for 25-30 minutes or until center is almost set. Remove from the oven; let stand for 5 minutes (leave oven on).

Combine topping ingredients; carefully spread over filling. Bake 5 minutes longer. Cool on a wire rack for 10 minutes. Carefully run a knife around edge of pan to loosen; cool 1 hour longer. Refrigerate overnight. Remove sides of pan just before serving. **Yield:** 2 servings.

■▪■▪■▪■▪■

MUSHROOM RIB EYES
(Pictured above)

Kathleen Hendrick, Alexandria, Kentucky
Who can resist a juicy rib eye steak topped with mush-
rooms and onions in a rich gravy? Simply add a
green salad and an impressive dinner is served.

    2 boneless rib eye steaks (8 ounces *each*)
1/4 teaspoon seasoned salt
1/8 teaspoon pepper
    2 teaspoons vegetable oil
    1 small onion, thinly sliced

    1 cup sliced fresh mushrooms
    1 envelope brown gravy mix
1/3 cup sour cream

Sprinkle steaks with seasoned salt and pepper. In a
large skillet, brown steaks on both sides in oil. Transfer to an 11-in. x 7-in. x 2-in. baking dish. In the skillet, saute onion and mushrooms until tender. Spoon
over steaks. Prepare gravy mix according to package directions; stir in sour cream. Pour over steaks.

    Cover and bake at 350° for 10-15 minutes or
until meat reaches desired doneness (for medium-
rare, a meat thermometer should read 145°; medium, 160°; well-done, 170°). **Yield:** 2 servings.

Potato Squash Casserole
(Pictured at left)

Tommy Haigler, Lexington, North Carolina

A combination of red potatoes, summer squash and cheddar cheese makes this stovetop specialty a favorite in my home. Bacon and onion lend a savory touch.

> 2 medium red potatoes, peeled and cubed
> 1 medium yellow summer squash, diced
> 3 tablespoons finely chopped onion
> 1 tablespoon butter
> Dash salt and pepper
> 1/2 cup shredded sharp cheddar cheese
> 3 bacon strips, cooked and crumbled

Place the potatoes in a small saucepan and cover with water. Bring to a boil. Reduce heat; cover and simmer for 5 minutes. Add squash; cover and simmer 5 minutes longer or until vegetables are tender. Drain. Place potatoes and squash in a bowl; mash.

In a small skillet, saute onion in butter. Add to potato mixture. Season with salt and pepper. Transfer to a greased 2-cup baking dish (dish will be full). Top with cheese. Bake, uncovered, at 350° for 10 minutes or until cheese is melted. Sprinkle with bacon. **Yield:** 2 servings.

Great Green Beans
(Pictured at left)

Janine Tueller Mickelson, Ames, Iowa

Garlic, rosemary and a little Parmesan cheese do wonders when dressing up fresh green beans in this versatile recipe. It's terrific alongside meat and poultry.

> 2 cups cut fresh green beans
> 1 cup chicken broth
> 1 garlic clove, minced
> 2 tablespoons butter
> 2 tablespoons minced fresh parsley
> 1 teaspoon minced fresh rosemary *or*
>   1/4 teaspoon dried rosemary, crushed
> 1/8 teaspoon garlic salt
> 1 tablespoon shredded Parmesan cheese

In a small saucepan, bring the beans and broth to a boil. Reduce heat; simmer, uncovered, for 10 minutes or until crisp-tender.

In a small skillet, saute garlic in butter until tender. Stir in the parsley, rosemary and garlic salt. Drain beans; drizzle with butter mixture and toss to coat. Sprinkle with Parmesan cheese. **Yield:** 2 servings.

Soft Valentine Cutouts
(Pictured at far left)

Helen Giroux, Hampton, New York

These from-scratch cookies are a buttery delight. Perfect for Valentine's Day, the treats practically melt in your mouth.

> 1/2 cup butter, softened
> 1 cup sugar
> 1 egg
> 1/2 cup sour cream
> 1/4 teaspoon lemon extract
> 1/4 teaspoon vanilla extract
> 2 cups all-purpose flour
> 1/2 teaspoon baking soda
> 1/8 teaspoon salt
> Red colored sugar

In a large mixing bowl, cream butter and sugar. Beat in the egg, sour cream and extracts. Combine the flour, baking soda and salt; gradually add to creamed mixture. Cover and refrigerate for 3 hours or until easy to handle.

On a lightly floured surface, roll out dough to 1/4-in. thickness. Cut with a floured 2-1/2-in. heart-shaped cookie cutter. Place 1 in. apart on ungreased baking sheets. Sprinkle with colored sugar. Bake at 375° for 8-10 minutes or until lightly browned. Remove to wire racks. **Yield:** about 2 dozen.

Corn 'n' Ham Fritters

Nancy Foust, Stoneboro, Pennsylvania

Nothing beats the down-home taste of golden-brown fritters. This version offers diced ham and kernels of corn, and it uses a biscuit mix for fast assembly.

> 1 cup biscuit/baking mix
> 1/2 teaspoon sugar
> 1 egg
> 1/2 cup milk
> 1 cup frozen corn, thawed
> 1/2 cup finely diced fully cooked ham
> Oil for deep-fat frying
> Maple syrup, optional

In a small bowl, combine the biscuit mix and sugar. In another bowl, whisk the egg and milk; stir into dry ingredients just until moistened. Fold in corn and ham.

In an electric skillet, heat 1-1/2 in. of oil to 375°. Drop batter by rounded tablespoonfuls, a few at a time, into hot oil. Fry until golden brown, about 1 minute on each side. Drain on paper towels. Serve warm with syrup if desired. **Yield:** 16 fritters.

HERBED TOMATO SALAD

(Pictured above)

Liane Davenport, Greensboro, North Carolina

Tomato, cucumber, red onion and feta cheese combine easily in this colorful salad. With basil and oregano, it packs big flavor in every bite.

        1 medium tomato, seeded and chopped
    1/3 cup chopped cucumber
    1/3 cup crumbled feta cheese
    1/4 cup chopped red onion
        2 tablespoons olive oil
        1 tablespoon minced fresh oregano
    1-1/2 teaspoons minced fresh basil
    1/4 teaspoon salt
    1/4 teaspoon pepper

In a small bowl, combine all ingredients; toss to coat. Cover and let stand for 15 minutes before serving. **Yield:** 2 servings.

EASY CHOPPED STEAK

(Pictured at far right)

Bette Persinger, Pasadena, Texas

You just can't beat the flavor or no-fuss convenience of these mouth-watering patties. Serve them with a salad from the deli department for a meal in minutes.

        1 egg, beaten
    3/4 cup soft bread crumbs
    1-1/2 teaspoons Worcestershire sauce
    1/4 cup finely chopped onion
    1/4 teaspoon salt
    1/8 teaspoon pepper
    3/4 pound ground beef

In a bowl, combine the first six ingredients. Crumble beef over mixture and mix well. Shape into two 1/2-in.-thick patties. Pan-fry or broil for 5-7 minutes on each side or until a meat thermometer reads 160°. **Yield:** 2 servings.

CREAMY SCALLOPED POTATOES

(Pictured at right)

Lucinda Isenberg, Fairmont, Minnesota

For a fantastic side dish that won't leave you with days of leftovers, try my scalloped potatoes. Whipping cream makes them a taste sensation.

        2 medium potatoes, peeled and sliced
    1/4 cup sliced onion
    1/4 teaspoon salt
    1/8 teaspoon pepper
    3/4 cup heavy whipping cream
    1/4 cup chicken broth *or* water
Paprika

Layer half of the potatoes in a greased 1-qt. baking dish. Top with onion; sprinkle with half of the salt and pepper. Top with the remaining potatoes, salt and pepper. Combine the cream and broth; pour over potatoes. Sprinkle with paprika.

Bake, uncovered, at 375° for 50-55 minutes or until the potatoes are tender and top is golden brown. **Yield:** 2 servings.

CRUMB-TOPPED BAKED TOMATOES

(Pictured at right)

Reba Chappell, Dunbar, West Virginia

Try these change-of-pace tomatoes in the summer when the vegetables are juicy and ripe! They're great with just about any main course.

        1 large ripe tomato
    1/8 teaspoon salt
Dash pepper
    1/4 cup crushed saltines
        1 tablespoon butter, melted
    1/4 teaspoon minced fresh basil *or* dash
        dried basil

Cut the tomato in half widthwise. Place cut side up in a shallow baking dish. Sprinkle with salt and pepper. Combine the cracker crumbs, butter and basil; sprinkle over tomatoes. Bake, uncovered, at 375° for 10-12 minutes or until crumbs are golden brown. **Yield:** 2 servings.

STRAWBERRY SHORTCAKE

(Pictured above right)

Janice Mitchell, Aurora, Colorado

When I was first married, my sister-in-law was a big help in sharing her recipes and cooking expertise. Many of her dishes remain our favorites, such as this yummy dessert for two.

1-1/2 cups sliced fresh strawberries
    1/3 cup sugar
BISCUITS:
    1 cup all-purpose flour
    7 teaspoons sugar, *divided*
    2 teaspoons baking powder
    1/4 teaspoon salt
    1/4 teaspoon cream of tartar
    1/8 teaspoon baking soda
    1/4 cup shortening
    1/3 cup buttermilk
    1/4 teaspoon vanilla extract
    1/2 cup heavy whipping cream

In a small bowl, mash the strawberries; stir in sugar. Cover and refrigerate until serving.

For biscuits, in a bowl, combine the flour, 4-1/2 teaspoons sugar, baking powder, salt, cream of tarter and baking soda. Cut in shortening until mixture resembles coarse crumbs. Stir in buttermilk and vanilla until moistened.

Turn dough onto a lightly floured surface; knead 8-10 times. Shape into two 4-in. circles. Place on an ungreased baking sheet. Bake at 450° for 12-14 minutes or until golden brown.

Split biscuits in half horizontally; spoon strawberry mixture over bottom halves. Replace tops. In a small mixing bowl, beat the cream until it begins to thicken. Add remaining sugar; beat until stiff peaks form. Dollop onto shortcakes. Serve immediately. **Yield:** 2 servings.

▰▰▰▰▰▰▰▰▰▰▰▰▰

TURKEY EGGS BENEDICT
(Pictured above)

Glenda Campbell, Kodak, Tennessee

An envelope of hollandaise sauce mix turns asparagus, deli turkey and English muffins into a special-occasion entree. The open-faced sandwiches easily impress.

  1/2 **envelope hollandaise sauce mix**
    2 **tablespoons butter**
  1/2 **cup water**
    1 **teaspoon white vinegar**
    2 **eggs**
    2 **slices deli turkey**
    1 **English muffin, split and toasted**
    4 **bacon strips, cooked**
    4 **asparagus spears, cooked and drained**

Prepare the hollandaise sauce with butter and water according to package directions.

Meanwhile, place 2-3 in. of water in a skillet, saucepan or omelet pan with high sides; add vinegar. Bring to a boil; reduce heat and simmer gently. Break cold eggs, one at a time, into a custard cup or saucer; holding the cup close to the surface of the water, slip each egg into water. Cook, uncovered, until whites are completely set and yolks begin to thicken (but are not hard), about 4 minutes.

Place a slice of turkey on each muffin half. With a slotted spoon, lift each egg out of the water; place over turkey. Top with bacon, asparagus and Hollandaise sauce. **Yield:** 2 servings.

Editor's Note: This recipe was tested with McCormick's Hollandaise Sauce Blend (1.25-ounce envelope).

Mozzarella Potato Skillet
(Pictured at left)

LaDonna Reed, Ponca City, Oklahoma

A few bacon strips lend a savory touch to my cheese-topped potatoes. After just one bite, you'll look for other menus to add the spuds to.

- 2 cups cubed cooked potatoes
- 2 teaspoons butter
- 1 cup (4 ounces) shredded part-skim mozzarella cheese
- 2 bacon strips, cooked and crumbled

In a skillet, cook potatoes in butter over medium heat for 6-8 minutes or until lightly browned. Sprinkle with cheese and bacon. Reduce heat; cover and cook for 2 minutes or until cheese is melted. **Yield:** 2 servings.

Pear Slushy
(Pictured at left)

Darlene Brenden, Salem, Oregon

Pears may not be a typical smoothie ingredient, but they sure lend a delightful flair to this beverage. The recipe is easy to double for guests, too.

✓ Uses less fat, sugar or salt. Includes Nutrition Facts.

- 1 cup chopped peeled ripe pear
- 1/4 cup orange juice
- 1/4 cup unsweetened pineapple juice
- 2 tablespoons honey
- 6 ice cubes

In a blender, combine all ingredients; cover and process until smooth. Pour into chilled glasses; serve immediately. **Yield:** 2 servings.

Nutrition Facts: 1 cup equals 144 calories, trace fat (trace saturated fat), 0 cholesterol, 2 mg sodium, 37 g carbohydrate, 2 g fiber, 1 g protein.

Sugar Cookie Tarts
(Pictured above left)

Barb White, Ligonier, Pennsylvania

Prepared sugar cookies get star treatment in this cute idea. I top them with cream cheese and then dress them up with sliced fruit and a simple citrus glaze.

- 5 tablespoons sugar, *divided*
- 1 teaspoon cornstarch
Dash salt
- 3 tablespoons water

- 2 tablespoons orange juice
- 1 tablespoon lemon juice
- 1 package (3 ounces) cream cheese, softened
- 4 large sugar cookies (3 inches)
- 1 cup sliced assorted fresh fruit (strawberries, kiwifruit *and/or* bananas)

For glaze, in a small saucepan, combine 3 tablespoons sugar, cornstarch and salt. Gradually stir in the water, orange juice and lemon juice. Bring to a boil over medium heat; cook and stir for 2 minutes or until thickened. Remove the mixture from the heat; cool.

In a small mixing bowl, beat cream cheese and remaining sugar until smooth. Spread over each cookie; arrange fruit on top. Drizzle with glaze. Refrigerate until chilled. **Yield:** 4 servings.

Mashed Potato-Topped Hot Dogs
(Pictured below)

Marcy Schewe, Danube, Minnesota

Instead of the hot dog-in-a-bun standby, I like to use up leftover mashed potatoes in this fun meal. The kid-friendly toppings can be adjusted to fit your taste.

- 4 hot dogs
- 1-1/3 cups mashed potatoes (prepared with milk and butter)
- 2 slices process American cheese, cut into quarters
Salsa and chopped green onions

Make a lengthwise cut three-fourths of the way through each hot dog. Open hot dogs and place cut side up on a baking sheet. Top with mashed potatoes and cheese. Bake at 350° for 5-10 minutes or until cheese is melted. Spread with salsa and sprinkle with onions. **Yield:** 2 servings.

Chicken Cheese Rolls
(Pictured above)

Leonora Wilkie, Bellbrook, Ohio

This entree is an elegant dinner for two, particularly on special occasions. The cheese filling is tasty and pairs well with the sweet-spicy chutney. It's an uncomplicated recipe that is impressive looking.

- 2 boneless skinless chicken breast halves (6 ounces *each*)
- 1/4 cup shredded cheddar cheese
- 2 tablespoons cream cheese, softened
- 1 tablespoon butter, melted
- 2 teaspoons chutney

Line a small baking pan with foil and grease the foil. Flatten chicken to 1/4-in. thickness. Combine the cheddar cheese and cream cheese; spread over chicken. Roll up and secure with toothpicks. Place in prepared pan.

Combine butter and chutney; brush over chicken. Bake, uncovered, at 350° for 25-30 minutes or until juices run clear. Discard toothpicks before serving. **Yield:** 2 servings.

Candied Sweet Potatoes
(Pictured above)

Ruby Williams, Bogalusa, Louisiana

This old-fashioned side dish is ideal for the holidays and just perfect for two. The touch of pineapple juice adds a nice flavor.

- 1 large sweet potato
- 1/4 cup packed brown sugar
- 2 tablespoons chopped pecans
- 1 tablespoon unsweetened pineapple *or* orange juice
- 1 teaspoon lemon juice
- 1/4 teaspoon ground cinnamon
- 1 tablespoon butter

Place sweet potato in a small saucepan; cover with water. Bring to a boil. Reduce heat; cover and simmer for 30-40 minutes or just until tender. Drain.

When cool enough to handle, peel and cut into 1/4-in. slices. Place in a greased shallow 2-cup baking dish.

In a small bowl, combine the brown sugar, pecans, pineapple juice, lemon juice and cinnamon; sprinkle over potato slices. Dot with butter.

Bake, uncovered, at 350° for 15 minutes or until bubbly and heated through. **Yield:** 2 servings.

CARROT 'N' BROCCOLI BAKE
(Pictured at left)

Debbie Raeubig, West St. Paul, Minnesota

This recipe was originally from my aunt, who gave it to my mother, who then gave it to me. For an extra bit of taste, I add onions. It's a delicious accompaniment to any meal.

- 2 small carrots, cut into 1/2-inch pieces
- 1 package (16 ounces) frozen chopped broccoli, thawed
- 1 small onion, chopped
- 2 ounces process cheese (Velveeta), cubed
- 1/4 teaspoon salt
- 1/8 teaspoon pepper
- 1/2 cup crushed butter-flavored crackers (about 12 crackers)
- 2 tablespoons butter, melted

Place carrots in a small saucepan; cover with water. Bring to a boil. Reduce heat; cover and simmer for 3-4 minutes or until crisp-tender. Drain.

In an ungreased 1-qt. baking dish, layer the broccoli, carrots, onion and cheese. Sprinkle with salt and pepper. Toss the cracker crumbs and butter; sprinkle over the top. Bake, uncovered, at 350° for 25-30 minutes or until bubbly and golden brown. **Yield:** 2-3 servings.

BUTTERSCOTCH DATE COOKIES
(Pictured above left)

Ellen Ball, Ilion, New York

Butterscotch has always been my favorite flavor, so when I found this recipe, I knew it would be a winner. The warm golden tones and crispy crust make it a very fine cookie for autumn.

✓ Uses less fat, sugar or salt. Includes Nutrition Facts.

- 1/2 cup shortening
- 1 cup packed brown sugar
- 1 egg
- 1/2 teaspoon vanilla extract
- 1/2 cup sour cream
- 2 cups all-purpose flour
- 1/2 teaspoon baking powder
- 1/2 teaspoon baking soda
- 1 cup butterscotch chips
- 1 cup chopped dates

In a large mixing bowl, cream shortening and sugar until light and fluffy. Beat in egg and vanilla. Add sour cream; beat just until combined. Combine the flour, baking powder and baking soda; gradually add to creamed mixture and mix well. Stir in butterscotch chips and dates.

Drop by tablespoonfuls 2 in. apart onto greased baking sheets. Bake at 425° for 8-12 minutes or until lightly browned and set. Remove to wire racks. **Yield:** 2 dozen.

Nutrition Facts: 1 cookie equals 197 calories, 8 g fat (4 g saturated fat), 13 mg cholesterol, 51 mg sodium, 29 g carbohydrate, 1 g fiber, 2 g protein.

RASPBERRY DESSERT SAUCE
(Pictured below)

Florence Wiggin, Stratham, New Hampshire

I like to serve this berry-citrus sauce over scoops of vanilla ice cream, but you could try it over angel food cake or even pound cake for dessert in a snap.

- 2/3 cup fresh or frozen raspberries, thawed
- 2 tablespoons sugar
- 1/2 teaspoon orange extract

Vanilla ice cream

In a blender, combine the raspberries, sugar and extract; cover and process on high until smooth. Strain and discard seeds. Serve raspberry sauce over ice cream. **Yield:** 2/3 cup.

CHOCOLATE BROWNIE COOKIES

(Pictured below)

Ruth Cain, Hartselle, Alabama

If you have a taste for cookies, but don't want to make dozens of them, try this chocolaty treat. It's the perfect goodie for two-person households.

☑ Uses less fat, sugar or salt. Includes Nutrition Facts.

- 1/2 **cup sugar**
- 1 **egg**
- 2 **tablespoons vegetable oil**
- 1 **square (1 ounce) unsweetened chocolate, melted and cooled**
- 1/2 **teaspoon vanilla extract**
- 1/2 **cup all-purpose flour**
- 1/2 **teaspoon baking powder**
- 1/8 **teaspoon salt**

Confectioners' sugar

In a mixing bowl, beat the sugar, egg, oil, chocolate and vanilla. Combine the flour, baking powder and salt; gradually add to creamed mixture. Chill for at least 2 hours.

Shape dough into 1-in. balls; roll in confectioners' sugar. Place 2 in. apart on lightly greased baking sheets. Bake at 350° for 10-12 minutes or until set. Remove to wire racks. **Yield:** about 1 dozen.

Nutrition Facts: 3 cookies equals 195 calories, 8 g fat (2 g saturated fat), 35 mg cholesterol, 94 mg sodium, 30 g carbohydrate, 1 g fiber, 3 g protein.

FRESH VEGETABLE PASTA SALAD

(Pictured above)

Mildred Sherrer, Fort Worth, Texas

This colorful pasta salad is a family favorite and one I make often because I love fresh vegetables. It's a meal in itself or a side dish compatible with any cut of meat. It's also a welcomed contribution to potluck suppers.

- 1/2 **cup uncooked small pasta shells**
- 1/4 **cup fresh cauliflowerets**
- 1/4 **cup fresh broccoli florets**
- 1/4 **cup thinly sliced fresh carrots**
- 1/4 **cup chopped sweet yellow pepper**
- 1/4 **cup chopped seeded tomatoes**
- 1/4 **cup creamy Italian salad dressing**

Leaf lettuce, optional

Cook pasta according to package directions. Meanwhile, in a small saucepan, cook the cauliflower, broccoli, carrots and yellow pepper in boiling water for 2 minutes. Rinse in cold water and drain well; place in a bowl. Drain pasta and rinse in cold water; add to vegetables. Cover and refrigerate for at least 30 minutes.

Stir in tomatoes. Add dressing and toss to coat. Serve on lettuce-lined plates if desired. **Yield:** 2 servings.

CHICKEN WRAPPED IN BACON

LaDonna Reed, Ponca City, Oklahoma

You'll only need six ingredients to whip up this classic main course. Stuffed with cheese, topped with green chilies and wrapped in bacon, these chicken breasts will quickly become a family favorite.

- 6 **bacon strips**
- 2 **boneless skinless chicken breast halves (5 ounces *each*)**
- 1 **package (3 ounces) cream cheese, softened**

2 garlic cloves, minced
1/2 teaspoon salt
1 can (4 ounces) chopped green chilies,
  drained

In a large skillet, cook bacon over medium heat until cooked but not crisp. Remove to paper towels to drain. Flatten chicken to 1/8-in. thickness. Spread with cream cheese; sprinkle with garlic and salt. Top with chilies. Roll up from a long side; tuck ends in.

Wrap three bacon strips around each piece of chicken; secure with toothpicks. Place in a greased 1-qt. baking dish. Bake, uncovered, at 350° for 35-40 minutes or until chicken juices run clear and bacon is crisp. Discard toothpicks before serving. **Yield:** 2 servings.

Broccoli Walnut Salad
(Pictured below)

Chriselda Tucker, Portland, Oregon

A handful of items is all that's required for this change-of-pace salad. The crunchy florets and nuts are a nice complement to the raisins and tangy dressing.

    2 cups fresh broccoli florets
    2 tablespoons chopped walnuts
    2 tablespoons raisins
    2 tablespoons mayonnaise
    2 teaspoons lemon juice

In a small bowl, combine the broccoli, walnuts and raisins. Combine the mayonnaise and lemon juice; add to broccoli mixture and toss to coat. Cover and refrigerate for 1 hour. **Yield:** 2 servings.

Marinated Carrots
(Pictured above)

Shannon Emmanuel, Charlotte, North Carolina

Here's a unique way to serve carrots that's sure to be a success at your dinner table. My chilled salad is a delicious alternative to the many pasta and mixed-vegetable varieties.

    1/2 pound fresh baby carrots
    1/4 cup chopped onion
    1/4 cup chopped green pepper
    1/2 cup tomato sauce
      2 tablespoons sugar
      2 tablespoons cider vinegar
      1 tablespoon vegetable oil
    1/2 teaspoon Worcestershire sauce
    1/4 teaspoon salt
    1/4 teaspoon pepper

Place 1 in. of water in a small saucepan; add carrots. Bring to a boil. Reduce heat; cover and simmer for 8-10 minutes or until crisp-tender. Drain.

In a small bowl, combine the carrots, onion and green pepper. In another bowl, combine the tomato sauce, sugar, vinegar, oil, Worcestershire sauce, salt and pepper. Pour over carrot mixture and stir to coat. Cover and refrigerate for several hours or overnight. Serve with a slotted spoon. **Yield:** 2 servings.

Get Creative with Carrots
Clean out the refrigerator with Marinated Carrots. Add leftover mushrooms, corn, peas or red pepper to the dish along with the carrots.

Meals in Minutes

These recipes make mealtime a breeze since most of them call for only a moment's worth of prep work.

Simply Elegant Sensations

NO ONE will believe how easily this menu came together. Starring pork chops from Joyce Brotzman of McVeytown, Pennsylvania and dessert from Tucker, Georgia's Theresa Mathis, it's a great spring meal. Round the supper with an unbelievable pilaf from Gene Brofka of Austin, Texas and a no-fuss salad dressing Sharon McClatchey serves in her Muskogee, Oklahoma home.

PENNSYLVANIA DUTCH PORK CHOPS

✓ Uses less fat, sugar or salt. Includes Nutrition Facts.

    6 bone-in pork loin chops (3/4 inch thick
      and 8 ounces *each*)
    2 tablespoons butter
  1/2 cup unsweetened pineapple juice
  1/2 cup ketchup
    2 tablespoons white vinegar
    2 tablespoons honey
1-1/2 teaspoons ground mustard
  1/4 teaspoon salt
    4 teaspoons cornstarch
    2 tablespoons water

In a large skillet, brown pork chops in butter. Using a slotted spoon, transfer to an ungreased 13-in. x 9-in. x 2-in. baking dish.

Combine the pineapple juice, ketchup, vinegar, honey, mustard and salt; add to drippings. Cook and stir until mixture comes to a boil. Pour over chops.

Cover and bake at 350° for 45 minutes. Uncover; bake 15 minutes longer or until a meat thermometer reads 160°. Remove the chops and keep warm.

In a small saucepan, combine cornstarch and water; stir in pan juices. Bring to a boil; cook

and stir for 1-2 minutes or until thickened. Serve with pork chops. **Yield:** 6 servings.

Nutrition Facts: 1 pork chop equals 151 calories, 7 g fat (4 g saturated fat), 29 mg cholesterol, 387 mg sodium, 16 g carbohydrate, trace fiber, 7 g protein.

MUSHROOM PILAF

    1 cup chopped onion
    1 cup uncooked long grain rice
  1/2 cup uncooked thin spaghetti, broken
      into 1-inch pieces
  1/4 cup butter
    1 can (14-1/2 ounces) chicken broth
    1 jar (6 ounces) sliced mushrooms,
      drained
  1/2 cup water
  1/4 teaspoon salt
  1/4 cup minced fresh parsley

In a large saucepan, saute the onion, rice and spaghetti in butter until onion is tender and spaghetti is golden brown.

Stir in the broth, mushrooms, water and salt. Bring to a boil. Reduce heat; cover and simmer for 20 minutes or until rice is tender. Remove from the heat; let stand for 10 minutes. Fluff with a fork; stir in parsley. **Yield:** 6-8 servings.

STRAWBERRY ANGEL DESSERT

1-1/2 cups sugar
    5 tablespoons cornstarch
    1 package (3 ounces) strawberry gelatin
    2 cups water
    2 pounds fresh strawberries, hulled,
      divided
    1 package (8 ounces) cream cheese,
      softened
    1 can (14 ounces) sweetened condensed
      milk
    1 carton (12 ounces) frozen whipped
      topping, thawed

1 prepared angel food cake (16 ounces),
　cut into 1-inch cubes

For glaze, in a large saucepan, combine the sugar,
cornstarch and gelatin. Add water and stir until
smooth. Cook and stir over medium-high heat
until mixture begins to boil. Cook and stir 1-2
minutes longer or until thickened. Remove from
the heat; cool completely. Cut half of the strawberries into quarters; fold into glaze.

In a small mixing bowl, beat cream cheese
until smooth. Beat in milk until blended. Fold
in whipped topping.

In a 4-qt. clear glass bowl, layer half of the cake
cubes, glaze and cream mixture. Repeat layers.
Cut remaining strawberries in half and arrange
over the top. Cover and refrigerate for at least 2
hours or overnight. **Yield:** 12-16 servings.

CHUNKY BLUE CHEESE DRESSING

　1 cup mayonnaise
　1/2 cup sour cream
1-1/2 teaspoons minced chives
　1/2 teaspoon garlic powder
　1/2 teaspoon pepper
　1/4 teaspoon Worcestershire sauce
　1/4 to 1/2 cup buttermilk
　1/2 cup crumbled blue cheese
Torn mixed salad greens

In a small mixing bowl, combine the first six ingredients. Stir in enough buttermilk to achieve
desired consistency. Stir in blue cheese. Cover and
store in the refrigerator. Serve with salad greens.
Yield: 2 cups.

Chowder Makes A Lunch-Time Lifesaver

HEARTY, flavorful bowls of soup make for a wonderful meal when time is tight. Consider this afternoon menu the next time you are trying to beat the clock.

Start the meal with a heartwarming serving of Oyster Corn Chowder. Ready in a snap, this rich-tasting specialty is shared by Lewy Olfson from Madison, Wisconsin. Chock-full of mushrooms, corn and oysters, the robust dish comes together easily with a can of cream-style corn and a little half-and-half cream.

Few things complement a bowl of steaming soup like a home-baked treat and Mini Focaccia is certainly no exception. "The trendy bread originated in Italy," explains Janice Bassing of Racine, Wisconsin. "Peasant cooks dimpled the dough with their fingers and topped it with whatever ingredients they had on hand." Featuring a tube of refrigerated biscuits, the savory, no-fuss rounds are just as good with salad or pasta as they are with soups, stews and chowders.

Sliced pound cake is an ideal dessert when the clock is ticking, particularly when it's dressed up with fruit and other simple fixings. "When I have leftover pound cake, I make my Peach Bliss Dessert," shares Parker, Colorado's Gail Van-Gundy. "The recipe came from a cookbook from the '60s, but it's a staple in my house. It's so quick and easy."

OYSTER CORN CHOWDER

2 cans (8 ounces *each*) whole oysters, undrained
1 can (14-3/4 ounces) cream-style corn
1 cup half-and-half cream
2 cans (4 ounces *each*) mushroom stems and pieces, drained
2 tablespoons butter
1/4 teaspoon Worcestershire sauce
1/8 teaspoon pepper

In a large saucepan, combine all ingredients. Cook, uncovered, over medium-low heat until heated through (do not boil), stirring occasionally. **Yield:** 4 servings.

MINI FOCACCIA

✓ Uses less fat, sugar or salt. Includes Nutrition Facts.

1 tube (11 ounces) refrigerated breadsticks
2 teaspoons olive oil
1 teaspoon Italian seasoning
2 tablespoons grated Parmesan cheese

Remove dough from tube; do not unroll breadsticks. Cut dough into eight slices. Press into 4-1/2-in. circles on greased baking sheets. Brush with oil; sprinkle with Italian seasoning and Parmesan cheese.

Bake at 375° for 10-15 minutes or until golden brown. **Yield:** 8 focaccia.

Nutrition Facts: 1 focaccia equals 126 calories, 4 g fat (trace saturated fat), 1 mg cholesterol, 313 mg sodium, 19 g carbohydrate, 1 g fiber, 4 g protein.

PEACH BLISS DESSERT

✓ Uses less fat, sugar or salt. Includes Nutrition Facts.

1 can (15-1/4 ounces) sliced peaches
1 tablespoon cornstarch
1/8 teaspoon ground cinnamon
1-1/2 teaspoons lemon juice
1/4 teaspoon almond extract
4 slices pound cake

Drain peaches, reserving juice; set peaches aside. Add enough water to juice to measure 1 cup.

In a small saucepan, combine cornstarch and cinnamon. Stir in lemon juice and peach juice mixture until smooth. Bring to a boil; cook and stir for 1-2 minutes or until thickened.

Remove from the heat. Stir in almond extract and reserved peaches. Serve warm over pound cake. **Yield:** 4 servings.

Nutrition Facts: 1 serving equals 211 calories, 6 g fat (3 g saturated fat), 66 mg cholesterol, 128 mg sodium, 37 g carbohydrate, 1 g fiber, 2 g protein.

ADD A PERSONAL TOUCH

Feel free to get creative when preparing Oyster Corn Chowder. Cooked and cubed ham or crumbed bacon make great additions to the recipe. Stir in a handful of frozen peas or consider adding some chopped onion. Mix in last night's potatoes or green beans as well.

Speedy Supper's Full of Surprises

THE BEST secrets are recipes, according to Deborah Elliot. "Everyone has to eat every day, so family cooks should all share their recipes with each other," writes the busy housewife from Ridge Spring, South Carolina.

"Someday, I hope to put together a cookbook based on all of the terrific recipes I've gotten from family and friends over the years," she says.

A chapter in that book will likely be devoted to time-saving specialties and fast fare. Even though her three children are grown and out on their own, Deborah continues to whip up dinners at a lively pace.

"I depend on meals that can be prepared in a flash so I can spend as much time outdoors as possible," she explains. "Gardening is a hobby of mine that I look forward to every year. I always plant many vegetables that I can cook with."

Perhaps that's why Stir-Fried Zucchini is so popular at her house—and in her neighborhood. "I'm happy to give extra zucchini to neighbors, and I often share this tasty way to prepare it as well," she adds. Italian seasoning, garlic and olive oil give this snappy side dish its zesty zip.

"A dear friend gave me the recipe for Chili Beef Noodle Skillet," Deborah writes. "My husband likes its hearty blend of beef, onions and tomatoes. I like it because it comes together easily on the stovetop which means that I can get the main course to the table quickly."

To cap off the meal, Deborah prepares Creamy Lemonade Cups. "Our daughters took my mother's recipe for a wonderful lemon pie and adapted it to serve in individual dessert dishes," she shares. "It's been a staple in our house ever since then." The creamy citrus taste of this easy-to-assemble treat is the perfect conclusion to any supper.

STIR-FRIED ZUCCHINI

✓ Uses less fat, sugar or salt. Includes Nutrition Facts.

- 2 pounds sliced zucchini
- 2 garlic cloves, minced
- 1/4 cup olive oil
- 1 teaspoon salt
- 1/2 teaspoon Italian seasoning
- 1/4 teaspoon pepper

In a large skillet, saute the zucchini and garlic in oil until zucchini is crisp-tender, about 5 minutes. Sprinkle with seasonings. Serve immediately. **Yield:** 8 servings.

Nutrition Facts: 1/2 cup equals 77 calories, 7 g fat (1 g saturated fat), 0 cholesterol, 299 mg sodium, 4 g carbohydrate, 1 g fiber, 1 g protein.

CHILI BEEF NOODLE SKILLET

- 1 package (8 ounces) egg noodles
- 2 pounds ground beef
- 1 medium onion, chopped
- 1/4 cup chopped celery
- 2 garlic cloves, minced
- 1 can (28 ounces) diced tomatoes, undrained
- 1 tablespoon chili powder
- 1/4 to 1/2 teaspoon salt
- 1/8 teaspoon pepper
- 1/2 to 1 cup shredded cheddar cheese

Cook noodles according to package directions. Meanwhile, in a large skillet, cook the beef, onion, celery and garlic over medium heat until meat is no longer pink and vegetables are tender; drain. Add the tomatoes, chili powder, salt and pepper. Cook and stir for 2 minutes or until heated through.

Drain noodles; stir into beef mixture and heat through. Remove from the heat.

Sprinkle with the cheese; cover and let dish stand for 5 minutes or until cheese is melted. **Yield:** 8 servings.

CREAMY LEMONADE CUPS

- 1-1/4 cups graham cracker crumbs (about 20 squares)
- 1/4 cup butter, melted
- 2 tablespoons sugar
- 1/2 cup finely chopped nuts
- 1 can (14 ounces) sweetened condensed milk
- 3/4 cup lemonade concentrate
- 1 carton (8 ounces) frozen whipped topping, thawed

In a large bowl, combine the crumbs, butter and sugar. Stir in the nuts. Set aside 1/4 cup for topping; press the remaining mixture onto the bottom of eight dessert dishes.

In another bowl, combine milk and lemonade concentrate; fold in the whipped topping. Spoon into prepared dishes. Sprinkle with reserved crumbs. Chill until serving. **Yield:** 8 servings.

Savory Dinner Is Big on Taste

EVEN THOUGH Patricia and Keith Fredericks live in Oak Creek—a city located in southeastern Wisconsin—you'll likely find them at their log cabin in the northern part of the state.

"That's where we spend weekends," notes Patricia. "Our children are grown and on their own, but they often join us at the cabin," she says. "When we eat together, I depend on recipes that need little preparation. This menu is a favorite.

"Italian Beef Sandwiches are ready in a snap," she adds. "I simply pick up sliced roast beef and sandwich buns at the deli." Served with an au jus created from a can of beef broth, the pepper-topped sandwiches make a savory dinner.

For a swift side dish, Patricia bakes a pan of tender Seasoned Oven Fries. "These potato wedges are as tasty as the deep-fried versions but with less mess," she reports.

Rounding out the meal are Breaded Tomato Slices. Garden-fresh tomatoes are sliced, breaded and browned for a flavorful change of pace. "The mozzarella cheese perfectly complements the simple, tasty coating," she notes.

Patricia says cleanup for this in-a-dash dinner is quick, too. "Keith and I make a good team in the kitchen—I do all of the cooking and he does all of the dishes!"

Italian Beef Sandwiches

1 can (14-1/2 ounces) beef broth
2 garlic cloves, minced
1 teaspoon dried oregano
1/8 teaspoon pepper
1 medium green pepper, thinly sliced into rings
1 pound thinly sliced deli roast beef
6 hoagie buns, split

In a large skillet, add the broth, garlic, oregano and pepper; bring to a boil. Add green pepper. Reduce heat; simmer, uncovered, about 5 minutes or until green pepper is tender. Remove green pepper with a slotted spoon; keep warm.

Return broth to a boil. Add roast beef; cover and remove from the heat. Let stand for 2 minutes or until heated through. Place beef and green pepper on buns; serve with broth for dipping. **Yield:** 6 servings.

Seasoned Oven Fries

6 medium baking potatoes
2 tablespoons butter, melted
2 tablespoons vegetable oil
1 teaspoon seasoned salt

Cut each potato lengthwise into thirds; cut each portion into thirds.

In a large resealable plastic bag, combine the butter, oil and seasoned salt. Add potatoes; shake to coat.

Place the potato wedges in a single layer on a greased baking sheet. Bake, uncovered, at 450° for 20-25 minutes or until tender, turning once. **Yield:** 6 servings.

Breaded Tomato Slices

✓ Uses less fat, sugar or salt. Includes Nutrition Facts.

1/2 cup seasoned bread crumbs
1 tablespoon finely chopped green onion
1 tablespoon grated Parmesan cheese
1 teaspoon salt
1 teaspoon Italian seasoning
1/4 cup milk
4 medium tomatoes, cut into 1/2-inch slices
2 tablespoons olive oil
1/3 to 1/2 cup shredded part-skim mozzarella cheese

In a shallow bowl, combine the bread crumbs, onion, Parmesan cheese, salt and Italian seasoning; mix well. Place the milk in another bowl. Dip the tomato slices in milk, then coat with the crumb mixture.

In a large skillet, heat oil. Fry tomato slices for 2 minutes on each side or until golden brown. Sprinkle with mozzarella cheese. **Yield:** 6 servings.

Nutrition Facts: 1 serving equals 126 calories, 7 g fat (2 g saturated fat), 7 mg cholesterol, 590 mg sodium, 12 g carbohydrate, 2 g fiber, 4 g protein.

Appealing Additions

Since this dinner offers lots of flavor, serve the meal with basic items such as milk or possibly iced tea. For dessert, consider something as simple such as vanilla pudding, sugar cookies or cups of butter pecan ice cream.

Our Most Memorable Meals

*All-time family favorites still bring
folks together for dinner memories.*

Flavorful Menu's Full of Fun

APPLESAUCE MEATBALLS

Betsy Smith, San Diego, California

These savory, from-scratch meatballs are always well-received. Folks really like the tangy sauce that uses hot pepper sauce to give the meatballs a little kick.

   1 egg, beaten
1/2 cup unsweetened applesauce
   1 cup soft bread crumbs
   1 teaspoon salt
1/4 teaspoon pepper
   1 pound ground beef
SAUCE:
   1 can (10-3/4 ounces) condensed tomato
     soup, undiluted
1/4 cup water
1/2 teaspoon sugar
1/2 teaspoon prepared horseradish
   3 to 5 drops Worcestershire sauce
   3 to 5 drops hot pepper sauce

In a large bowl, combine the first five ingredients. Crumble beef over mixture and mix well. Shape into 1-1/2-in. balls. In a large skillet, gently brown meatballs over medium heat; drain. Transfer to an ungreased 2-qt. baking dish.

Combine sauce ingredients; pour over meatballs. Cover and bake at 325° for 45-50 minutes or until meat is no longer pink. **Yield:** 4 servings.

STUFFED ICEBERG WEDGES

Rosemarie Surwillo, Lake St. Louis, Missouri

These eye-appealing servings are sure to break up the same-old-salad doldrums you may be facing. Filled with ham, cheese and more, wedges make great lunch entrees.

   1 medium head iceberg lettuce
1/3 cup mayonnaise
1/4 teaspoon curry powder
   1 cup (4 ounces) shredded cheddar
     cheese
1/2 cup coarsely chopped fully cooked ham
1/2 cup chopped celery
1/4 cup minced fresh parsley
   1 jar (2 ounces) diced pimientos, drained
Salad dressing of your choice

Remove core from the head of lettuce. Carefully hollow out lettuce, leaving a 3/4-in. shell (save removed lettuce for another use).

In a small bowl, combine the mayonnaise and curry powder. Add the cheese, ham, celery, parsley and pimientos; mix well. Spoon into lettuce shell. Tightly wrap in plastic wrap; refrigerate for at least 3 hours. Cut into wedges. Serve with salad dressing. **Yield:** 4-6 servings.

GRANDMA'S EGG NOODLES

Mary Stout, Topeka, Indiana

It's hard to beat the down-home comfort of from-scratch egg noodles. This recipe captures that magic for me every time I prepare it.

   2 cups all-purpose flour
1/2 teaspoon salt
   2 egg yolks
   1 egg
1/3 cup water
   1 tablespoon olive oil
   6 cups chicken broth

In a small bowl, combine the flour and salt. Make a well in the center. In another bowl, beat the egg yolks, egg, water and oil; pour into well. Stir to form a stiff dough.

Turn dough onto a well-floured surface; knead 8-10 times. Divide into thirds. Roll each portion to 1/8-in. thickness. Cut noodles into 1/4-in. strips; cut the strips into 2-in. lengths. Cook immediately in boiling broth for 5-7 minutes or until tender; drain. **Yield:** 5 servings.

WALNUT CHERRY CAKE

Carol Wessels, Harbor Beach, Maryland

Here's my version of a country classic. A homemade cherry cake is updated with a finger-licking topping.

- 2 cups sugar
- 2 tablespoons butter, softened
- 2 eggs
- 1 teaspoon salt
- 2 cups all-purpose flour
- 2 teaspoons baking soda
- 2 cans (14-1/2 ounces *each*) pitted tart cherries
- 1 cup chopped walnuts

TOPPING:
- 2 cups heavy whipping cream
- 1/4 cup confectioners' sugar
- 1/2 cup sugar
- 2-1/2 teaspoons cornstarch
- 1/8 teaspoon red food coloring, optional

In a large mixing bowl, beat sugar and butter until crumbly; stir in the eggs and salt. Combine flour and baking soda; stir into sugar mixture until combined.

Drain cherries, reserving 1/2 cup juice; set juice aside. Gently stir the cherries and walnuts into the sugar mixture.

Pour into a greased 13-in. x 9-in. x 2-in. baking dish. Bake at 350° for 40-45 minutes or until a toothpick inserted near the center comes out clean. Cool completely on a wire rack.

For topping, in a small mixing bowl, beat cream and confectioners' sugar until soft peaks form. Spread over cake; refrigerate for 2 hours.

In a small saucepan, combine sugar and cornstarch. Stir in reserved cherry juice until smooth. Stir in food coloring if desired.

Bring to a boil over medium heat; cook and stir for 2 minutes or until thickened. Cool. Just before serving, drizzle over whipped cream. Refrigerate leftovers. **Yield:** 12-15 servings.

Hearty Spring Supper's a Breeze

▰▰▰▰▰▰▰▰▰▰▰

PINEAPPLE STEAKS

Rita Sholtz, Tonawanda, New York

It's a snap to dress up ham steaks with just a handful of kitchen staples. You won't believe how easily and quickly this entree comes together before it's time to simply pop it in the oven.

✓ Uses less fat, sugar or salt. Includes Nutrition Facts.

> 1 can (8 ounces) unsweetened crushed pineapple
> 1 tablespoon whole cloves
> 2 bone-in fully cooked ham steaks (1/2 inch thick and 1 pound *each*)
> 1/4 cup packed brown sugar
> 1/2 teaspoon ground mustard

Drain pineapple, reserving juice. Insert cloves into edges of ham steaks. Place one ham steak in a greased shallow baking pan. Spread pineapple over ham; top with the second ham steak. Pour reserved pineapple juice over ham. Combine brown sugar and mustard; sprinkle over the top.

Bake, uncovered, at 350° for 45 minutes or until heated through, basting occasionally with pan juices. Discard cloves before serving. **Yield:** 6-8 servings.

Nutrition Facts: 3 ounces equals 155 calories, 7 g fat (3 g saturated fat), 30 mg cholesterol, 765 mg sodium, 11 g carbohydrate, trace fiber, 11 g protein.

▰▰▰▰▰▰▰▰▰▰▰

CRUMB-TOPPED ASPARAGUS

Nancy Brown, Janesville, Wisconsin

Here's a lovely vegetable side that requires only a handful of ingredients. The bright colors make it perfect for spring get-togethers.

> 2 pounds fresh asparagus spears, trimmed
> 2 tablespoons butter
> 2 teaspoons lemon juice
> Dash pepper
> 1/4 cup seasoned bread crumbs
> 1 hard-cooked egg, chopped

Place the asparagus in a large skillet; cover with water. Bring to a boil. Reduce heat; cover and simmer for 2-3 minutes or until crisp-tender.

Meanwhile, in a small saucepan, melt butter. Add lemon juice and pepper. Stir in bread crumbs; cook and stir until crumbs are lightly browned. Drain asparagus; arrange on a serving platter. Sprinkle with crumb mixture and egg. Serve immediately. **Yield:** 6-8 servings.

▰▰▰▰▰▰▰▰▰▰▰

CHEESE-STUFFED DOUBLE BAKERS

LeeAnn Johnson, Joliet, Illinois

Two types of cheese, sour cream and a little garlic powder make these twice-baked potatoes a success in my house. After one bite, you'll want to make them time and again.

> 4 large baking potatoes
> 1/2 cup sour cream
> 2 tablespoons butter
> 3/4 teaspoon salt
> 1/8 teaspoon *each* garlic powder, onion powder and pepper
> 1 cup (4 ounces) shredded cheddar cheese, *divided*
> 1 cup (4 ounces) shredded part-skim mozzarella cheese, *divided*
> 1/4 cup chopped green onions

Scrub and pierce potatoes. Bake at 375° for 1 hour or until tender. When cool enough to handle, cut each potato in half lengthwise; scoop out pulp, leaving a thin shell.

In a large mixing bowl, beat the pulp with sour cream, butter, salt and seasonings. Stir in 3/4 cup each cheddar and mozzarella. Spoon or pipe into potato shells. Sprinkle with remaining cheeses.

Place on a baking sheet. Bake at 375° for 15-20 minutes or until heated through. Top with green onions. **Yield:** 8 servings.

▰▰▰▰▰▰▰▰▰▰▰

BLUEBERRY SOUR CREAM TORTE

Corinne Jagocki, Palm Coast, Florida

For a pleasant taste of summer, consider my berry specialty. Cinnamon and nutmeg lend a hint of spice to the berry filling, but lemon peel offers a refreshing bit of citrus.

> 3/4 cup butter, softened
> 1/4 cup sugar
> 2 egg yolks
> 2 cups all-purpose flour

1 teaspoon baking powder
1/2 teaspoon salt
FILLING:
4 cups fresh *or* frozen blueberries
1 cup sugar, *divided*
1/4 cup quick-cooking tapioca
1/2 teaspoon ground cinnamon
1/2 teaspoon grated lemon peel
1/8 teaspoon ground nutmeg
2 egg yolks
2 cups (16 ounces) sour cream
1 teaspoon vanilla extract

In a mixing bowl, cream butter and sugar. Add egg yolks; mix well. Combine the flour, baking powder and salt; add to the creamed mixture. Press onto the bottom and 1 in. up the sides of a greased 9-in. springform pan. Place pan on a baking sheet.

Bake at 400° for 10-12 minutes or until lightly browned. Cool on a wire rack.

In a large saucepan, gently toss the blueberries, 1/2 cup sugar, tapioca, cinnamon, lemon peel and nutmeg. Let stand for 15 minutes. Cook, uncovered, over medium heat until mixture comes to a boil. Cook and stir for 2 minutes. Remove from the heat; pour into crust.

In a mixing bowl, beat the egg yolks, sour cream, vanilla and remaining sugar. Spoon over blueberry mixture. Return pan to baking sheet. Bake at 350° for 35-40 minutes or until center is set. Cool on a wire rack for 10 minutes. Carefully run a knife around edge of pan to loosen; cool 1 hour longer. Refrigerate for at least 4 hours before serving. Remove sides of pan. Refrigerate leftovers. **Yield:** 10-12 servings.

▞▞▞▞▞▞▞▞▞▞▞▞

SEASONED TURKEY SANDWICHES

LaVonne Hegland, St. Michael, Minnesota

This delicious, savory turkey tucked in homemade buns will steal the show at any potluck or family reunion. It's been a huge hit at football dinners, graduation parties and other get-togethers.

HOMEMADE SANDWICH BUNS:
- 2 packages (1/4 ounce *each*) active dry yeast
- 2 cups warm water (110° to 115°), *divided*
- 1/2 cup sugar
- 1 egg
- 3 tablespoons shortening
- 1 teaspoon salt
- 6-1/2 to 7 cups all-purpose flour
- 3 tablespoons butter, softened

GRILLED TURKEY:
- 2 teaspoons salt
- 2 teaspoons garlic powder
- 2 teaspoons pepper
- 1 turkey (14 to 16 pounds)
- 1/2 cup butter, cubed

In a large mixing bowl, dissolve yeast in 1/2 cup warm water. Add sugar, egg, shortening, salt, remaining water and 2 cups flour; beat until smooth. Stir in enough remaining flour to form a soft dough (dough will be sticky).

Turn onto a floured surface; knead until smooth and elastic, about 6-8 minutes. Place in a greased bowl, turning once to grease top. Cover and let rise in a warm place until doubled, about 1 hour.

Punch dough down. Turn onto a lightly floured surface; divide in half. Divide each portion into 12 pieces. Shape each into a ball. Place 3 in. apart on greased baking sheets. Brush with butter. Cover and let rise until doubled, about 30 minutes.

Bake at 400° for 8-10 minutes or until golden brown. Remove to wire racks to cool.

Meanwhile, combine the salt, garlic powder and pepper; rub over turkey. Place butter inside turkey cavity; tie drumsticks together. Prepare grill for indirect medium heat. Tuck wings under turkey and place with breast side up in a disposable roasting pan; place on grill rack.

Grill, covered, for 1 hour. If using a charcoal grill, add 10 briquettes to coals. Baste with pan drippings. Cover and grill 1-1/2 to 2 hours longer

or until a meat thermometer reads 180°, adding 10 briquettes to maintain heat and brushing with pan drippings every 30 minutes. (Cover loosely with foil if turkey browns too quickly.)

Cover and let stand for 20 minutes before carving. Split buns in half; fill with sliced turkey. **Yield:** 24 sandwiches.

▞▞▞▞▞▞▞▞▞▞▞▞

TANGY WATERMELON SALAD

Alisha Duncan, Blanchard, Oklahoma

I rely on this refreshing blend of watermelon, onion and a hint of orange to do me proud at summer picnics and potlucks. I prepare it a day ahead so the flavors have a chance to blend and marinate. Use a bottle of citrus vinaigrette to cut preparation time.

- 14 cups cubed seedless watermelon
- 1 medium red onion, halved and thinly sliced
- 1 cup chopped green onions
- 3/4 cup orange juice
- 5 tablespoons red wine vinegar
- 2 tablespoons plus 1-1/2 teaspoons honey
- 1 tablespoon finely chopped sweet red pepper
- 1/2 teaspoon salt
- 1/4 teaspoon onion powder
- 1/4 teaspoon garlic powder
- 1/4 teaspoon ground mustard
- 1/4 teaspoon pepper
- 3/4 cup vegetable oil

In a large bowl, combine the watermelon and onions. In a small bowl, combine the orange juice, vinegar, honey, red pepper and seasonings; slowly whisk in the oil.

Pour over watermelon mixture; toss gently to coat. Cover and refrigerate for at least 2 hours, stirring occasionally. Serve with a slotted spoon. **Yield:** 16 servings.

▞▞▞▞▞▞▞▞▞▞▞▞

SWEET PEPPER PESTO PASTA

Karen Hentges, Bakersfield, California

What's a family gathering or summer supper without at least one pasta salad? This covered-dish mainstay can be served hot or cold. It's great freshly made or served a day or two later.

- 4-1/2 cups uncooked bow tie pasta
- 1 large sweet red pepper, chopped
- 1 large sweet yellow pepper, chopped
- 2 teaspoons olive oil
- 1/2 teaspoon garlic powder

1 cup prepared pesto
1 can (2-1/4 ounces) sliced ripe olives, drained
1/3 cup grated Parmesan cheese

Cook pasta according to package directions. Meanwhile, in a bowl, combine the peppers, oil and garlic powder; toss to coat. Arrange in a single layer in a greased 15-in. x 10-in. x 1-in. baking pan. Bake at 350° for 15-18 minutes or until peppers are tender.

Drain pasta and rinse in cold water. In a large salad bowl, toss the pasta, pesto, olives and pepper mixture. Refrigerate until serving. Sprinkle with Parmesan cheese. **Yield:** 8 servings.

BUTTERSCOTCH PEANUT BARS
(Not pictured)

Margery Richmond, Fort Collins, Colorado

With lots of peanuts and butterscotch flavor, plus a rich, buttery crust, these bars are oh-so good.

✓ Uses less fat, sugar or salt. Includes Nutrition Facts.

1/2 cup butter, softened
3/4 cup packed brown sugar
1-1/2 cups all-purpose flour
1/2 teaspoon salt
3 cups salted peanuts
TOPPING:
1 package (10 to 11 ounces) butterscotch chips
1/2 cup light corn syrup
2 tablespoons butter
1 tablespoon water

Line a 15-in. x 10-in. x 1-in. baking pan with aluminum foil. Coat the foil with cooking spray; set aside. In a small mixing bowl, cream butter and brown sugar. Add flour and salt; mix well. Press into prepared pan. Bake at 350° for 6 minutes. Sprinkle with peanuts.

In a large saucepan, combine topping ingredients. Cook and stir over medium heat until chips and butter are melted. Spread over hot crust. Bake for 12-15 minutes or until topping is bubbly. Cool on a wire rack. Cut into bars. **Yield:** 4 dozen.

Nutrition Facts: 1 bar equals 147 calories, 9 g fat (4 g saturated fat), 7 mg cholesterol, 99 mg sodium, 15 g carbohydrate, 1 g fiber, 3 g protein.

Lamb Dinner's Simply Divine

RACK OF LAMB WITH FIGS

Sylvia Castanon, Long Beach, California

Your Easter dinner guests are sure to enjoy this special main course that my grandmother prepared. Roasted lamb is served with a full-bodied sauce made with port wine and figs, and topped with a sprinkling of chopped walnuts. I always ask my butcher for a French-cut rack of lamb.

✓ Uses less fat, sugar or salt. Includes Nutrition Facts.

2 racks of lamb (2 pounds *each*)
1 teaspoon salt, *divided*
1 cup water
1 small onion, finely chopped
1 garlic clove, minced
1 tablespoon vegetable oil
2 tablespoons cornstarch
1 cup port wine *or* 1/2 cup grape juice plus 1/2 cup reduced-sodium beef broth
10 dried figs, halved
1/4 teaspoon pepper
1/2 cup coarsely chopped walnuts, toasted

Rub lamb with 1/2 teaspoon salt. Place meat side up on a rack in a greased roasting pan. Bake, uncovered, at 375° for 25-30 minutes or until meat reaches desired doneness (for medium-rare, a meat thermometer should read 145°; medium, 160°; well-done, 170°).

Remove to a serving platter; cover loosely with foil. Add 1 cup water to roasting pan; stir to loosen browned bits from pan. Using a fine sieve, strain mixture; set drippings aside.

In a small saucepan, saute onion and garlic in oil until tender. Stir in cornstarch until blended; gradually add the wine, drippings, figs, pepper and remaining salt. Bring to a boil. Reduce heat to medium-low; cook, uncovered, until figs are tender and sauce is thickened, about 10 minutes.

Sprinkle walnuts over lamb; serve with fig sauce. **Yield:** 6-8 servings.

Nutrition Facts: 2 chops equals 273 calories, 11 g fat (2 g saturated fat), 33 mg cholesterol, 332 mg sodium, 23 g carbohydrate, 3 g fiber, 13 g protein.

GARLIC MASHED POTATOES

Jennifer Adams, Plymouth, Massachusetts

If you're looking for a new twist on potatoes, try this idea. I mash them with garlic, then create a creamy, olive oil topping that's drizzled on top.

✓ Uses less fat, sugar or salt. Includes Nutrition Facts.

2 pounds potatoes, peeled and cut into chunks
8 garlic cloves, peeled
1 teaspoon salt
1/4 teaspoon coarsely ground pepper
1/4 cup olive oil, warmed

Place the potatoes and garlic in a large saucepan; cover with water. Cover and bring to a boil. Cook until tender, about 20 minutes. Drain, reserving 3/4 cup cooking liquid.

In a large mixing bowl, mash the potatoes and garlic. Beat in the salt, pepper and enough reserved cooking liquid to achieve a creamy consistency. Drizzle with oil. **Yield:** 6-8 servings.

Nutrition Facts: 2/3 cup equals 130 calories, 7 g fat (1 g saturated fat), 0 cholesterol, 298 mg sodium, 16 g carbohydrate, 1 g fiber, 2 g protein.

EASTER FRUIT SALAD
(Not pictured)

Deanna Richter, Elmore, Minnesota

Featuring pastel marshmallows, this Easter fruit salad is sure to attract young and old alike.

1 can (20 ounces) unsweetened pineapple chunks
3/4 cup sugar
2 tablespoons all-purpose flour
2 eggs, lightly beaten
1 tablespoon lemon juice
1 cup heavy whipping cream, whipped
1 can (11 ounces) mandarin oranges, drained
1 package (10-1/2 ounces) pastel miniature marshmallows
1 jar (10 ounces) maraschino cherries, drained and chopped

Drain pineapple, reserving juice; set pineapple aside. In a heavy saucepan, combine the sugar, flour, eggs, lemon juice and reserved pineapple juice until smooth. Cook and stir over medium-low heat until mixture is thickened and reaches 160°. Cool to room temperature.

Fold in whipped cream. In a large bowl, combine the oranges, marshmallows, cherries and re-

served pineapple; fold in cooked dressing. Refrigerate until chilled. **Yield:** 12 servings.

■▪■▪■▪■▪■▪■▪■▪■▪■

LEMON SORBET TORTE
(Not pictured)
Sarah Bradley, Athens, Texas

Oohs and aahs are sure to be the reaction when you bring this elegant torte to the table. It all starts with the unique almond and cinnamon-flavored crust topped with a layer of strawberry jam, then filled with prepared lemon sorbet. The torte is served with a rhubarb-strawberry sauce.

    3 cups slivered almonds, toasted
  1/2 cup sugar
  1/4 teaspoon ground cinnamon
    5 tablespoons butter, melted
  1/3 cup seedless strawberry jam
    3 pints lemon sorbet, softened
STRAWBERRY-RHUBARB SAUCE:
  1/2 cup sugar
  1/4 cup water
2-1/2 cups sliced fresh *or* frozen rhubarb

2-1/2 cups frozen unsweetened strawberries, partially thawed and sliced
  3/4 teaspoon vanilla extract
    1 pint fresh strawberries, sliced

Place the almonds, sugar and cinnamon in a food processor; cover and process until finely chopped. Stir in the butter. Press onto the bottom and 2 in. up the sides of an ungreased 9-in. springform pan.

Place pan on a baking sheet. Bake at 350° for 15-20 minutes or until lightly browned. Cool completely on a wire rack.

In a small saucepan over low heat, melt jam; spread over bottom of crust. Top with sorbet. Freeze until firm.

Meanwhile, for sauce, combine sugar and water in a large saucepan. Bring to a boil. Add rhubarb; return to a boil. Reduce heat; cover and simmer for 5-8 minutes or until rhubarb is tender. Add thawed strawberries; bring to a boil. Remove from the heat; cool to room temperature. Stir in vanilla. Cover and refrigerate.

Just before serving, remove sides of springform pan. Spoon 1/2 cup sauce onto center of torte; top with fresh strawberries. Serve with remaining sauce. **Yield:** 12 servings.

Country Menu's Sure to Please

●▪▪▪▪▪▪▪▪▪▪▪▪▪●

BEEF AND MUSHROOM ROLL

Amy Stoddard, Upland, California

My mom used to make this, and it was always a favorite of mine. I remember watching her make it and snitching bits of the meat that were leftover in the pan. I always had several tastes before she realized what I was doing.

- 1 pound ground beef
- 1 small onion, chopped
- 1 can (4 ounces) mushroom stems and pieces, drained
- 1/4 cup dill pickle relish
- 1 teaspoon salt
- 1/4 teaspoon ground mustard
- 1/4 teaspoon pepper
- 2 tablespoons all-purpose flour
- 1/3 cup water

PASTRY:
- 2 cups all-purpose flour
- 2 teaspoons baking powder
- 1 teaspoon salt
- 1/2 teaspoon poultry seasoning
- 1/4 cup shortening
- 3/4 cup plus 2 tablespoons milk, *divided*

GRAVY:
- 2 tablespoons butter
- 3 tablespoons all-purpose flour
- 1/2 teaspoon salt
- 1/4 teaspoon pepper
- 2 cups milk

In a large skillet, cook beef and onion over medium heat until meat is no longer pink; drain. Add the mushrooms, relish, salt, mustard and pepper. Combine flour and water until smooth; stir into beef mixture. Bring to a boil; cook and stir for 2 minutes or until thickened. Set aside.

For pastry, in a large bowl, combine the flour, baking powder, salt and poultry seasoning. Cut in shortening until mixture resembles coarse crumbs. Stir in 3/4 cup milk to form a soft dough. Turn onto a floured surface; pat dough into a 12-in. x 9-in. rectangle.

Set aside 1/4 cup meat mixture. Spread remaining mixture over dough to within 1 in. of edges. Roll up, starting with a long side; pinch seam to seal. Place seam side down on a greased baking sheet; brush with remaining milk. Bake at 425° for

15-20 minutes or until golden brown.

For gravy, melt butter in a saucepan over medium heat. Stir in the flour, salt and pepper until smooth. Gradually add milk.

Bring to a boil; cook and stir for 2 minutes or until thickened. Stir in reserved meat mixture; heat through. Slice roll; serve with gravy. **Yield:** 4-6 servings.

●▪▪▪▪▪▪▪▪▪▪▪▪▪●

CARROTS IN LEMON-PARSLEY BUTTER

Wanda Pentor, Franklinton, Louisiana

This simple side dish offers surprising flavor with its touch of lemon and fresh parsley. The great color makes any dinner plate pleasing to the eye.

✓ Uses less fat, sugar or salt. Includes Nutrition Facts.

- 1-1/2 pounds fresh carrots, sliced
- 1/4 cup butter, cubed
- 2 tablespoons minced fresh parsley
- 2 tablespoons lemon juice
- 1/4 teaspoon salt

Place 1 in. of water in a large saucepan; add carrots. Bring to a boil. Reduce heat; cover and simmer for 7-9 minutes or until crisp-tender. Drain; set carrots aside.

In the same pan, melt butter over medium heat. Stir in the parsley, lemon juice and salt. Return carrots to the pan and heat through. **Yield:** 6 servings.

Nutrition Facts: 1/2 cup equals 117 calories, 8 g fat (5 g saturated fat), 20 mg cholesterol, 216 mg sodium, 12 g carbohydrate, 3 g fiber, 1 g protein.

●▪▪▪▪▪▪▪▪▪▪▪▪▪●

TARRAGON COLESLAW

George Volrich, Medina, Tennessee

A tangy, tart dressing contributes to making this slaw more flavorful overnight or even on the third day. Slightly colored by paprika, it's an attractive addition with barbecue meats or any other main course.

✓ Uses less fat, sugar or salt. Includes Nutrition Facts.

- 1/2 cup sugar
- 1/2 cup tarragon vinegar
- 2 tablespoons olive oil
- 1 teaspoon salt
- 1 teaspoon paprika
- 1 garlic clove, minced

8 cups shredded cabbage (about 1
    medium head)
2 tablespoons minced fresh parsley

In a jar with a tight-fitting lid, combine the sugar, vinegar, oil, salt, paprika and garlic; shake well. Place cabbage and parsley in a large bowl. Add dressing and toss to coat. Cover and refrigerate for at least 2 hours before serving. **Yield:** 8 servings.

Nutrition Facts: 3/4 cup equals 97 calories, 4 g fat (trace saturated fat), 0 cholesterol, 308 mg sodium, 17 g carbohydrate, 2 g fiber, 1 g protein.

▪▪▪▪▪▪▪▪▪▪▪▪▪▪

DATE-NUT APPLE CAKE

Sue Mackey, Galesburg, Illinois

We've enjoyed this recipe for many years. It looks like a standard fruit cake, but the rich, moist texture of apples, dates, raisins and nuts makes it a satisfying dessert. A slice of this cake, topped with whipped cream, whipped topping or a big scoop of ice cream keep guests coming back for more.

1 package (8 ounces) chopped dates
1 cup raisins

2-1/2 cups all-purpose flour, *divided*
1/2 cup butter, softened
2 cups sugar
2 eggs
1 teaspoon vanilla extract
2 teaspoons baking soda
1 teaspoon salt
1-3/4 cups boiling water
1 cup chopped peeled tart apple
1 cup chopped walnuts
Confectioners' sugar, optional

In a small bowl, combine dates and raisins. Add 1 tablespoon flour and toss to coat; set aside.

In a large mixing bowl, cream butter and sugar. Add eggs, one at a time, beating well after each addition. Beat in vanilla. Combine the baking soda, salt and remaining flour; add to creamed mixture alternately with boiling water. Stir in the apple, walnuts and reserved date mixture.

Transfer to a greased and floured 10-in. fluted tube pan. Bake at 350° for 65-70 minutes or until a toothpick inserted near the center comes out clean. Cool for 10 minutes before removing cake from pan to a wire rack to cool completely. Dust with the confectioners' sugar if desired. **Yield:** 10-12 servings.

Make Meals Special Again

▪▪▪▪▪▪▪▪▪▪▪▪▪▪

HONEY-GLAZED CHICKEN

Pat Dube, Phoenix, Arizona

When I was a young girl, this was my oldest sister's Sunday dinner. The tradition has continued, as I make this dish twice a month and my four daughters serve their families with this favorite dish, too. It has an old-fashioned, subtle flavor everyone enjoys.

  1/4 cup butter, melted
  1/4 cup orange juice
  1/4 cup honey
  1/2 teaspoon salt
    1 broiler/fryer chicken (3 to 4 pounds),
      cut up

In a shallow bowl, combine the butter, orange juice, honey and salt. Remove 1/3 cup and set aside for basting. Dip chicken pieces in remaining butter mixture; place in a well-greased 13-in. x 9-in. x 2-in. baking dish.

Bake, uncovered, at 350° for 1 hour or until juices run clear, basting occasionally with reserved butter mixture. **Yield:** 6 servings.

▪▪▪▪▪▪▪▪▪▪▪▪▪▪

GREEK POTATO SALAD

Roberta Webster, Hampton, Florida

Oregano adds a mouth-watering twist to potato salad with this recipe. Served on a bed of lettuce, it's a great change-of-pace lunch.

    5 cups cubed peeled potatoes
  1/2 cup white wine vinegar
  1/3 cup sugar
    1 tablespoon olive oil
3-1/2 teaspoons dried oregano, divided
1-1/2 cups mayonnaise
  1/2 teaspoon salt
    1 bunch leaf lettuce, shredded
Cherry tomatoes, halved, optional

Place potatoes in a large saucepan and cover with water. Bring to a boil. Reduce heat; cover and cook for 10-15 minutes or until tender. Drain and cool to room temperature.

In a small bowl, combine the vinegar, sugar, oil and 1/2 teaspoon oregano; set aside. In a large bowl, combine the mayonnaise, salt and remain-

ing oregano. Add potatoes and toss to coat. Cover and refrigerate until chilled.

Just before serving, toss lettuce with the vinegar mixture; place on a serving platter. Top with potato salad. Garnish with cherry tomatoes if desired. **Yield:** 10 servings.

▪▪▪▪▪▪▪▪▪▪▪▪▪▪

CREAMY 'N' FRUITY GELATIN SALAD

Elaine Schmit, Mifflintown, Pennsylvania

I remember looking forward to eating this pretty salad when I was a child. It has all the ingredients youngsters like. My grandmother served it during the holidays and on other special occasions and my mother did the same.

☑ Uses less fat, sugar or salt. Includes Nutrition Facts.

    2 packages (3 ounces *each*) orange gelatin
    1 cup boiling water
    1 pint orange *or* pineapple sherbet
    1 can (11 ounces) mandarin oranges,
      drained
    1 can (8 ounces) crushed pineapple,
      drained
    1 cup miniature marshmallows
    1 cup heavy whipping cream, whipped

In a large bowl, dissolve gelatin in boiling water. Add sherbet; stir until smooth. Stir in the oranges, pineapple and marshmallows. Fold in whipped cream. Pour into a 6-cup serving bowl. Cover and refrigerate for 3-4 hours or until set. **Yield:** 10 servings.

Nutrition Facts: 1/2 cup equals 158 calories, 5 g fat (3 g saturated fat), 18 mg cholesterol, 42 mg sodium, 28 g carbohydrate, trace fiber, 2 g protein.

▪▪▪▪▪▪▪▪▪▪▪▪▪▪

RED RASPBERRY PIE

Patricia Morrow, Mapleton, Minnesota

Made easy with a refrigerated pie crust, this lovely desserts offers the best of summer flavor. A hint of lime complements the sweet raspberries so well.

1-1/2 cups plus 1/2 teaspoon sugar, *divided*
  1/3 cup quick-cooking tapioca
  1/4 teaspoon salt
    6 cups fresh raspberries
    1 teaspoon lime juice
Pastry for double-crust pie (9 inches)
    1 tablespoon butter
    1 teaspoon milk

In a large bowl, combine 1-1/2 cups sugar, tapioca and salt. Add raspberries and lime juice; toss gently to coat. Let stand for 15 minutes.

Line a 9-in. pie plate with bottom pastry; trim even with edge of plate. Add filling; dot with butter. Roll out remaining pastry to fit top of pie; place over filling. Trim, seal and flute edges. Cut slits in top. Brush with the milk; sprinkle with the remaining sugar.

Cover edges loosely with foil. Bake at 450° for 10 minutes. Reduce heat to 350°; remove foil and bake 35-40 minutes longer or until crust is golden brown and filling is bubbly. Cool on a wire rack. Store the pie in the refrigerator. **Yield:** 6-8 servings.

General Recipe Index

A

APPETIZERS & SNACKS

Cold Appetizers
Black Forest Ham
  Pinwheels, 6
Marinated Mushrooms and
  Cheese, 11

Dips & Spreads
Curried Vegetable Dip, 10
✓Garlic Eggplant Spread, 8
✓Greek Salsa, 5
Mocha Fondue, 18
Nutty Caramel Apple Dip, 8
✓Pastrami Artichoke
  Spread, 6
Sesame Salmon Spread, 17
Warm Crab Dip, 14

Hot Appetizers
Artichokes with Lemon-Mint
  Dressing, 19
Brie with Apricot Topping, 8
Buffalo Wing Poppers, 12
Chorizo-Queso Egg Rolls, 15
Cranberry Camembert
  Pizza, 19
Curried Chicken
  Turnovers, 16
Festive Baked Brie, 16
Fontina Asparagus Tart, 12
Hearty Rye Melts, 7
Spicy Pork Baguette
  Bites, 12
Sweet Sausage Puffs, 5

Snacks
Almond Snack Cake, 18
✓Chunky Fruit 'n' Nut
  Fudge, 7
Cranberry Mousse, 9
✓Eggnog Truffle Cups, 14
Faux Chicken Nuggets, 15
Poppy Seed Coffee Cake, 10
Raspberry Apple Cake, 9

APPLES
Applesauce Meatballs, 160
✓Chunky Rhubarb
  Applesauce, 80
Cinnamon Apple Dumplings, 132
Country Style Pork Medallions, 48
Creamy Cranberry Apple
  Salad, 43
Date-Nut Apple Cake, 169
Dutch Apple Sour Cream
  Pie, 114
✓Fruity Apple Salad, 26
Nutty Caramel Apple Dip, 8
Raspberry Apple Cake, 9
Speedy Apple Butter, 80
Sweet Shoppe Caramel
  Apples, 122
✓Wassail Bowl Punch, 17
✓Westerfield Wassail, 11

ARTICHOKES
Artichokes with Lemon-Mint
  Dressing, 19
✓Pastrami Artichoke Spread, 6

ASPARAGUS
✓Black Bean Asparagus
  Salad, 31
Crumb-Topped Asparagus, 162
Fontina Asparagus Tart, 12

B

BANANAS
✓Banana Crunch Muffins, 96
Southern Banana Pudding, 124

BEANS
✓Black Bean Asparagus
  Salad, 31
✓Calico Black Bean Salad, 34

✓Cranberry Baked Beans, 85
Great Green Beans, 143
Green 'n' Red Potato Salad, 137
Green Bean 'n' Corn Bake, 84
Green Bean Bundles, 82
Green Bean-Tomato Salad, 21
Quick Baked Beans, 86
Spicy Two-Bean Chili, 42
Summer Bean Salad, 28
Yankee Bean Soup, 39

BEEF *(also see Ground Beef)*
Asian Barbecued Short Ribs, 64
Beef Pinwheels, 62
✓Easy Oven Stew, 54
✓German-Style Short Ribs, 71
Glazed Corned Beef and
  Cabbage, 68
Grilled Fajitas with Pico de Gallo, 71
Grilled Steak and Mushroom
  Salad, 38
Italian Beef Sandwiches, 158
Mushroom Rib Eyes, 142
✓Pastrami Artichoke Spread, 6
✓Pineapple Steaks, 162
Southern Barbecued Brisket, 53

BEETS
Sweet-and-Sour Beets, 78

BEVERAGES
Fruity Sangria, 5
Mango Tango Smoothies, 14
✓Mocha Fireside Coffee, 18
✓Pear Slushy, 147
✓Wassail Bowl Punch, 17
✓Westerfield Wassail, 11

BLACKBERRIES
Berry Peach Tossed Salad, 25
Black 'n' Blue Berry Grunt, 123

*✓Recipe includes Nutrition Facts
and Diabetic Exchanges*

*✓Recipe includes Nutrition Facts
and Diabetic Exchanges*

*✓Recipe includes Nutrition Facts
and Diabetic Exchanges*

✓*Recipe includes Nutrition Facts
and Diabetic Exchanges*

Alphabetical Recipe Index

✓*Recipe includes Nutrition Facts
and Diabetic Exchanges*

✓*Recipe includes Nutrition Facts*
and Diabetic Exchanges